Robert Detobel
Shakespeare and the Concealed Poet

Robert Detobel

Shakespeare and the Concealed Poet

Verlag Uwe Laugwitz

Editor:
Jan Scheffer

English version
assisted by K. C. Ligon (1949-2009)

Special issue no. 8 of NEUES SHAKE-SPEARE JOURNAL
All rights for this edition reserved by Verlag Uwe Laugwitz,
Matthias-Claudius-Weg 11B, 21244 Buchholz, Germany
www.laugwitz.com

ISBN 9783-933077-55-9

Contents

Introduction

This book arrives on the heels of a spate of new Shakespearean biographies, all clearly seeking to place the man´s life within striking distance of his immortal works, an endeavor that has, due to the apparent paucity of the documentary record, been conducted primarily in the realm of speculation and fiction. It is our observation that this relatively recent explosion of searching for a connection between Shakespeare´s life and his art is in direct response to increased public awareness of a growing body of evidence that the man traditionally accepted for centuries as the Bard of Avon may not in fact have been the true poet.

Apparently in hopes of dispelling all doubt in the Stratford player and sharcholder´s identity as ´Shakespeare,´ traditional biographers have stepped up their attempts to locate the life of the incumbent bard in a literary historical context, presumably poring over all extant contemporary documents in the quest of any salient detail that might have escaped detection until now. Nevertheless it is our contention, based upon our own research, that a number of key primary source documents have not been throroughly examined and placed within their rightful historical context by previous scholars and historians of the era. In our view searching for Shakespeare (according to the traditional biography) is like waiting for Godot. Godot, we note, is actually a pseudonym, in everyday life his name is God. For many, certainly, Shakespeare is also a deity, a god. And was Shakespeare in everyday life called Shakespeare, or was the name a pseudonym? Who was Shakespeare?

Pozzo (*peremptory*): Who is Godot?

Estragon: Godot?

Pozzo: You took me for Godot.

Estragon: Oh no, sir, not for an instant, sir.

Pozzo: Who is he?

Vladimir: Oh, he´s a... he´s a kind of acquaintance.

Estragon: Nothing of the kind, we hardly know him.

Vladimir: True... we don´t know him very well... but all the same.

The traditional biographer/Vladimir would certainly challenge our parallel here: 'We know more about Shakespeare than we do about the majority of contemporary authors. True, we wish we knew more about him *as a writer*. We have no letters *from* him because none are extant. But we do have letters *to* him, well…we have *one* anyway. It was found among his papers, that is, the papers of the man who wrote to Shakespeare. It was his neighbor Richard Quiney who sent the letter, or more exactly, intended to send it. But he never did. But all the same.'

Beckett's play is staged in a barren landscape, except for one tree – which is withered. At the end of the play the sun sets, the moon rises, lending the withered tree a spectral nimbus.

Vladimir: Well? Shall we go?

Estragon: Yes, let's go.

(*They don't move*)

Vladimir and Estragon rather famously stay put, never advancing a single step. So ends many a biography of Shakespeare, searching for the man behind the works without progress; even though these 'biographies' may move 'upward' by imagining his life, or 'downward,' toward the underground, concentrating on the atmosphere influencing those who lived and worked around him. The proponents of the bard-as-secret-Catholic theory, for example, argue that in the Tudor and Stuart police state Shakespeare was forced to lie low. He dared not speak too much too openly, due to his religion. Yet can this be the reason Shakespeare's real life in the *literary* world is virtually invisible?

* * *

We too will be following an underground route, or subway. It will take us but three stations to meet the author of the Shakespearean works. The first stop is St Paul's Churchyard, at the sign of the Half Eagle and the Key, the shop of William Jaggard, printer of the First Folio. The next is not far off, Stationer's Hall, the building of the Stationer's Company, where Shakespeare's works were registered for printing. Finally we arrive at Botolph Lane, where Francis Meres resides. We call it "subway" because the primary concern will not be to find the author. His identity at this moment is only a by-product of our first goal: to find answers to problems related to publication in general and of Shakespearean works in particular. These questions are of a technical nature. Some have thus far been unsatisfactorily answered by scholars, others haven't been addressed at all. To begin with, how is the prefatory material to the First Folio to be understood? Secondly, what was the true role of the printer James Roberts in the publication of Shakespeare's plays between 1598 and 1604? Finally, what is the significance of Francis Meres' "Comparative Discourse", a symmetrized namedropping of ancient and English authors, in which Shakespeare's tragedies and comedies are set upon a par with the hallowed classic tragedies of Seneca and the comedies of Plautus?

At the end of part I the identity of the author will be known, but of his personality we shall have learnt hardly anything. The advantage of a formal approach, a trip by subway, is also its limitation. The goal is all, it is firmly traced between the walls of a tunnel, eye and mind undistracted by a variegated landscape. Contrary to Vladimir and Estragon we'll have made headway, but our scene will still be no less barren than theirs. Having attained our goal of identifying the author (in our estimation unequivocally) by a very formal procedure, we still cannot claim to know anything of him as a man, the singular individual who would one day be named 'the soul of the age.'

But orthodox theorists have claimed to know at least something personal about him. Therefore (before pursuing our own way in part III) we will look at what is universally regarded as their principal evidence, said to be found in Robert Greene's infamous invective against Shakespeare as "Shake-scene" in a letter in *Greene's Groatsworth of Wit*. Is it possible that all puzzling aspects of this letter have not been thoroughly examined within the proper historical framework? To contextualize this question we have reviewed a wider base of contemporary information, including an examination of the possible role of the distinguished but controversial scholar Gabriel Harvey in the transmission of Greene's papers, among them the famous letter in *GGW*. According to traditional biographers, this letter provides the first glimpse of the personality of Shakespeare, as penned by an embittered playwright and poet who was envious of his fellow's success. Yet after careful review of the events surrounding the publication of this pamphlet, and of the language in related documents, our conclusion is that 'Shake-scene' was anything but a playwright, though he was most certainly an actor whose prominence as a player would have made his identity instantly recognizable to any contemporary reader and/or theatregoer. On the other hand, some unorthodox theorists have concluded that the man from Stratford was a cold-hearted moneylender, based in large part upon a legal record known as the Clayton suit. We will also examine this document, one that has in our view been misunderstood by orthodox and unorthodox theorists alike.

The subject of part III is the concealed poet, without quotation marks, for his presence is no longer a mere scent in the wind, he is now visible, palpable, and he is less concealed than not named. He first comes into view in one of Greene's pastoral romances, reappearing later in a brief report by another author as the foremost poet of the 1580s. We see him in the midst of the famous literary quarrel raging in the first half of the 1590s between Harvey and Thomas Nashe, the outstanding satirist of his time, though Shakespeare is strangely absent from the *contretemps* (or is he?). We witness that he is repeatedly apostrophized by both Harvey and Nashe as the dominant figure amongst the London literati of the 1580s and 90s, a prolific patron and premier poet in his own right. Curiously, he has remained a blind spot in English literary history.

He will turn out to be the same person we identified as the poet Shakespeare at the end of part I, and here we find him, the pre-eminent literary light at the teeming centre of the world of English literature for the last two decades of the sixteenth century.

Part I
The Subway To Shakespeare

Chapter I
Shakespeare: The Courtier

The First Folio is prefaced by a dedication to the earls of Pembroke and Montgomery and the epistle to "the great variety of readers", together about 900 words. Of these only a fraction is generally quoted, the description of the author as "gentle Shakespeare" and of his art: "His mind and hand went together: And what he thought, he uttered with that easiness, that we have scarce received a blot in his papers." About 3% is considered of interest, the remaining 97% is, one must presume, either so plain or so insignificant as to require no comment. Yet is there really nothing more to ask about the prefatory matter of the Folio? Certainly we might wonder why Heminges and Condell, supposing they are the real authors of these texts (more than one scholar has suggested that Ben Jonson authored the prefaces), would write in the dedication to Pembroke and Montgomery that Shakespeare´s plays are "trifles" that the earls have deigned to favour, but in the epistle to the readers praise the plays as a phenomenal intellectual achievement. "Read him, therefore," they exhort the reader, "and again, and again." The trifles? And why do they affirm in the dedication to the earls that they are publishing the First Folio "without ambition either of self-love or fame", and display in the epistle to the readers a radically opposite, commercial, profit-oriented attitude: "Especially, when the fate of all books depends upon your capacities: and not of your heads alone, but of your purses. Well! it is now public, & you will stand for your privileges we know: to read, and censure. Do so, but buy it first. That doth best commend a book, the stationer says." Why, at the portal of the First Folio, this presumably high-minded literary venture, do we find this Janus-face?

The same Janus-face is put on by Sir George Peckham, the author of a prologue to another sort of venture – it, too, momentous: "There was no doubt in the minds of contemporaries that two quite separate social groups were combining in overseas enterprises. In 1583, writing in support of a project for the colonization of Newfoundland, Sir George Peckham considered it ´convenient that I do divide the adventurers into two sorts: the noblemen and gentlemen by themselves, and the merchants by themselves.´ He said he had heard that in fact two companies were going to be established, one for each class. And he shaped the propaganda accordingly. For the gentry he stressed the fine climate, the conditions favorable to landowners, the crops that could be produced, and the excellent hunting, including a description of a moose. For the merchants he provided a list of over 70 commodities which could bring them profit – with leopards, silkworms, pepper, and rubies quite unabashedly claimed for Newfoundland. This was the popular impression of the differences between the aims and interests of the two classes, and it was fairly accurate in gauging the temper of most merchants, whose prime concern was, naturally, for trade."[1] Yet a few pages later the same historian suggests that more than "popular impression" may have lain at the basis of Peckham´s differentiations. "... the composition of the companies reveals that trade alone, despite its more reliable assurance of profit, could not attract the gentry as easily as could a colony or an exploration. Certainly they were interested in making money... But they rarely if ever came to depend on commerce for their livelihood. There was a glamour in overseas enterprise that inspired motives beyond the desire for profits... The motivation of the merchant was generally less complicated. He did rely on trade for living, and the return on his investment had to be his chief concern."[2] What is reflected in the dedication to the earls of Pembroke and Montgomery and Sir George Peckham´s advertisement alike is the difference of the social roles allocated to gentry and merchants. To each class corresponded another set of attitudes and patterns of behaviour which was as much constitutive of class as a consequence of it.

Thus, in the dedication to the Folio **aristocratic** values are stressed, in the epistle **mercantile** values are. Printing and publishing were regarded as "mercenary" by members of the nobility. Members of the nobility were not necessarily peers and possibly not even knights. Nearness to the court and compliance with an unwritten behavioral code were other criteria. Philip Sidney, not a titled knight in the early 1580s, took strong aristocratic views, especially with respect to the publishing of poetry. After his death Fulke Greville oversaw the publication of his friend's works. In a letter to Sidney's father-in-law, Sir Francis Walsingham, Greville writes: "besides he has most excellently translated among divers other 'notable' works Monsieur du Plessis' books against atheism, which is since done by another as both in respect of the love between Plessis & him besides other affinities in their works, but especially Sir Philip's incomparable judgement, I think fit there be made a stay of that mercenary book ... many other works as Bartas' *Semaines*, 40 psalms translated into meter, etc which require the care of his friends, not to amend ... but only to see to the paper & other common errors of mercenary printing."[3]

This "anti-mercenary" attitude can be traced back to feudal times. However, the feudal complexion of the aristocracy in the 16th century did not belong so much to the natural skin as to its makeup. In the 16th century the aristocracy was irrevocably metamorphosed from a feudal into a courtly class.

Two leisure-time poets: Hartmann von Aue and William Shakespeare

Hartmann von Aue was a German author of chivalric romances, a contemporary of Chrétien de Troyes, writing about the turn of the 13th century. Nothing is known of him besides what he reports about himself in his romances. He is a knight serving his lord. And, a rarity in those times, he was a knight who could read and was proud of it, as he tells us in the opening lines of his romance *Der arme Heinrich (Poor Henry)*:

A knight so learned was,
that he read in books,
what he therein found written,
he was called Hartmann,
Serving man at Aue.

A serving man, a "sergeant"in old English terminology, was a knight serving his lord beyond military service. In the opening lines of another romance, *Yvain*, he says he sometimes even writes poems himself:

A knight who learned was,
And from the books did read,
When he had no better use

for his hours,
also wrote poems.

Sir Philip Sidney, too, only wrote during such 'idle' hours. In the dedication to his sister the Countess of Pembroke Sidney calls *Arcadia* "this
idle worke of mine... being but a trifle, and that triflingly handled...
read it then at your idle tymes." And it was in these idle times, by his
own description, that William Shakespeare wrote. In his dedication of
Venus and Adonis to the earl of Southampton the poet vows "to take
advantage of all idle hours, till I have honoured you with some graver
labour."

Another who only took to literary production in his 'idle hours' was
the French aristocrat Georges de Scudéry, brother of Mademoiselle
Madeleine de Scudéry. In 1629 he publishes his play *Ligdamon et Lidias*
and writes in the preface: "thinking to be but a soldier I found myself a
poet... poetry is only a delightful pastime to me, not a serious occupation; if I am rhyming, then because I do not know what else to do and
the only purpose of this kind of work is my private contentment; and
far from being mercenary, the printer and the actors can witness to the
fact that I sold them nothing, which at any rate they cannot pay for."
He then asks the reader to pay no heed to the errors he himself had
overlooked, because "he is more accustomed to the fuse of the harque-
bus than to the wick of the candle and apter at arranging soldiers than
words and at squaring battalions than periods."[4] Magendie, the author
of the work on the theory of honesty from which the lines are quoted,
qualifies this preface as "vaniteuse", "conceited". He might be right in
one sense, in another he misses the significance of Scudéry's words.
Scudéry was by no means indifferent to literary fame. Seven years later
he would explode with envy at Pierre Corneille's success with *Le Cid*
and heap reproaches of plagiarism and faulty style on him. But what
Scudéry displays in his preface is not primarily an individual subjective
attitude; he delivers his business card or, more exactly, his non-
business card. In plain text he affirms that he is a member of the courtly
aristocratic elite: 'I, Scudéry, am first of all a soldier, and poetry is
something I enjoy in my idle hours, but it is not my occupation, and I
don't take money for my writings.'

Serving the lord, serving the prince

Hartmann von Aue lived in feudal times. He had a reason to restrict his writing and reading to idle hours. The relationship between vassal and lord was one of loyalty. It was conceived as a personal relationship based on honour. The idea of profitable exchange was absent from the relationship or at least kept as remote as possible, the idea of serving put in the foreground. The vassal was devoted, not hired to the service of his feudal lord. Any activity other than military or other service to the lord had to be reserved for idle hours.

In Scudéry's, actually by Sidney's time, the rules had changed. Learning was no longer considered superfluous or a debasement for an aristocrat, altering the long-standing tradition of the majority of the nobility who had opposed letters and learning. The exhortation of a Spanish marquis in the last quarter of the 15th century reveals why: "La ciencia no emboda el fierro de la lanza nin face floxa el espada en la mano del cavallero".[5] ("Science neither blunts the sword nor slackens the spear in the hand of the knight.") Even at the beginning of the 16th century many nobles thought learning incompatible with nobility. J. H. Hexter cites the answer the diplomat and humanist Richard Pace (1483-1536) received from "an unnamed gentleman on learning. 'It becomes the son of gentlemen to blow the horn nicely, to hunt skilfully, and elegantly to carry and train a hawk.' He added that 'the study of letters was for rustics,' that it was stupid, and that all learned men were beggars. 'Rather should my son hang,' than be learned, he concluded."[6] Hexter further indicates that the proportion of students of common to gentle origin at the university of Oxford in the third quarter of the sixteenth century was about five to three and five to six at the beginning of the seventeenth century, but that this proportion is biased because the presence of members of the latter group was not always registered. "An undeterminable number of gentle-born did not bother to matriculate in Oxford at all, although they had lodgings in a college."[7] Still, nearly forty years after Sir Thomas Elyot had claimed in his *Book of the Governor* (1531), a handbook on the education of the aristocracy from whose ranks alone Elyot held the rulers of the state could come, that learning and "honesty" (good manners) were two essential criteria. In his own book on the education of the youth, *The Scholemaster*, Roger Ascham warned young aristocrats not to persist in their neglect of learning and "honest" living as they would risk being overrun by learned commoners in the competition for offices of state.[8]

In fact, Ascham's admonition had been taken to heart by members of the aristocracy. Military function, still proclaimed their main occupation, was nevertheless on the wane in favor of their role as officers and statesmen in the administrative service of the Prince, which in a centralizing realm had displaced service to the regional lord. The old honor still mattered, but it was complemented by another notion, derived from the Latin word for honor: "honestas", "honesty", a word covering a large range of meanings: honor, good manners, refinement, uprightness, civil behavior, etc. Ascham uses it a score and a half times on about the same number of pages in varying meanings.

Historians have not come into consensus with respect to the precise nomenclature of this 'new' aristocracy. Some stress the radical break with the old feudal nobility; others emphasize the continuity between the two aristocracies with appellations such as "refeudalization of society" or "bastard feudalism". Our own preference lies with the designation of Norbert Elias, "courtly aristocracy".[9] The center of power had definitely shifted from regional allegiances to the sovereign and the court. It was the court which had taken up the reins of the civilizing process and which was seen as the fountain of all values. In his play *Poetaster* (IV.ix) Ben Jonson has the banished Ovid complain:

> Within the court is all the kingdom bounded,
> And as her sacred sphere doth comprehend
> Ten thousand times so much, as so much place
> In any part of all the empire else;
> So every body moving in her sphere
> Contains ten thousand as much in him
> As any other her choice orb excludes.[10]

The words reflect not Ovid's own thought but Ben Jonson's own "Augustan values" as the editor and others term it.[11] On the surface, the term "Augustan" seems wholly inappropriate. Augustus was anxious to maintain every semblance of continuity of his reign with the past republican commonwealth. Consuls were still elected yearly, the senate was still considered the supreme governing body. Monarchic symbols were anxiously repressed. Augustus had no crown, no court, he lived not in a palace but in a house in Rome and called himself not king or emperor but *princeps*, 'the first'. However, it was in the symbolic order that the republican institutions survived in a ritualized and idealized mode, while the monarchic character, obfuscated in the **symbolic** order, shaped the **social** and **politic** order. On the contrary, for the Elizabethan court, as for other courts of the Renaissance and early modern times, the display of kingly power, glory and splendor was an essential instrument of power sustenance. Yet on a more abstract level of functionality the epithet "Augustan" is quite apt and in some respects the Augustan term *principate* for the Roman empire might perhaps better describe the reality of the Elizabethan state than the more usual "absolute monarchy".

Under the aspect that matters most in the present context the term "Augustan" is even apposite. To legitimize his comprehensive powers, Augustus had to hold up the appearances of the republican tradition. In early modern times, to legitimize the power of the monarch and the aristocratic claim to the natural leadership in the realm, a continuity had to be established with the feudal past to sustain the notion that leadership was 'traditionally' and 'naturally' rooted in the aristocratic class. As republican traditions lived on in a ritualized form in Augustus' *principate*, so feudal traditions survived in the absolute monarchy (for the Tudor feudal revival see Roy Strong, *The Cult of Elizabeth. Elizabethan Portraiture and Pageant*. London: Thames and Hudson, 1977).

The feudal military function of the aristocracy had grown obsolete, partly due to technological inventions, partly due to the political discredit the feuding aristocracy had suffered in the Wars of the Roses. Though the courtly aristocrat was still eager to affirm that arms was his primary occupation, he likely handled them more often in joustings than in wars. According to the principles of the feudal relation of loyalty between vassal and lord, culminating in the ceremony of homage and the oath of fealty, the notion of "exchange", or of a transaction based on mutual profit, was mercenary and profane. Mercenary activities were seen as irreconcilable with the rank of a feudal aristocrat as manual labor would be. It has been pointed out by sociologists[12] that the rejection of acquisitiveness was an essential pre-requisite of the feudal aristocracy to distance itself from other social groups. Some seldom noticed particularities of the courtly society may have their roots herein: the cult of presents at court, the fact that annuities were most often formulated as grants without mentioning of services in return.[13] The semantic metamorphosis of exchange into grant is satirized in Molière's comedy *Le Bourgeois-Gentilhomme* (1670). Monsieur Jourdain, who wishes to become a courtier, is still fearing that his and his father's trade will prove an unsurmountable obstacle to his ambition. The ingenious servant Covielle convinces him that his father had never been a cloth merchant (IV.iii):

Covielle. Yes. He was a very honorable gentleman.
Jourdain. What did you say?
Covielle. I said that he was a very honorable gentleman.
Jourdain. My father?
Covielle. Yes.
Jourdain. And you knew him very well?
Covielle. Assuredly.
Jourdain. And you knew him as a gentleman?
Covielle. Without doubt.
Jourdain. Then I don't know what is going on!
Covielle: What?
Jourdain: There are some fools who want to tell me that he was a
tradesman.
Covielle: Him, a tradesman! It's pure slander, he never was
one. All that he did was to be very obliging, very
ready to help; and, since he was a connoisseur in
cloth, he went all over to choose them, had them
brought to his house, and gave them to his friends
for money.

A similar mockery of courtly diction is found in II.iv of *The Return from Parnassus* (published in 1606 but acted some years earlier at Cambridge):

Stercutio: Son, is this the gentleman that sells us the living?

Immerito: Fie, father! thou must not call it selling: thou must say: Is this the gentleman that must have the *gratuito*? ...

Stercutio: O, is this the grating gentleman? And how many pounds must I pay?

Immerito: O, thou must not call them pounds, but thanks.

Academico: Not pounds, but thanks! See, whether this simple fellow that hath nothing of a scholar, but that the draper hath blacked him over, hath not gotten the style of the time?

The 12th-century feudal knight Hartmann only wrote poems in his leisure time, his main occupation was military and political service to his lord. This was the field where he had to win his spurs. The same holds true for the 17th-century French aristocrat Georges de Scudéry. But in the latter's case the only lord was the overlord, the Prince, the king of France. What once had been an element of the feudal aristocratic ideology was now a basic element of the courtly aristocratic ideology. On the publication of Baldasar Castiglione's *Book of the Courtier* in 1528 Peter Burke comments: "By the standards of the time, writing a book and having it printed was a somewhat ambiguous activity for a courtier. Publication was associated with profit as well as fame... This made association with the press inappropriate for noblemen, at least in the eyes of some contemporaries... These prejudices were not universal. As we have seen Ariosto published his poem *Orlando Furioso* in 1516, and Bembo published his dialogues in 1505 and 1525."[14] Indeed, in the *Book of the Courtier*, composed of book I-IV, Castiglione had pictured an ideal courtier who was not only skilled at arms but also accomplished in different sciences, under which is mainly to be understood letters and other arts such as music, painting, dancing, and had acquired in all these disciplines and in his behaviour as well a natural grace, an "effortlessness" which he coined *sprezzatura*. The etymology of the word *sprezzatura* itself is indicative of the aristocracy's contempt for the mercenary spirit. *"Sprezzatura* was not, literally speaking, a new word at all, but rather a new sense given to an old word, the basic meaning of which was 'setting no price on'".[15] In Book IV, however, Castiglione insists that all these accomplishments do not have their end in individual perfection but in the service to the Prince. The ideal courtier should win by them the favor and the confidence of the Prince, "so that he can and always will tell him the truth about all he needs to know, without fear or risk of displeasing him."[16] It was one of the ideological tenets on which the aristocracy based its right to rule. "La noblesse expose sa vie pour le salut de l'État et pour la gloire du souverain." (The nobility stage their lives for the commonwealth and the glory of the sovereign.")[17] In this view the merchant, for naturally seeking profit, could assume no responsibility for the whole. The aristocracy was the visible hand which directed the pursuit of individual profit toward the overall interests of the community, a view which Adam Smith's axiom of the "invisible hand" was to center in the individual two and a half centuries later. The service of the Prince and the commonwealth also sets the limits of the "stigma of print". Bembo's platonic dialogues, like Castiglione's book itself, could be conceived as a work of public interest. Ariosto's epic poem *Orlando Furioso* was at the same time a dynastic poem in honor of the Este family, serving a major purpose of any Prince, the representation of his glory and power. However, Ariosto's comedies were not published during his lifetime.

Hence Georges de Scudéry's insistence on writing poetry only for his private pleasure during his idle hours, and on caring not much for errors as this was not his profession (his true fame being that of a soldier), and on seeking no profit from the publication of his play. These were merely stock phrases, clichés employed to emphasize that his behaviour did not violate the courtly aristocratic code. And it can be seen that similar catchphrases are being utilized in the dedication of the First Folio.

The plays were "trifles" to the earls, as such they had to have been publicly regarded by aristocrats like themselves and Sidney. And apparently they would have been deemed "trifles" by Shakespeare, something accomplished as a pastime in his "idle hours", as he himself stated in the dedication to *Venus and Adonis*. This means that Shakespeare either adopted the attitude of a courtier or actually was one.

And Heminges and Condell do assure the reader: "We have but collected them, and done an office to the dead, to procure his Orphans, Guardians; without ambition either of self-profit, or fame: only to keep the memory of so worthy a Friend, & Fellow alive, as was our SHAKE-SPEARE". For commoners, members of a commercial playing company, whose manager Heminges was, it would have been both hypocritical and politically incorrect to declare they had not done it for profit and to subscribe the epistle to the readers, the first part of which is precisely that, a commercial promotion of the project. Yet Heminges and Condell are speaking as representatives of their "worthy friend and fellow SHAKESPEARE", and if he were in truth a courtier their statement is perfectly in line with the attitude he would be obliged to take toward literary works of a private character.

Yet another statement, found in the epistle, can be interpreted as a confirmation of Shakespeare's courtier status. Castiglione had defined the behavior of the ideal courtier in purely aesthetical categories. All the examples used to illustrate the *sprezzatura* or "effortlessness" of the ideal courtier are taken from art, so that it is sometimes difficult to distinguish whether Castiglione is writing about behavior or an artistic work. "Then again, in painting, a single brush stroke made with ease, in such a way that it seems the hand is completing the line by itself without any effort or guidance, clearly reveals the excellence of this artist, about whose competence everyone will then make his own judgment." And without transition he turns to the behaviour of the courtier: "The same happens in almost every other thing. Our courtier, therefore, will be judged to be perfect and will show grace in everything, and especially his speech, if he shuns affectation."[18] Castiglione, Burke notes, practised this rule for his own book. He claimed "to have written it 'in a few days' (I.i), although we know that he rewrote and elaborated it over a number of years."[19] In III.iv of John Lyly's play *Campaspe*, Alexander the Great, trying his hand at painting his beloved Campaspe, is criticized by the painter Apelles: "Your eye goeth not with your hand, your hand goeth not with your mind." And in the Folio epistle we find: "His mind and hand went together: And what he thought, he uttered with that easinesse, that we have scarce received from him a blot in his papers." The statement could apply to either the playwright Shakespeare, or to the "effortlesness", the *sprezzatura*, of the courtier Shakespeare. In any case it would not mean that Shakespeare never blotted out a line, but that the end version of his plays created the same impression as Apelles' painting, to have been written "with one stroke of the hand".

The courtier and editorship

Today the Spanish author Francisco de Quevedo (1580-1645), courtier, diplomat, soldier, is best known for his picaresque novel *El Buscón* (*The Rogue*) and his lyrics, though he also wrote religious tracts. When it came to editing his works, however, he recognized his religious material but rejected what are now considered his greatest literary achievements. "Ironically, those writings that Quevedo sought to withhold from public view during his own life-time and in some cases openly denounced (for example, the picaresque novel *El Buscón*, 'renounced at the request of the author, who does not recognize it as his own') are today the basis upon which we have constructed his reputation for 'authenticity' and 'originality', qualities undoubtedly privileged far less in the seventeenth century than in post-romantic culture."[20] The rejection is ambiguous, though. Outwardly, the author distances himself from those works and is at the same time confirmed as author by the publisher: "renounced at the request of the author."

Customs with regard to printing were changing. In the 17th century the veil aristocratic authors were using had grown thinner, but there were still many authors reluctant to openly appear as editor of their own works. Balthasar Gracián (1601-1658), a Jesuit, only wrote one work, on a religious subject, under his own name. His more worldly works, *Oraculo manual y arte de prudencia* (*The Art of Worldly Wisdom*) or *El Discreto* (*Prudent Man*), precepts on how to behave at court, which still enjoy a wide readership, were edited by and under the name of his brother Lorenzo. Pedro Calderón de la Barca (1600-1681), the famous playwright, also a courtier, started the edition of his works in 1636, but his brother Joseph acted as editor. It is known that Calderón supervised the edition by his brother, but he himself did not want to come into the open as such. It is very likely that Gracián also supervised the edition by his brother, but he did not publicly assume the editorship. The more one goes back into the 16th century, the more conspicious appears the "disregard" of Spanish authors for the edition of their works. Of the lyrics of Fray Luis de León (1527-1591) no authorized version exists. "This defective situation is common for our lyric poets of the Golden Age".[21] Juan Boscán (c. 1490-1542) translated Castiglione's *Book of the Courtier*, which is published under his own name. None of his own lyrics, however, were printed during his lifetime. Toward the end of his life he prepared what would be the posthumous edition of his lyrics (an unauthorized version was published shortly before his death).

Travelling the same road back in England's history one obtains a similar picture. In 1645 the poems of the courtier-poet Sir Edmund Waller (1606-1687) were published in his absence, Waller being in exile in France after an abortive conspiracy against Parliament. Back in 1651 he undertook no attempt to re-issue a corrected edition. It was not until 1664 that he gave his consent for a corrected version. Even then he did not figure as editor. It is the printer who wrote the preface. "When the author of these verses (written only to please himself, and such particular persons to whom they were directed) returned from abroad some years since, he was troubled to find his name in print; but somewhat satisfied to see his lines so ill rendered that he might justly disown them,... Having been ever since pressed to correct the many and gross faults (such as use to be in impressions wholly neglected by the authors) his answer was, that he made these when ill verses had more favour, and escaped better; ... These are the reasons which, for above twelve years past, he has opposed to our request;... Not so much moved with these reasons of ours (or pleased with our rhymes), as wearied with our importunity, he has at last given us leave to assure the reader, that the Poems which have been so long and so ill set forth under his name, are here to be found as he first writ them...".[22] In 1628 Lord

Brooke, better known as Sir Fulke Greville, died, apparently having spent many years preparing what would be a posthumous edition of his complete works.[23] Only one was published, surreptitiously and without his name on the title-page, during his lifetime. This was his closet drama *Mustapha* in 1609. Sir Philip Sidney disdained publication of any of his work during his lifetime, expressing contempt in his *Apology for Poetry* for those who cause their work to be printed. "Upon this necessarily follows, that base men with servile wits undertake it, who thinke it enough if they can be rewarded of the Printer:... so these men no more but setting their names to it, by their own disgracefulness, disgrace the most gracefull Poesie."[24]

In the epistle to the reader in the First Folio it is said that Shakespeare was prevented from overseeing his work by death. "Overseeing" would have been what the author Calderón did, certainly what Gracián would have done, and as Waller would have in 1664. In the dedication, however, it is stated that Shakespeare did not have the "fate to execute" his own writings, a phrase borrowed from testamentary language. Yet here there seems to be a contradiction: the overseer and the executor were not the same person, the former supervised or watched the latter. So while at first sight it could appear that the epistle simply repeats what had already been expressed in the dedication, in fact the dedication has put forward an entirely different idea:

"But since your L.L. have been pleas'd to think these trifles something, heretofore; and have been prosecuted both them, and their Author living, with so much favour: we hope, that (they outliving him, and he not having the fate, common with some, to be the executor to his own writings) you will use the like indulgence toward them, you have done unto their parent."

If we leave out the apposition "common with some" the contradiction disappears: Shakespeare did not have the fate to "execute" or to edit his own plays because of his untimely death. It is generally agreed that the editions of his two long poems *Venus and Adonis* (1593) and *The Rape of Lucrece* (1594) must have been carefully supervised by the poet. Thus we naturally conclude that he would have certainly wished to as fastidiously edit his plays in a volume of complete works but that he died before he could accomplish this. Yet we cannot ignore the apposition "common with some," and if we read it in context, logically, the meaning is that Shakespeare did not have the fate to edit his own work while alive; and, this fate is common to some. We should repeat: it is, according to the epistle's logic, common for some not to die before they can edit their work, for others it is not common not to die before they can edit their work: This is patently nonsensical: Death does not know such a custom. Yet here is the sensible truth conveyed by this apparently nonsensical declaration: it was indeed not common for courtiers to publish their literary works during their lifetime or altogether; but on the contrary, it was common for commoners to do so. As the author of *The Arte of English Poesie* observed: "And in her Majesty's time that now is are sprung up another crew of courtly makers, noblemen and gentlemen of her Majesty's own servants, who have written excellently well, as it would appear if their doings could be found out and made public with the rest, of which number is first that noble gentleman *Edward* Earl of Oxford."[25]

Why should it not have been common for Shakespeare of Stratford to be "the executor" of his own plays? As far as we know the question remains unanswered, and until now, unasked too.

s

Chapter II
Shakespeare: The Lord Chamberlain

"...And he by death departed from that right..."

"It had been a thing, we confess, worthy to have been wished, that the Author himself had liv'd to have set forth, and overseen his own writings; but since it hath bin ordain'd otherwise, and he by death departed from that right, we pray you do not envy his Friends, the office of their care, and paine, to have collected & publish'd them; and so to have publish'd them, as where (before) you were abus'd with diverse stolen and surreptitious copies, maimed, and deformed by the frauds and stealths of injurious impostors, that expos'd them: even those, are now offer'd to your view cur'd, and perfect of their limbs".

Heminges and Condell, from the preface to the First Folio

As we have seen, this statement in the epistle (addressed to "the great variety of readers") contradicts the language of the dedication, as the verb "to execute," used in the sense of 'edit,' is not meaningfully associated with "death." Yet the epistle tells us Shakespeare could not *oversee* the folio edition as death robbed him of that possibility, and most readers have understood this to be a confirmation of the statement in the dedication that Shakespeare did not have "the fate to execute" his writings. As we have shown in the preceding chapter, according to the logic of the dedication's language, Shakespeare was prevented from editing his own works in his lifetime not by death, but by his status as a courtier. The two verbs, "to execute" in the dedication, and "to oversee" in the epistle (each borrowed from testamentary language), denote *different* functions. It is only reasonable to conclude (especially in light of other distinctions of tone and content we have observed between the two parts of the preface), that by using a different verb and metaphor the author(s) of the dedication and the epistle intended to convey a *different* meaning in the two parts of the preface, respectively. In the will of Augustine Phillips, an actor and shareholder in Shakespeare's company, we find that there are appointed an executrix and overseers [emphases are ours]: "And I ordain and make the said Anne Phillips, my loving wife, sole **executrix** of this my present testament and last will, provided always that if the said Anne my wife do at any time marry after my decease, that then and from thenceforth she shall cease to be any more longer **executrix** of this my last will and testament. And that then and from thenceforth John Hemminges, Richard Burbage, William Slye and Timothy Whitehorne shall be fully and wholly my **executors** of this my last will and testament, as though the said Anne had never been named. And of the **execution** of this my present testament and last will I ordain and make the said John Hemminges, Richard Burbage, William Slye and Timothy Whitehorne **overseers** of this my present testament and last will."[26] Anne Phillips was to be 'overseen' by Hemmings, Burbage, Sly and Whitehorne; if she remarried, the overseers would become executors, and this was in fact what happened: Anne Phillips did remarry and thus ceased to be executrix. Now as we observed earlier, some authors were hindered by status from editing their own works but not from overseeing their editions, thus the messages in dedication and epistle are logically consistent: Shakespeare could not have edited his own works but he could have overseen the edition. From the former right he was barred by status, from the latter by death. Yet clearly the Stratford man's status would not have barred him from editing his own works, and all the evidence argues that he did not at any time oversee the folio edition of the Shakespeare plays.

Orthodox biographers tell us that Shakspere (as the man's name was often spelled) returned to Stratford after writing *The Tempest* in 1611, though little evidence exists for this assumption. Why he would have left London in 1611 and not in 1609, or 1613, is hardly clear. In 1613 he is mentioned in a legal record as residing in Stratford-on-Avon, but he is already living there according to a legal record of the previous year (the suit Bellott v. Mountjoy, to which he had been summoned as a witness). The details of this litigation need not concern us here, we only note the date the citizen of Stratford made his deposition, 11 May 1612, when he is clearly identified as "William Shakespeare of Stratford upon Avon".[27] Shakspere had then declared that he had known both plaintiff and defendant (the latter being the father-in-law of the former), but that he could not recall the exact year, stating that it was "ten years or so" ago. The action brought by Steven Bellot against his father-in-law was about the amount of the portion. Shakspere had acted as a go-between and somehow negotiated the portion at the request of his host Mountjoy. Stephen Bellott married Mary Mountjoy on 19 November 1604. At some time before November 1604 Shakspere must have lodged in Mountjoy's house. It was not his residence, however. One witness deposed that he "lay in that house", which implies that in 1603-4 Shakspere had no permanent abode in London. In every extant record between 1604 and 1612 Shakspere appears as citizen of Stratford: as in a document from early in 1611 about the Stratford tithes, a business in which Shakspere was heavily involved,[28] and also in 1609, when one "Willielmus Shackspeare" sues one "Johannem Addenbrooke" for a debt of £6.[29] He is again referred to as citizen of Stratford ("Stratford Burgus" and "Willielmus Shackspeare, burgus predicti"). He was not a London resident in 1603-4, and this fact is confirmed by another document dated 1602 in which he is identified as "William Shakespere of Stretford uppon Avon".[30] In February 1598 he was visited by inspectors on the suspicion of hoarding grain.[31] Evidence of grain-hoarding would presumably be assessed over some previous period of time, so it appears likely that his permanent residence was in Stratford some time before February 1598.

1597-1604

Thus, between 1597 and 1611 the documentary evidence is that Shakspere was domiciled in Stratford, not in London. Strangely, the only evidence for his ever having had a residence in the capital is found in the reports of the tax collectors in the autum of 1597 and the following years, and what we learn from them is that he no longer resided at that address.[32] Yet even if one grants the most favourable date, 1611, the information from the epistle seems without rhyme or reason if applied to the Stratford man. In the five remaining years before his death in 1616 he would have taken no action to provide authentic versions of the "maimed" texts, the so-called bad quartos; that is, between the year of his traditionally alleged departure from London and his death, he would have left it to his colleagues Heminges and Condell (and Burbage, who died in 1619) to gather his plays together and to restore them to their original state. If we take Heminges and Condell at their word and accept that this man was the poet Shakespeare, it was not death which "departed" the author from the right to oversee his work, it was supreme indifference or sheer neglect.

Nevertheless, there is evidence that the poet Shakespeare had at one time fully exercised his "right" to oversee his works, the right that Heminges and Condell say "death" took from him. In 1598 the text of *Love's Labour's Lost,* though poorly printed, was published in a consistent version, indicating that it was the author who corrected the text but had for some reason abstained from proofreading it. The play, as its title page states, was "Newly corrected and augmented by W. Shakespere" from a version now lost. In 1597 a bad text (Q1) was published of *Romeo and Juliet*. In 1599 a new edition of this play (Q2) was published as "Newly corrected, augmented, and amended". "The fairly full stage-directions of Q2, with notes for the use of properties, suggest an author's hand..."[33] In fact, between 1598 and 1604 a number of good texts were published, suggesting that they were printed from the author's manuscript or at least with his cooperation: *A Midsummer-Night's Dream* (1600), *The Merchant of Venice* (1600), *Much Ado About Nothing* (1600), *2 Henry IV* (1600), and, finally, the second edition (Q2) of *Hamlet* (1604), "Newly imprinted and enlarged to almost as much againe as it was, according to the true and perfect Coppie."

Shakespearean publication: What happened in 1604?

Let us consider this period of active revision, correction and amendment of Shakespearean texts between 1598 and 1604, and for the moment simply compare the lifespans of the two major claimants for the authorship of the canon (William Shakspere of Stratford and Edward de Vere, 17th Earl of Oxford), in relationship to the communication in the epistle of the First Folio. If the author were the Stratford player and shareholder, then he did actively correct and augment the editions until 1604 but afterwards lost any interest in them, though he lived on until 1616. The statement in the Folio becomes then a pious lie to avoid an embarrassing truth: the poet had grown so indifferent to his own works that he no longer felt inclined to correct "the frauds and stealths of injurious imposters," after 1604. Indeed, years before his plays became "orphans" they would have been left by the author in a "state of abandonment". Alternatively, if the author were Edward de Vere, he would have engaged in revision and correction of his plays published in quarto editions beginning in 1598 but would have been prevented from continuing to do so by his death in June 1604.

This would certainly explain why the stream of publication of Shakespeare's plays was suddenly interrupted at that time, and clearly Heminges and Condell would have been telling the truth when they wrote:

"It had been a thing, we confess, worthy to have been wished, that the Author himself had liv'd to have set forth, and overseen his own writings; but since it hath bin ordain'd otherwise, and he by death departed from that right…"

One man, a stationer, played a major role in the publication of Shakespeare's plays in the period 1598-1604. In July 1598 it is he who enters Shakespeare's *The Merchant of Venice* (his first-ever registration of a play) in the Stationers' Register. In the second half of 1604 he prints Shakespeare's *Hamlet* (his last printing of a play). Thus the period of James Roberts' involvement in the printing of Shakespeare's plays is more or less congruent with the period of the author's own overseeing of his works in quarto editions

James Roberts

Roberts received his freedom from the Stationers' Company in 1564. The end of the apprenticeship was fixed at the completion of the twenty-fourth year, regardless of how long before that date it had started. This was an educational measure the Common Council of London City had decreed in 1556 to prevent overhasty marriages of young people without adequate material means at the end of their apprenticeship.[34] It is therefore probable that James Roberts was born in 1540. As the minimum duration of apprenticeship was seven years and the possibility exists that he entered the apprenticeship after the age of seventeen, allowance must be made for a birthyear later by a few years. Since the 1570s he held, jointly with Richard Watkins, a lucrative privilege, a royal patent for the printing of *Almanacs and Prognostications*, renewed by the queen in 1589. In 1594 he acquired another lucrative privilege, the printing of the playbills formerly belonging to John Charlewood, whose widow Alice he had married. Another printer of Shakespearean works also succeeded to a printing business by marrying a widow. Richard Field, printer of *Venus and Adonis* and *The Rape of Lucrece,* married Jacqueline, widow of Thomas Vautrollier, and took over the latter's business and patents (privileges). This kind of marriage was not unfrequent and profited both husband and wife. The number of printers in London was restricted. A stationer who married the widow of an authorized printer acquired *eo ipso* this authorization himself. If, as in the case of Charlewood/Roberts and Vautrollier/Field, the husbands had been granted some privileges, the match was the more valuable. Both Jacqueline Vautrollier and Alice Charlewood are known to have done some printing in the wake of their husbands' death. This the Stationers' Company allowed for some time. After a while, however, widows, if they had no son who was a stationer, would have had to sell. The only sure way then to stay in the business was to remarry another stationer.

It is not until 1594 that we see James Roberts start printing noteworthy literary works (he had printed some ballads before). From 1594 on he is a prolific printer. He prints nearly all the poetry of Michael Drayton and Samuel Daniel, as well as the satires of John Marston, but not plays (apart from the anonymous *Arden of Feversham* in 1599 and Samuel Daniel's *Cleopatra*, though the latter was a "closet drama", not a stage production). Then, in 1600, we have a doubly dramatic turn, actually more of a U-turn, to dramatic literature.

It was A.W. Pollard in the first decades of the twentieth century who drew attention to the role of James Roberts in the publication of the plays belonging to the repertory of the Lord Chamberlain's Men, and who advanced the conception of James Roberts as an agent of this company.[35] Though the theory has been rejected by such eminent scholars as E. K. Chambers, Charles Sisson and others, it never gave way completely and seems to have found a biotope in the Arden editions of Shakespeare. In Pollard's own day the theory gained some momentum. Previously Roberts had been regarded as a piratical printer, one who procured and printed copy in plain disrespect of the proprietary rights of the author. Pollard demonstrated the extreme improbability, if not absurdity, of this view. He pointed to Roberts' close business relationship with the players as a printer of their playbills, making it unlikely that he would act against their interests which, according to Pollard, was to keep their plays unprinted for as long as possible. Apparently Pollard held the rather odd assumption that the potential reader of a play would be disinterested in doing so after seeing it performed onstage. As Peter W.M Blayney quipped, "For that theory to work, the market in printed plays would have to have been lively enough, and the plays themselves deadly enough, to create so many hundred disappointed readers in such a short time that their collective absence from the playhouse was noticeable."[36]

Nevertheless Pollard assigned a key role to James Roberts in the history of the publication of Shakespeare's plays, and highlighted some occurrences which those scholars who have justly rejected his overall interpretation have unjustly neglected to re-interpret. In formulating his theory Pollard was led by two concerns. First of all he wanted to demonstrate that the versions of Shakespearean texts that have come down to us are for the most part in 'good' quarto editions because the players had successfully prevented the unscrupulous from pirating them. The other factor which informed Pollard's theory was that between 1598 and 1604 James Roberts entered five plays from the repertory of the Lord Chamberlain's Men in the Stationers' Register but either did not print them at all or protracted their publication. Of the five plays performed by the Lord Chamberlain's Men he entered, one is lost, while two were printed respectively two and six years later by others. Entering the texts gave Roberts control over publishing and, as he was a printer, the right to print them. It must be understood that the publisher was generally another stationer than the printer, and it was the publisher who owned the right of publishing. We want to avoid the term "copyright" here, as this could prompt the reader to form the incorrect representation that this right (granted by the Stationers' Company) was more or less the same as a modern copyright. It was not, it was in the very etymological sense a right to copy, literally to multiply the work the publisher had entered in the Stationers' Register, but it did not encompass all the rights attached to the modern notion of copyright.[37]

The five plays of the repertory of the Chamberlain's Men that Roberts entered in the Stationers' Register are: 1) On 27 May 1600 the anonymous *A Morall of Clothe Breeches and Velvet Hose*. This play was almost certainly based on Robert Greene's *Quip for an Upstart Courtier*.[38] It is not known whether it was ever printed. If so, it is no longer extant. It was entered upon the condition of getting "further authority"; 2) On 29 May 1600 he entered *Allarum to London.*, also an anonymous play. Again, more authority was required by the wardens of the Stationers' Company, "PROVIDED that yt be not printed without further Aucthoritie"; the play was printed two years later but not by Roberts. 3) On 22 July 1600 he entered Shakespeare's *The Merchant of Venice*; again the entry was conditional, not on the obtention of "further authority" but of the "license of the Lord Chamberlain" to print it; it was printed by Roberts in the last quarter of 1600. 4) on 26 July 1602 he entered *Hamlet*; this time no condition was imposed, not explicitly at least; Roberts printed it toward the end of 1604. Yet a much abridged and altered version had been printed in 1603 by Valentine Sims for the publishers Nicholas Ling and John Trundle. We will later examine how this was possible. 5) on 7 February 1603 he entered *Troilus and Cressida* "in a full Court holden this day" on the condition to print it "when he hath gotten sufficient authority for it"; he never printed that; it was re-registered and printed in 1609. Of these five plays he published none and printed only two: Shakespeare's *The Merchant of Venice* and *Hamlet*, but with the considerable delay of over two years, a rare phenomenon in the printing trade. This caught Pollard's attention. Though Roberts did not publish the plays, by entering them he could control their date of publication. This manoeuvre can best be observed from his handling of *The Merchant of Venice*. He registered it on 22 July 1598, assigned the right to Thomas Hayes on 28 October 1600 and printed it the same year (it is even possible he had already printed it when Thomas Hayes received the right to publish). It is not known when he transferred his right in *Hamlet* to Nicholas Ling for whom he printed it in 1604. Roberts' record as publisher is a poor one:

"Roberts's name appears in the imprints of about 150 known books, but in the great majority of cases it is as printer, not as publisher. During the years 1593 to 1606 he made only ten entries in the Stationers' Register apart from the plays already mentioned and an assignment of Charlewood's stock. Among them were three copies that belonged to the Stationers' Company and that he printed to its order or by its leave, one that he eventually printed for someone else, and one that seems to have been a song or ballad. We are left with only five copies of any substance over a period of fourteen years. Another five of the sort he issued without entrance, but not all of these were certainly his original copies. It is clear that Roberts was mainly a trade-printer, printing books for other stationers and only occasionally venturing on a serious publication of his own."[39]

Why did Roberts register these five plays from the repertory of the Lord Chamberlain's Men, and not the other six plays from the same repertory entered between 1599 and 1603? We note that all of the latter six were printed within a few months after entrance. Nothing can be stated about *Cloth Breeches*, which is lost. But the four others, all entered by James Roberts, were only printed after over two years. Here is the remarkable fact which Pollard saw and which apparently he alone had thus far thought important: Roberts was a dilatory registerer of plays. On this cognition Pollard built his theory of the "conditional blocking entries". According to Pollard, Roberts created this delay in three instances by having the wardens of the company require "further/

sufficient authority" and in one case, the license of the Lord Chamberlain. Only *Hamlet* would be an "unconditional entry".

On the face of it this might appear a lucid insight but in reality it was a hotchpotch. What was "sufficient authority" and whose authority was deemed sufficient? Article 4 of the Star Chamber Decree of 23 June 1586, the first comprehensive press act in English history, had vested the power of licensing for the press in the Archbishop of Canterbury and the Bishop of London. In 1588 this power of licensing was extended to their deputies, in most cases clerics, among others: Abraham Hartwell, the secretary of the Archbishop of Canterbury, later Samuel Harsnett, chaplain to the Bishop of London. Zachariah Passfield, a prebendary of St Paul's, was another frequent licensor. When the wardens required "further authority", or "sufficient authority" it always meant that the book in question had not yet been examined by one of these episcopal censors. In the case of *Alarum for London, A Moral of Cloth Breeches and Velvet Hoses* and of *Troilus and Cressida* it was what the wardens required James Roberts to do: to submit it to an episcopal censor before printing it. The "full court" which requested such authority for *Troilus and Cressida* is the Court of Assistants, the governing body of the Stationers' Company. A Court of Assistants was the governing body of every London livery company: drapers, ironmongers, etc. The organization of the medieval and early modern corporation was, in fact, not so very different from that of a modern corporation. The Court of Assistants can be readily likened to the modern board of directors, the master and the two wardens (upper warden and under warden) to the management in charge of the day-to-day business. The wardens, elected annually at the end of June or the beginning of July, were *ex officio* members of the Court of Assistants and remained so after the end of their term. No mystery or extraordinary circumstance need be sought to explain this licensing by the Court of Assistants and their request of "sufficient authority" It means no more than that the Court of Assistants just happened to be holding a session that day. In 1599 the same happened eight times; in 1600, two; in 1601 and 1602, five times each; and in 1603, four times. Nor should we suppose the requirement of "sufficient authority" is unusual. Several entries show such a requirement. It is, as stated above, absent from the entry of *Hamlet*. However, the trivial reason why no further authority was required for *Hamlet* is that this had already been obtained. The play had been perused by the episcopal censor Zachariah Passfield. It would not make sense to ask James Roberts to submit the play to an episcopal censor when he had already done so before presenting it to the wardens. However tiresome, it is worthwhile to dwell a little longer on this triviality, for even today the spectre of A.W. Pollard's "conditional blocking entries" is haunting some quarters. Even a careful editor like Harold Jenkins was dazzled by Pollard's theory[40] and E.K. Chambers, though he rejected it, was not entirely immune to Pollard's terminological concoctions, to the point that he once adopts the term coined by Pollard: "That his other entries, except in the case of *Hamlet*, were conditional, is hardly relevant. They are not, like that for *Merchant of Venice*, distinguishable in form from many entries by other publishers, in which the further authority required was pretty clearly the allowance of an episcopal licenser."[41] To be precise, when Roberts presented the manuscript of *Hamlet* to the wardens of the Stationers' Company for entrance, it bore the signature of an episcopal censor for approval, the *Imprimatur*. Consequently it is illogical to call the entry of *Hamlet* an "unconditional" one. The condition which the full court of the Stationers' Company required to fulfill **after** entrance of *Troilus & Cressida* was the same which Roberts had already fulfilled for *Hamlet* **before** entrance. It is true, though, that unlike their earlier policy, during the period of 1601-1603 the wardens more often requested that a work not yet submitted to an episcopal censor (referred to as "authority") be submitted to them. It was the end of the reign and political nervosity was mounting. The wardens were less inclined to incur risks by letting a work pass without legal authorization (which they could and often did). On 1 June 1599, a few days after Roberts' entrances of *Alarum for London* and *A Moral of Cloth Breeches and Velvet Hoses* the Archbishop ordered the Stationers' Company to burn all the works of Thomas Nashe and Gabriel Harvey, the satires of John Marston, Marlowe's translation of Ovid's *Elegies* and a number of other works.

We have stated that the Star Chamber Decree of 1586 had vested the licensing power for the press in the Archbishop of Canterbury and the Bishop of London, and have used the same word "license" in connection with the wardens of the Stationers' Company. Indeed, the entry of *Hamlet* was done under the hand of Master Passfield, a censor, and of Simon Waterson, then under warden, as well. The two licenses, the one of the censors and the other of the Stationers' Company are entirely independent of one another. Yet, it is useful to deal with this issue when we come to the entry of *The Merchant of Venice*, which, as Chambers points out, is of a different nature than the four others; and for us first to return to Pollard's theory on James Roberts' role. Pollard remains entirely silent on how Roberts could have "enticed" the wardens into requiring "further authority". What is undeniably true is that Roberts waited an unusually long time to print *The Merchant of Venice*, *Hamlet*, and *Troilus and Cressida*, which play he had still not printed when he went out of business in 1606 or 1608. Thus it might be that Pollard was onto something about Roberts, as indeed we believe he was.

The stayed plays in August 1600

Pollard was also correct in his observation that it was James Roberts the stationer who on 4 August 1600 tried to enter four plays, three of them by Shakespeare. The four were: *Much Ado About Nothing*, *Henry V*, *As You Like It*, and Ben Jonson's *Every Man in His Humour*. The plays were 'stayed,' and Pollard saw this is as another successful attempt by the players to prevent the printing of their plays, grossly ignoring that one of the plays, *Henry V*, was registered only ten days later in a version which fulfills his own criterion of an out-and-out 'bad quarto,' and possibly already printed at its registration. "Here we have the 'Lord Chamberlen's men' themselves taking action with the Stationers' Company direct, despite the fact that they had no status in it, to protect their own property. The fact that the Stationers permitted them to do this is significant of the influence which as the Lord Chamberlain's servants they possessed..."[42].

Regardless of Pollard's botched attempt to explain the role of Roberts, it certainly seems important enough to deserve more attention than it has hitherto received. If he actually were the stationer who presented the four stayed plays to the wardens for registration, at least nine plays of the Lord Chamberlain's Men's repertory would have gone through his hands between 1598 and 1603 (three plays by others, but at least six plays by Shakespeare). Some more non-Shakespearean plays of the Lord Chamberlain's Men were entered in that period, but only three more plays of Shakespeare: *A Midsummer Night's Dream* and *2, Henry IV*, both good texts, and the bad text of *The Merry Wives of Windsor*. As a rule, good texts presuppose a certain degree of cooperation by the author, but the possibility that James Roberts was acting as an agent of Shakespeare himself has never been examined. The possibility that he was acting as agent of the Chamberlain's Men, as Pollard hypothesized, has been rightly rejected. The stayed plays of August 1600, with which Pollard sought further to vindicate his theory, falsify it. Had Pollard looked into the Stationers' Register for the entries in August 1600 he would have seen that, far from being prevented from printing, two of the plays (*Every Man in His Humour*, *Henry V*) were orderly entered 10 days later, one (*Much Ado*) was entered nineteen days later. One (*As You Like It*), was not entered and was for the first time printed in 1623. Jonson's *Everyman in His Humour* was printed in 1601, *Henry V* and *Much Ado* in 1600, the same year. Moreover, as stated above, *Henry V* was a "bad quarto". In 1960 C. J. Sisson wrote :

"I have little doubt that the 'entry' of the 4 August 1600 on a spare leaf of Register C is a mere memorandum of the Clerk's and not an entry, and that the words 'to be staied' mean that the desired entry is to await further consideration. The absence of any Stationer's name from the margin is significant. A provisional entry would certainly impede any subsequent, alternative claim to the same 'copy' or 'book' by another Stationer. It is difficult to see any necessity for interpreting the entries in question as evidence that Roberts, for instance, was a mere agent of the Lord Chamberlain's Men in a device to prevent the entry of copies of their plays to other Stationers desirous of printing them. The problem obviously requires more detailed examination than can be given here, but it cannot yet be taken as settled."[43]

At this juncture it may be useful to look at this fly-leaf, at the same time noting Sissons´ remark that the entry had to await "further consideration."

	My lord chamberlens menns plaies Entred
27 may 1600	
To master	*Viz*
Robertes	*A moral of ´clothe breches and velvet hose´*
[See *p.*161.]	
	Allarum to London/
27 May	
[1600]	[The next entry has nothing to do with the preceding. The ink of it is now of a different colour.]
To hym [*i.e.*	
J. **Robertes**.	
See *p.* 161.]	

4. August [1600]

[The year is fixed by the subsequent entries at *pp.* 169 and 170.]

As you like yt/a booke |

HENRY *the* FFIFT/a booke |

[See *pp.* 169	*Every man in his humour*/a booke	
and 204]	to be staied
	The commedie of ´muche A doo	
[See *p.* 169]	*About nothing´*
	/a booke
[See *p.* 170]	

Peter W. M. Blayney has remarked about Pollard´s theory, "But no matter how flimsy the narrative has proved when subjected to scholarly scrutiny, as a story it has proved all too durable. Like a folktale, it continues to surface in whole or in part in most introductory accounts of the relations between the early theatre and the book trade."[44] The problem of the stayed plays "cannot be taken as settled", Sisson wrote in 1960. The subject continues to puzzle scholars. What happened on 4 August 1600? In 1997 Blayney undertook another attempt at explaining it:

> "Having written out the registration ("provided that [Roberts] is not to putt it in prynte Without further & better Aucthority" [Arber, 3:161], the Stationers' clerk, Richard Collins, did something unprecedented. He turned to the beginning of the register, wrote the heading, "my lord chamberlens mens plaies Entred" at the top of a blank flyleaf, and made a brief entry below it: the date, Roberts's name, and the title of the play (3:37). When Roberts provisionally registered a second play two days later, after writing the registration itself Collins turned back to his list in its original form – but what is significant is that he started it at all. Its purpose was probably to keep track of an expected string of provisional entries, so that whenever the required "Aucthority" for one of the plays was produced, he could find the list as finding aid. But even its precise purpose is relatively unimportant; what matters is that on May 27 Collins heard something – presumably from Roberts the playbill printer – that made him expect the imminent arrival of enough Chamberlain's plays to make a list desirable. As things turned out, only eight of the plays registered during the second glut belonged to the Lord Chamberlain's Men – but the significance of the list and its heading lies not in the outcome but in the expectation. The single play that Roberts brought in on May 27 was correctly recognized as the first of many."[45]

Blayney's explanation is perhaps not a "folktale" but it is not satisfactory either. First, many entries were subjected to obtaining further authority. Why should the clerk have made a special list in this case as a "finding aid"? The entries were all listed chronologically in the register of entries and easy to find. Moreover, the fact that some orderly entries were sometimes cancelled after months due to a prior right of another stationer indicates that the wardens and/or the Court of Assistants regularly checked the register for duplicate entries. Then, the procedure of evidencing that authority had been obtained was the same as in the case of assignments from one stationer to another. Either the transferor could orally witness to the transferee before the court or the transferee had to present to the court a signed declaration of assignment. An entry of November 23, 1602 to Walter Dight "but not to be printed untill he bringe further Aucthoritie for yt"[46] suggests that the stationer had to "bring" the authority, to come to Stationers' Hall in order to prove that he had obtained the requested authority (in cases where this authority was received soon after entrance, it was added to the entry; in the great majority of cases no such note was added). In another entry the process of proving authority is more completely described:

15 Januarij [1588][47]

Edward Aldee	Entred unto him *the first foure bookes of AMADIS de Gaule* To be translated into English and so to be printed for his copie so that he first get it to be lawfully and orderly allowed as tolerable to be printed and Do shew[e] aucthoritie thereof at a Court to be holden.

Secondly, what was the "authority" status of the six plays and what was requested for each of them? Nothing permits the assumption that the four stayed plays were written down on a fly-leaf[48] because the authorization by the censors was outstanding. Blayney, like Pollard, seems not to have noted what the ulterior fate of the stayed plays was. Jonson's play had already been authorized by an episcopal censor when it was entered on August 14 and , in all likelihood, had already obtained this authorization on August 4, when James Roberts presented it for entrance. No further authority at all was required by the wardens for the two other plays, *Much Ado* and *Henry V*. It is important to note that two were **not** stayed; their status was different from the four stayed plays. It was for the two plays that had been duly entered into the register that further authority was required. For them Roberts did have the publishing right; on the contrary, the publishing right of the four other plays was held in suspension by the stay.

A key to the solution is offered by Sisson's remark that the "desired entry was to await further consideration". When the wardens of the Stationers' Company ordered a stay it was evidently in cases which fell within the purview of their specific responsibility, the right of a stationer to a copy, the publisher's copyright. A stay meant that there was a contest over such rights and it had to be "further considered" by the Court of Assistants. "Further consideration" was also requested in another case. On June 1602 the copyright of the stationer John Barnes for Riding's dictionary is suspended and a remark is added "to be further considered of". Indeed, on 6 December 1602 it was definitively entered to John Barnes by a full court.[49] However, when several works were presented at the same time, either for first registration or transfer, the Court of Assistants not only checked the books presented for entry or transfer that day but added to the lot recent entries, if any, by the same stationer. On 3 November 1600 were entered to the stationer Hugh Astley a number of works first entered to him on 1 March 1596 but crossed out afterwards, because Astley was not a member of the Stationers' Company by then (he was translated from the Drapers' Company to the Stationers' Company in July 1600).[50] On 3 November, 1600 they were definitively entered to him by the Court of Assistants.[51] On 11 August 1600 Astley had separately received the copyright for *Belvedere, the Garden of the Muses*.[52] On 3 November 1600 this single work, separately entered about twelve weeks before, was added to the lot checked by the Court of Assistants. In the same way, the two works Roberts had entered about ten weeks before 4 August 1600 were put together with those presented for entry but stayed that day. If it were not James Roberts who had presented the four stayed plays, it would not be the two plays recently entered to him which would have been joined with them. The different status of the two plays and the four stayed plays is clearly marked out. The four stayed plays are joined by a brace, the two plays are outside it. For the latter, orderly entered, James Roberts possessed the right. The lack of authority had no impact on this right which Roberts could only lose if another stationer proved to have an older right in it. Because he had the right in these two plays, his name was written in front of them. Because he had not yet a right in the stayed plays, his name was not placed in front of them. This indicates that the six plays had been written on a fly-leaf in order to submit the case to the decision of the Court of Assistants.[53] Why was it ultimately not done? It is, again, the date of 14 August which should retain our attention. On that date there are three entries. Two of them were signed by both wardens, Thomas Dawson and Edward White. The formula of the third entry is very unusual. Whereas all other entries of the day were licensed by both wardens, this entry was licensed by only one of the wardens to Thomas Pavier:

"by Direction of master White, warden, under his handwriting."

The clause "These Copies following being things formerly printed and set over to the said Thomas Pavier" clearly suggests that the fact of being formerly printed and transferred was considered to constitute a copyright for all these plays among which was *Henry V*. It was Pavier's copyright which had been opposed to James Roberts on 4 August 1600 and had caused the staying of the plays. The other warden, Thomas Dawson, seems to have been reluctant to accept it. Why was Edward White pressing ahead? Thomas Pavier and Edward White were partners for at least one play: *Titus Andronicus*, a play James Roberts printed the same year for Edward White alone (perhaps in compensation). On 10 April 1602 there is a registration of the copyright transfer of three books by John Myllington to Thomas Pavier, among them *Titus Andronicus* and the first and second part of *Henry VI*, that is the *Contention Between the Houses of Lancaster and York*.[54] Furthermore, among the copies assigned to Pavier was *The Spanish Tragedy*, which had been Edward White's copy since 1599 when it was assigned to him by Abel Jeffes.[55] Edward White used his function as under warden to protect the publishing right of his occasional partner Thomas Pavier in *Henry V*. There was no intervention of an invisible hand, there was instead the well-seen hand of Edward White. Above all there was no attempt by the players to protect their property, as Pollard, in a cascade of exhortative phrases, proclaimed.

Why was *As You Like It* withdrawn, and not entered until November 1623? It was certainly not this play which caused the stay. No other publishing right was opposed to it as in the case of *Henry V*. *AYLI* was most likely returned by James Roberts to the author Shakespeare. As to the reason, we can only speculate.

Walter W. Greg´s prophetic soul

Far from proving the influence of the players with the Stationers´ Company and their success in stopping the printing of the plays, the case of the four stayed plays dramatically underscores the futility of Pollard´s theory. And yet, despite his "folktale", his bungling of logic, his "conditional blocking entries" pieced together from different materials, Walter W. Greg, in his last publication, paid this tribute to his former mentor A.W. Pollard:

> "It cannot be said that, taken individually, there is much in the form of Roberts´s registrations to suggest that they are ´blocking entries´, and the critics of Pollard´s theory have perhaps had the best of it. But when we look at the situation as a whole we get a somewhat different impression. Let me repeat. Here we have a man, known to have been in touch with the players, but who never before or after concerned himself with dramatic copy, making, over a period of five years, five entrances of plays belonging to one particular company..."[56]

Was Greg´s warning that in the end Pollard might not have been completely amiss merely a pious commemoration, an attempt to rescue Pollard´s credit? Or was it the expression of a sincere feeling that the last word might not yet have been spoken? Six more plays of the Chamberlain´s Men were entered in the period 1598-1603, but not by Roberts. Three or more works from the repertory of the Chamberlain´s Men, now the King´s Men, were entered after 1603, but none by Roberts. Roberts continued registrating works in the register after that date, three in all. It is perplexing that no scholar, in particular Greg himself, has ever taken note of another striking connection of Roberts´ endeavours, either with respect to the Lord Chamberlain´s Men and their plays or in relationship to Shakespeare and his plays. After 1604 Roberts, in the remaining two or four years he was in business, never again concerned himself with dramatic copy. If we look at Roberts´ history of printing as set out in the table in Appendix IV (set up from Vol. V of Arber's transcript), we see Roberts' printings from 1594, when he started with literary works, up until 1604. There is a marked shift in 1600. Between then and 1604 Roberts seems to have almost uniquely concentrated on the printing of Shakespeare. He printed hardly anything else. Even the miscellany *England's Helicon* of 1600 is not unrelated to Shakespeare, as it contains a correction of William Jaggard's *Passionate Pilgrim* (published in the previous year). Two poems ascribed by Jaggard to Shakespeare are grouped in *England's Helicon* with a song from *Love's Labour's Lost,* and assigned to "Ignoto". Another poem ascribed to Shakespeare in *The Passionate Pilgrim* is reassigned to Christopher Marlowe, followed by two others signed "Ignoto".[57]

The printer James Roberts did not act as an agent of the Lord Chamberlain's Men but on behalf of their main author Shakespeare.

In the remaining years he was in business James Roberts never concerned himself again with the company that the Lord Chamberlain's Men had become, the King's Men, nor with Shakespeare. Edward de Vere had died in June 1604. Then or soon afterwards Roberts started the printing of *Hamlet*. We have seen that Roberts' involvement in the printing and publishing of Shakespeare's plays coincides with the period the author was overseeing editions of his plays. The fact that in the remaining years he was in business Roberts never printed *Troilus and Cressida* suggests that between 1600-1604 he only printed what Shakespeare wished him to, and that after 1604 he was no longer receiving orders because the author had "been departed from the right to oversee his own writings."

And that the epistle to the *First Folio* spoke true.

The entry of The Merchant of Venice

On 22 July 1598 James Roberts paid sixpence to the Stationers' company for the entrance of Shakespeare's *Merchant of Venice*. The entry reads:

xxijo Iulij 1598
Iames Robertes./Entred for his copie under the handes of bothe the wardens, a booke of the Marchaunt of Venyce or otherwise called the Iewe of Venyce./ Provided that yt bee not printed by the said Iames Robertes; or anye other whatsoever without lycence first had from the Right honorable the lord Chamberlen vjd

As in the case of *Troilus and Cressida,* and contrary to *Hamlet,* the play had not been submitted before to an episcopal censor, but no "further authority" was required by the wardens. A few weeks before, new wardens had been elected. Isaac Bing as upper warden and William Ponsonby as under warden were serving their one-year term. William Ponsonby was Spensers's and Sidney's publisher. It may be due either to him or to Bing or to both that the second title of the play, *The Jew of Venice,* was mentioned in the entry, precluding any duplicate entry resulting from a different title. Such a mishap had occurred three years before to Ponsonby. On 29 November 1594 he had entered Sir Philip Sidney's *The Defence of Poesy.* This manuscript was also known under the title *An Apology for Poetry,* and it was under this title that Henry Olney had entered the work on 12 April 1595. "Both entries were made under the same Wardens' hands, which might be thought to imply some lack of vigilance but the titles differed and the second did not name the author. The identity was not discovered till after Olney's edition at least had appeared; but that no blame was imputed is clear from the terms under which the second entry was cancelled: 'This belongeth to Mr. Ponsonby by a former entrance, and an agreement is made between them whereby Mr. Ponsonby is to enjoy the copy.'"[58] The wardens from July 1594 to July 1595 were Gabriel Cawood, upper warden, and Isaac Bing, under warden. Thus both Bing, as warden, and Ponsonby, as publisher, were aware of the potential fallacies lurking in double titles. Without the mention of the second title it was by no means assured that another stationer would not register and print the same play under the title *The Jew of Venice.* The risk was minimal during Bing and Ponsonby's term, but in the event Roberts would wait more than one year — as he did — the next wardens would possibly not notice that the play had already been entered to Roberts. It was unusual for a publisher to delay printing for so long a time; generally, a book was printed within 3 months after entrance. But Roberts did wait over two years, and given the precaution taken, it seems as if he anticipated the possibility of entrance under another title. Of course, as in the the the case of Sidney's *Apology of Poetry*, the error would have become manifest after the publishing of *The Jew of Venice* by the other stationer. However, the desire of the Lord Chamberlain not to see any version of the play printed before he had given his consent would have been bypassed. This could not happen in the case of *The Merchant of Venice*. The next wardens would know that *The Merchant of Venice* and *The Jew of Venice* were one and the same play and that the right in it was James Roberts'. Shakespeare's play was safe-guarded against printing at an earlier date than the Lord Chamberlain would allow. If so, we note, the clause "that it be not printed by the said James Roberts or any other whatsoever without license first had from the Right Honorable the Lord Chamberlain" is puzzlingly redundant. The possibility that any other stationer could have printed it seems to have been ruled out by the modalities of the entry. As Chambers remarked in objection to Pollard's theory, "an unconditional entry would have served Professor Pollard's assumed purpose as well."[59] The remark implies, though, that Roberts' right was beyond contest, once the copy was entered to him. Why then this additional clause that Roberts had to have the license of the Lord Chamberlain before printing and that neither any other stationer should print it?

We must first ask: from whom did the wardens and the clerk, who registered it, receive the information that the Lord Chamberlain alone would determine the date of printing? Leo Kirschbaum, after having noted that the entry is unusual, recurred to the following makeshift: "When Roberts entered the play he must have brought a warrant from the Lord Chamberlain that the play was never to be published without the latter's consent."[60] This hypothesis is not plausible. As Greg observes: "When later the book-entries were taken over by the Clerk the procedure became more formal, and we then find Collins [the clerk] duly recording some licenses as contained in covering letters or given by word of mouth. Thus in 1589 two copies were 'allowed by a letter or note under Mr. Hartwell's hand' and another two entered 'upon the Bishop of London's letters in that behalf directed'; in 1584 a copy was 'allowed by th'Archbishop of Canterbury by testimony of the Lord Chenie and in 1587 two were 'authorized' by the same 'as reported by Mr. Cosin'."[61] Had there been a written warrant by the Lord Chamberlain the wardens would have acknowledged it, either as a note beneath the entry or in the records of the Court of Assistants.[62] The only plausible premise is that James Roberts himself instructed the wardens of the company "by word of mouth". Then, unfortunately, the clause is doubly redundant. If Roberts told the wardens he had to wait for the license or permission of the Lord Chamberlain, why was it necessary to state that Roberts himself should not print the play till the Lord Chamberlain had given his consent? This would have been a matter solely concerning the Lord Chamberlain and James Roberts, not the Stationers' Company. Was there perhaps another reason why the clause was necessary in this form to prevent any earlier printing by another stationer?

But what is meant by "the license of the Lord Chamberlain"? The licensing *power* lay with the Archbishop of Canterbury and with the Bishop of London or their deputies, the censoring authorities, controlling the conformity of a work with the political, religious and moral order. When the wardens used phrases such as "further authority" or "better authority" for a book not yet submitted to the censors it is to this episcopal authority they refer, as appears from the following entries on 4 January 1602:

Master Man	Entred for his Copye under th[e h]andes of master PASFEILD and master **Seaton** warden A booke Called *A Defence of Tobacco*...
Master Man	Entered for his Copye under the lyke Aucthoritie *Tenne sermons* of master BURTONS *uppon... the 6 Chap[ter] of MATTHEWE*...

As the wardens could not know in advance which censor would peruse the book, the requirement of "further authority" was always indefinite.

In the case of *MoV*, however, it was the license, the permission of the Lord Chamberlain that was required, which, as E.K. Chambers remarked, is different from the "normal conditional entries".[63] The Lord Chamberlain reserved the right to decide when the play would go into print. This license had nothing to do with the episcopal *Imprimatur*.

Neither was it the license granted by the wardens, which was nothing more than the granting of the publishing right to one stationer as against the right of any other, today commonly called (but as seen, not wholly exactly), the copyright. This license was totally independent of the episcopal license. The publishing right was created by the permission given by the wardens or sometimes the Court of Assistants of the Stationers' Company. Once entered, the lack of episcopal authority was no bar to this license. In 1603, for instance, James Roberts acquired the publishing right of *Troilus and Cressida* and could print it as soon as he had the authorization of an episcopal censor. Even in the event another stationer later presented the same play authorized by a censor before Roberts showed his authorization to the Stationers' Company, the authority obtained by this other stationer would have attached to Roberts' right, as is expressly stated in the following entry:

John Trundell yf he gett sufficient Aucthoritie. for. *The copy of A letter sent from a gent[leman] of the report of the Late bloody fight at sea betwene the Spaniardes and the Hollanders before Dover.* And shewe his aucthority to the wardens Then yt is to be entred for his copy/Or yf any other bringe the Aucthority. yet it is to be the said **John Trundelles** copy...

We can even find cases in which a copyright for which the authority requested by the wardens had not yet been delivered was transferred to another stationer. "Moreover copyright in a book for which the enterer was still to acquire authority was transferable. On August 1, 1603 (III, p. 243), John Hardy entered a copy and paid the fee of sixpence. The condition 'Provided that yt be licensed' appears. On August 9, he assigned this copy to Pavier, 'The seid Thomas pavier to have the same in the lyke manner that it is entred to John hardy' (III, p. 244)."[64]

The authority of the Lord Chamberlain must have been of some other kind. Besides the legal authority of the episcopal censors two other extra-legal sources of authority, existed. First, some discretion was left to the wardens of the company themselves. They could decide that no authority was required for certain books, thereby themselves authorizing it by implication. This is what happened in the case of *The Merchant of Venice*. The wardens did not require Roberts to submit the play to an episcopal censor before printing it.

The other source of authority was that of "experts", as Greg aptly terms it.[65] It was an authority closely related to the specific office. Such an "expert" was, for instance, Sir Thomas Smith (ca. 1558-1625), from 1609-1620 treasurer of the Virginia Company. On 24 February 1612 the following entrance was made[66]:

Master Welbye.	Entred for his Copy under th[e h]andes of Sir THOMAS SMITHE knighte and Master **Lownes** warden, A booke or thinge called, *The publicacon of the lotary* [*i.e.* lottery] *for Virginia*...

The wardens had no reason not to accept the publication of a lottery for a company of which Smith was the treasurer and one of the founders; nor the authority of the French ambassador in December 1590 for reports on the civil wars in his country;[67] nor the joint authority of the Archbishop of Canterbury, the Lord Admiral, the Lord Chamberlain of Her Maiesties House in October 1590 for the entrance of *The tables and mappes of the Spaniardes pretendid Invasion*.[68] It must be stressed that in each case this kind of "expert" authorization was attached to the document or book before it was presented for entrance; in no case did the wardens refer to such an authority when they required "further authority" (or "lawful", "sufficient", etc.). However, even such "expert authority" could be judged insufficient by the wardens and required by them to be supplemented by "sufficient authority". A case in point is the licensing of plays for the press by the Master of the Revels from 1607 to mid 1637. This licensing was based on no formal authority, but on the Master's licensing power of plays for the stage, for which he did possess official authority. Even so, from 1607-1637 the Master's formal authority only attached to the licensing for the stage and did not displace the formal authority of the episcopal censors. Otherwise it would be inconceivable that certain plays were still licensed by episcopal licensors, the most notorious case being the licensing by Dr. Worrall in November 1623 of the remainder of Shakespeare's plays to be (for the first time) printed in the *First Folio*. In November 1621 the wardens required "more sufficient authority" for a romance (not a play) of the famous Spanish playwright Lope de Vega licensed by the Master of the Revels (Sir George Buc).[69] Further, had the Master of the Revels possessed, for the press, formal and not just factual authority tolerated by the wardens, it would not have been possible to withdraw it from him after enactment of the Second Chamber Decree of 11 July 1637 without explicit reassignment, and by simply renewing the provisions regarding licensing of plays of the Star Chamber Decree of 1586. "Thus the decree of 1637, by merely reaffirming the provisions of 1586, put an abrupt end to the activities of the Master of the Revels as a licenser of plays for press, from which we may conclude that these activities lacked official sanction."[70]

Thus, in the case of *The Merchant of Venice,* it was not the license of the Stationers' Company, the publishing right, which was required. This had been granted by the wardens Bing and Ponsonby. Neither was it the *Imprimatur*, the formal authority of an episcopal censor. In this case the clause would have been "provided he get sufficient authority", as it was, for instance, for *Troilus and Cressida*. It was not the license of the Master of the Revels or his superior the Lord Chamberlain of the Royal Household. What sort of licensing authority could this license of the Lord Chamberlain then have been?

Another source of authority must now also be considered: that of the author himself. It cannot be ruled out *a priori* that indeed it was the author's authority upon which the Lord Chamberlain's claim was based. Far from being a non-entity in the publishing process, we shall soon see that the author did possess a kind of veto right.

The authority of the author

That the Stationers' Company recognized certain authorial rights is apparent from several records in the Court Books B and C and the book of entries, the part of the Stationer's Registers reserved for the registration of books, *e.g.* from the following entry of 11 March 1607:

John	Entred for his copie under the handes of the wardens. a
Browne	book called *musicke of sundry Kyndes* sett forthe in Two
	Bookes &c Composed by THOMAS FFORD

> yt is agreed 13 marcij *Anno supradicto* [1607]. that this copye shall never hereafter be printed agayne without the consent of master FFORD the Aucthour
>
> **John Browne**

Clearly, the author has made the reprinting of his work dependent upon his consent. Yet it is not the author who addresses the wardens, it is instead the owner of the copy, the publisher John Brown, who declares that he needs the consent of the author. The addition is a memorandum. More similar memoranda can be found in the book of entries. The word "memorandum" is sometimes explicitly stated. As in an entry of 22 September 1628:

> "Entred for his Copie under the handes of Master THOMAS TURNOR [episcopal corrector] and Master **Weaver** [warden of the Stationers' company] warden.A booke Called *A Just Apologie for the Jesture of kneeling in the Act of receiving the Lordes supper.* by Master THOMAS PAYBODYE./
> MEMORANDUM That I the afore said **William Jones** Doe promise not to reimprinte the same booke againe with out the Authors Consent./ and that I the said **William Jones** shall surrender up the said Coppie to him againe, when he shall require it.
>
> By me **William Jones**"

Again, it is not the author who has sent a letter to the wardens that he must give his consent to a reprint. It is the publisher William Jones who signs a declaration that he is bound to ask the permission of the author for reprinting when the book goes out of print. Such a memorandum was sometimes also written in the margin, sometimes incorporated within the entry. All these entries resemble the clause in the entry of *The Merchant of Venice*, with the difference that it is not the Lord Chamberlain, a case absolutely unique in the registers from 1557 to 1640, who makes the printing dependent upon his consent, but the author who gives his consent to the reprinting.

Whose intent was served by such memoranda? And to what purpose? If it was neither the intent of the author nor of the publisher, it could only have been that of the third party, the wardens of the Stationers' Company. Would a verbal declaration not have worked as well? It might have worked for the incumbent wardens, but in July 1629 new wardens were to be elected, in July 1630 again, and so on. Without a written memorandum the successors of the current wardens would not have known that those books could not be reprinted without authorial consent. As for the purpose, the wardens had to be informed that they could not apply paragraph 5 of the company's ordinance of 1588.

The ordinance of 1588

The ordinance is printed in Arber's Transcript of the Stationers' Registers.[71] It bears no date. Arber tentatively dates it Spring of 1588, and it was certainly issued in the first half of that year. The period is determined by the signature of the then master of the company, John Judson, who served only one term as master, 1587/88. The records of the Court of Assistants contain an entry of 4 December 1587 about forms kept standing and the maximal numbers of copies to be printed[72] which reappears as paragraphs 1 and 2 of the ordinance. The ordinance has six paragraphs of which the fifth reads:

> And lastly that yf it shall happen at any tyme hereafter the copy of any man to be out of prynt and that after warninge shalbe gyven him and registred in the hall book at a Court of Assistentes for the reprynting thereof, the owner of the same doo not within Sixe monethes (after suche warning and regestring in the said book)

reprynt or begyn to reprynt the same and procede orderly with the ympression to ye finishing thereof **as he conveniently may so that the Aucthor of any suche copy be no hinderance thereunto** [our emphasis] That then it shalbe Laufull for the Journemen of the said Company to cause and gett any suche book or copy to be printed to ye use of ye Company during the Impression then to be printed of ye same copy. Savinge and alowinge to the owner of the copie a ratable parte with them in ye same Impression in proffitt and charge as yt shall fall out to every severall partener in every suche Impression According to the order and discretion of the Master. and Wardens of the Company for the tyme beynge.[73]

In his *History of English Law* W.S. Holdsworth gives a more readable account of this paragraph 5:

"Copyright is protected by the imposition of penalties upon those who infringed it. It is assigned, sold, settled, given in trust; and limited grants are made. Its duration is nowhere stated, unless it is expressly created for a limited period. It is therefore most probable that it was perpetual, unless a general enactment or order could be pointed to which expressly limited it. Nowhere can such general enactment or order be found. The only limitation on the right of the owner of the copy was an order of 1588 that, if a book was out of print, and, after warning, the owner did not reprint within six months, any member of the company could do so, provided that the author did not refuse and the owner of the copyright was given such part of the profit as the Master and Wardens of the company might order."

Consider the hypothetical case of the entry to John Browne without the memorandum. Ford´s book goes out of print. John Brown does not reprint it. Either another stationer or the wardens notes that the book is out of print but not reprinted. The wardens urge John Brown to reprint it. If within six months he has not started reprinting, the wardens can give one impression, the printing of one edition, to any other stationer. The wardens fix the share John Brown will have in the proceeds; the same would apply for William Jones in the absence of the memorandum. Jones would be urged to reprint it and if within six months he has not started reprinting any other stationer can print an edition on the same conditions. Jones would have a share in the proceeds to be determined by the wardens. However, with the memoranda – and that is indeed their purpose – the wardens were informed that those books, when out of print, were not eligible for the application of paragraph 5. The application is blocked. If any entry fits A.W. Pollard's term "conditional blocking entry", it is this kind. They are blocked upon the condition stipulated in paragraph 5: the outstanding consent of the author, the "hindrance of the author".

The memoranda differs from the clause in *MoV* in form but not in substance. The clause in *MoV* is an exact negation of the clause in paragraph 5 of the ordinance of 1588. The wardens are warned that if the play is not yet printed after a certain time James Roberts should not be urged to start printing it and no other stationer "whatsoever" can be given the printing of an edition: "Provided that it be not printed by the said James Roberts; or any other whatsoever without license first had from the Right Honorable the Lord Chamberlain."

Objection: first printing versus reprint

Paragraph 5 addresses the delaying of the reprint of books out of print but not, at least not explicitly, the case of the first printing of a book. However, the purview of a law depends upon more than the letter: the intention of the legislator must also be taken into account and this intention must be understood within the historical context. The situation to which the ordinance of 1588 responded was the climate of unrest within the Stationers' Company in the late 1570s and throughout the 1580s, stirred up by the privileges (patents) of certain of its members.

The most contested patents were those for such best-selling items as the *ABC and Catechisms* (John Day), *Almanacs* and *Prognostications* (James Roberts and Richard Watkins), *Bibles* and *Testaments* (John Jugge), law books (Richard Tottel), Latin books used in the grammar schools (Thomas Marsh), some Latin books and *The New Testament* (Thomas Vautrollier, later Richard Field), psalters, primers, and prayer books (William Serres), Latin grammars and accidences (Francis Flowers) and music books (William Byrd, the composer, who had been granted a royal patent for music books).[74] The latter two were not members of the Stationers' Company. The competitive edge such patents gave the holders over other stationers reached farther than the privilege as such. "A profitable copyright enables one to purchase other copyrights and since power breeds power, it is not difficult to see how perpetual copyright could enable a small group to establish their control over the trade by controlling the most profitable copyrights."[75]

But not only did the printing monopoly of such bestsellers deprive other stationers from present and future income and working opportunities, the problem was aggravated by the large number of apprentices freed of the company and becoming journeymen between 1571 and 1576[76] and, additionally, by such illicit practices as the employment of strangers or unpaid apprentices to further lower the expenditures. It was the very *raison d´être* of a corporation to ensure a fair distribution of trading chances, and though the privileged printers were among the most influential in it, the company as a body had to take measures to remedy the situation or at least to show off its preparedness to do so. In October 1577 it was ordered that bookbinders should give priority of employment to English people over strangers and should work promptly,[77] an indication that privileged stationers were sometimes accumulating tasks which they were not able to carry out within a reasonable term. On 27 January 1578 is recorded a petition by the poor men of the company for relief.[78] Among the claims we find are: that the company should take the necessary steps to provide more work, that people not belonging to the company (or foreigners) should not be given work, and that the numbers of apprentices attached to one stationer should be limited so as to prevent an excessive employment of apprentices at the expense of journeymen.

The ordinance of 1588 was probably the company´s most comprehensive attempt to cope with these grievances and to palliate the inequalities. In paragraph 1 it was stipulated that no forms of letters should be kept standing; in paragraph 2, that the number of books per issue (impression) was to be limited; in paragraph 3, that no apprentices should be employed to replace journeymen; in paragraph 4 were noted some exceptions to paragraph 3; in paragraph 5, as seen, if a book were out of print and not reprinted within a suitable time by the copy owner, one impression could be given to any stationer. Paragraph 6 is the stick to the carrot of the preceding paragraphs: if journeymen were still not content, the consequence would be the repeal of the entire ordinance.

The objective of paragraph 5 was to keep piling up of copy within limits. However, monopolizing of copies by delaying the first printing had the same effect as delaying the reprinting of a sold-off edition or, being the malpractice addressed in paragraph 2, the printing of huge quantities. It would have been illogical not to include first printing in the application of paragraph 5. Empirical evidence may be found in the Stationers' Register and the Court Books B and C, that the paragraph was extended to first printing. In an entry of December 5, 1606 we find the clause: " PROVYDED that this copye must be prynted before Mydsommer next".[79] This is somewhat longer than six months but given the fact that the custom was to fix time limits between two feast days, the term of six months was approximated to as close as the interval between two feast days permitted. Paragraph 5 also helps to solve another bibliographical and legal puzzle: the printing of the first quarto of *Hamlet*.

Hamlet: *Q1 (1603) and Q2 (1604)*

The publication history of Q1 and Q2 of *Hamlet* is another riddle which scholars have been unable to explain satisfactorily. James Roberts, to whom the play was entered on 26 July 1602, held *ipso facto* the right of publishing. He did not print it until the latter half of 1604. The publisher was Roberts' long-standing partner Nicholas Ling, to whom at some time between July 1602 and 1604 Roberts must therefore have transferred his right by virtue of the entry of July 1602. It has been passingly mentioned above in connection with the evidencing procedure for authority after entrance that registration of such a transfer was a possibility but not a necessity. But in 1603 a quarto, very different from that printed by Roberts in 1604, was published by John Trundle and

Nicholas Ling and printed not by Roberts but by Valentine Sims. If James Roberts still possessed the publishing right, this publication of 1603 constituted an infringement of Roberts' right. It would normally have been punished by the Stationers' Company, which could not and did not tolerate such breaches of their regulations. The exclusivity of the right of publishing was essential to the orderly functioning of the company, which is why infringements of the right of others were called "disorderly printing". In August 1592 the press of Roger Ward was defaced for printing a book belonging by patent to another stationer.[80] In December 1592 Edward White was penalized for printing *The Spanish Tragedy*, which was Abel Jeffes' copy; Abel Jeffes was penalized for printing the play *Arden of Feversham*, which was Edward White's copy; both were threatened with imprisonment.[81] In February 1593 Edward White was ordered to stop publishing of a book which belonged to another.[82] In June 1595 Andrew Wise (who in the course of the following 5 years was to publish five plays of Shakespeare: *Richard III*, *Richard II, 1 and 2 Henry IV*, and *Much Ado*) was fined for printing a sermon in which he had no right.[83] In May 1604 Felix Kingston was fined 10s. for infringing the right of John Windet.[84] But no trace can be found of a fine imposed on John Trundle. The presence of Nicholas Ling complicates the matter. In 1604 Nicholas Ling had been assigned the right in *Hamlet* by Roberts. Ling would have violated the publishing right of his partner John Roberts, though it was likely that the latter would assign it to him. It is possible, likely even, that Ling had already been assigned this right in 1603. By publishing an unauthorized text then, Ling, oddly enough, would have "pirated" his own copy. In his introduction to the Arden edition of the play Harold Jenkins notes: "The participation in Q1 of Trundle, a very much junior partner, with Ling, an established bookseller, together with Trundle's disappearance when the bad quarto was succeeded by the better, has sometimes led to a guess – it can be no more – that it was he who secured the unauthorized copy...When Roberts entered *Hamlet*, then, in July 1602, with or without the Lord Chamberlain's men's blessing, it is to be supposed that what he hoped to print was what he later did print, the genuine text. But before he could do so, he was anticipated by Q1, which led to Ling's having publication rights and subsequently partnering Robert in Q2".[85] It is outside the scope of the present work to examine in detail Jenkins' lengthy account of the publication history. We will instead give a brief account of the misconceptions we observe and then argue that the enigmatic aspects disappear when paragraph 5 is taken into consideration.

The fundamental error in Jenkins' analysis lies in his assumption that Trundle and Ling would have established publishing rights by mere publishing, defeating Roberts' right by virtue of his entrance of July 1602. In a statement of about 1620 the stationer John Bill declares: "**Bishop** gave to DOCTOR FULKE as also for **40**[li] which Bishop gave him and his Assignees, and this appears by witnesses as also the registry of the Stationers' Hall where this was entered before the master and wardens of the Stationers at a Court then holden as all copies which are bought by Stationers are. **And this entry in the hall book is the common and strongest assurance that Stationers have, for all their copies, which is the greatest part of their estates.**" [our emphasis]. Ling and Trundle could not defeat the entry to Roberts by mere publishing. There were only three ways the right to a copy established by entrance could be defeated. First, if it afterwards appeared that a previous entry existed (as in the above case of Olney's entry which was crossed out in favor of the previous entry by Ponsonby). Second, if the author complained that he had not given his authorization.[86] Third, if a publisher unduly delayed the printing or reprinting of a work. Jenkins' afterthought that the manifest proviso in *MoV* is perhaps also latent in *Hamlet* is a lucid insight, but eventually misses the true causality. It is because the proviso was absent from the entry of *Hamlet* that Trundle could publish the so-called bad quarto in 1603. That it was in fact Trundle who procured the copy of Q1 is much more than "a guess," it is a certitude. That Trundle did not incur a penalty need not surprise us. It simply means that he had not acted contrary to the regulations of the Stationers Company. That he did not is clear from paragraph 5 of the ordinance of 1588. In 1603 more than six months had elapsed, and Roberts had not yet printed *Hamlet.* Since the entry lacked a clause similar to that of *The Merchant of Venice,* Roberts' or rather Ling's right could be suspended for one impression if Trundle got hold of a manuscript of *Hamlet*. Obviously, Ling or Roberts had again to wait for the permission of the author, but this was not expressly stated in the entry of *Hamlet*. All Ling and Roberts (who must have already have assigned the right to Ling), could do was either refuse to publish or to print respectively, and to let Trundle have the right for one impression. Ling actually had two options: either he could desist and receive a part of the proceeds (to be fixed by the wardens), or he could directly share in the publication with Trundle. But Ling could not prevent Trundle from publishing one edition of *Hamlet*. When Q2, markedly different from Q1, was published in the second half of 1604, Trundle might have conserved his right in Q1 (if it were not already out of print), but this was now valueless.

Hamlet provides another proof that paragraph 5 was also applied to first printing, as logically follows from the intent of the ordinance of 1588.

Conclusion

Even on the flimsy hypothesis that it was the administrative authority of the Lord Chamberlain which was required, the clause in *The Merchant of Venice* makes no sense. In that case James Roberts would have to wait for this authority but would have kept the right of publishing against any other stationer, such authority being entirely independent of the right to the copy granted by the Stationers' Company. The second part of the proviso, that it should neither be printed by "any other whatsoever," would have been superfluous. This clause uniquely refers to paragraph 5 of the ordinance of 1588. While such a proviso was included in the entry of *The Merchant of Venice* but not in that of *Hamlet*, the unauthorized version Q1 could be published in 1603 against the publishing right of Ling. As the only condition to make void the application of this paragraph 5 was the opposition, the "hindrance" of the author, the logical conclusion is that the Lord Chamberlain, who made the printing conditional upon his license, was in fact the author himself.

Thus, what actually happened on 22 July 1598 at Stationers' Hall was that James Roberts, like John Browne on 11 March 1607 and William Jones on 22 September 1628 (for reprinting), told the wardens that the author reserved the right of the date when the play should be printed, so that paragraph 5 could not be applied, and that the author was the Lord Chamberlain. The clerk then inserted a clause that the permission or license of the Lord Chamberlain was required and chose a wording which made it plain that this paragraph was put out of effect: "not to be printed by James Roberts nor by any other whatsoever", so that Roberts could not be urged to start printing and no other stationer could be given the right to print one edition. The wardens were advised that the sole condition of non-application was fufilled: pending permission of the author, which was indicated by "license of the Lord Chamberlain". It was by no means the purpose of the clerk of the Stationers' Company to reveal to anyone the identity of the author. Yet for the wardens to know they could not apply paragraph 5 it was necessary that some reference be made to the only person whose pending permission could bar the application, and that was the author. Thus a trade regulation of the Stationers' Company brings us closer to the identity of the author of *The Merchant of Venice*.

Which Lord Chamberlain?

Finally, who was this Lord Chamberlain? Without doubt, many will answer George Carey, 2nd Baron of Hunsdon. He then would be our author, though nothing in his known history would lend credence to this conclusion. Yet a handy rule of thumb, not without some currency even among historians, has it that the title 'Lord Chamberlain' always refers to the Lord Chamberlain of the Royal Household. When a tenet, be it ever so widespread, leads us to absurd conclusions, it should be re -examined. Not only did Edward de Vere, 17th Earl of Oxford, sign a declaration as "Lord Chamberlain" in 1603, we also find that Edward Seymour, Earl of Hertford and Lord Great Chamberlain of England, signed the probation of Henry VIII's will[87] in 1547 as "Lord Chamberlain" – to cite only two such cases. Accounts of coronation ceremonies reveal further instances, and Charles Wisner Barrell and Ruth Loyd Miller have both provided sufficient evidence that Edward de Vere, 17th

Earl of Oxford Lord Great (or High) Chamberlain of England was sometimes referred to as Lord Chamberlain.[88]

In his classic *The King's Council in England during the Middle Ages* James Foswick Baldwin stated that at the Duke of Gloucester's death in 1447 William de la Pole, Earl of Suffolk, had succeeded him as chamberlain. In a footnote he added: "The chamberlain was the officer who regularly received all petitions addressed to the king, and would be the one to transmit them to the council in the case this was done."[89] In fact, the Dukes of Gloucester and Suffolk were Great Chamberlains of England. R.Virgoe remarked that Baldwin had made a mistake here, the offices of great chamberlain and chamberlain of the household being quite different offices.[90] Who was right and who wrong? Baldwin had studied the documents of the period, Virgoe was just reciting a rule of thumb. Baldwin was right, for throughout the Lancaster and the York period the Great Chamberlain of England was indeed the principal officer of the royal household. Either he or the chamberlain to the king or the vice-chamberlain received the petitions to the king. The same holds true for the period 1540-1553 after Thomas Cromwell's household reform in 1540, as David Starkey has shown.[91]

The automatic identification of "Lord Chamberlain" as "Lord Chamberlain of the Royal Household" will in most cases be correct; but as any Lord who held an office of chamberlain could be spoken of as "Lord Chamberlain" it will sometimes be wrong, as in the following case. In his letter of 20 July 1616 John Chamberlain writes: "On Sunday the King gave order at Tiballs [Theobalds, the residence James I bought from the Cecils] that the earle of Arundell shold be sworne a counsaillor which was done upon Tewsday at Whitehall...The Queene hath long laboured the same honour for the Lord Carew [Baron George Carew of Clopton], so that going to Tiballs on Monday to take her leave of the King that is now gon on his progresse, she brought a warrant to sweare him this day or to morow: ytt was objected to as an incongruitie that he shold preferred to that place before her Lord Chamberlain but that is salved with a distinction, that he is not made as her vicechamberlain but as a master of the ordinance."[92] In a footnote the editor mechanically identifies this lord chamberlain as "William Herbert, third Earl of

Pembroke", that is, the lord chamberlain of the king's household. Yet not only does John Chamberlain say it is *her* lord chamberlain (the lord chamberlain of the *queen's* household), but in a letter of 6 April 1616 he writes that the vice-chamberlain of the king's household had been sworn of the council: "The day of the Kings going Sir John Digbie was sworne vicechamberlain and of the privie counsaile: what composition he hath made with the Lord Stanhop I know not..."[93] Pembroke was a privy councillor then, thus there was no incongruity in appointing his vice-chamberlain. Robert Sidney, Viscount of Lisle, was not yet a privy councillor, though his vice-chamberlain Lord Carew was. Therefore the Lord Chamberlain in this case was the Lord Chamberlain of Queen Anne's household, not of the King's household.

In 1598 there are only two possible Lord Chamberlains as candidates for the authorship of *The Merchant of Venice*: the unlikely George Carey, 2nd Baron Hunsdon, and Edward de Vere, 17th Earl of Oxford.

Chapter III
Shakespeare: The Earl Of Oxford

"As early as 1598 a shameless name-dropper named Francis Meres began the liturgical chant, claiming that 'As Plautus and Seneca are accounted the best for Comedy and Tragedy among the Latines: so Shakespeare among the English is the most excellent in both kinds for the stage."[94]

"In truth, Meres was neither a profound nor industrious gatherer of commonplaces; in many respects the *Palladis Tamia* seems to be the work of a hack who had a contracted obligation to fulfil."[95]

"This chapter uses the simile format to compare classical authors to their contemporary English counterparts, and it constitutes a unique and extremely valuable survey of English literature at the end of the sixteenth century."[96]

Who was Francis Meres really? An attentive observer of the London literary scene who recognized Shakespeare's incommensurable genius and left an "extremely valuable survey" of contemporary English literature? Or was he a "shameless name-dropper," the first high-priest of bardolatry, reeling off names of ancient and English authors like names of saints in a litany? And what kind of work is this *Palladis Tamia,* more particularly the "Comparative Discourse" in which Shakespeare is likened to Plautus for comedy and to Seneca for tragedy? The reputable scholar G. E. Bentley puts it in a row of popular commonplace books of the age. "John Cotgrave's *English Treasury of Wit and Language*, 1655, is a book of quotations much in the tradition of earlier commonplace books like *Politeuphuia*, *Wits Commonwealth*, 1597, *Palladis Tamia*, *Wits Treasury*, 1598, *Wits Theatre of the Little World*, 1599, *Belvedere*, 1600, and *Wits Labyrinth*, 1648. Like the other five, it consists of a large number of quotations from a variety of authors, classified according to subjects — Adversity, Beauty, Chastity, Envy, Heaven, Sin, Women."[97] In Bentley's chronological listing it stands between two other commonplace books, the first and third part of the series *Wit's Commonwealth*. The first part of *Wit's Commonwealth*, *Politeuphia*, opens with a section "Of God"; the third part of *Wit's Commonwealth*, *Theatre of the Little World*, opens with a section "Of God"; the second part of *Wit's Commonwealth*, Francis Meres's *Palladis Tamia – Wit's Treasury*, opens with a section "Of God". What distinguishes Meres's commonplace book from the other two of the series is the presence of a section on art, mainly literature, in which Meres heaps praise on four contemporary poets: Michael Drayton, Samuel Daniel, Edmund Spenser and above all William Shakespeare, and simply lists a great number of others, in the overwhelming majority of cases without mentioning more than their bare names. The heading "A comparative discourse of our English Poets, with the *Greeke, Latine, and Italian Poets*." is misleading. The first paragraph contains no "discourse" at all, only a simple symmetric arrangement of names of ancient and English authors. The second paragraph contains only a short piece of discourse: " As *Homer* is reputed the Prince of Greek Poets; and *Petrarch* of Italian Poets: so *Chaucer* is accounted the God of English Poets." Yet, this morsel is not Meres'own but a quotation from William Webbe's *Discourse of English Poetry*, published in 1585, thirteen years before Meres's *Palladis Tamia*: "*Chaucer*, who for that excellent fame which he obtained in his Poetry was always accounted the God of English Poets." Apparently G.E. Bentley did not hold Meres' discourse to be of a sufficiently distinctive quality to set his commonplace book apart from the other ones. Nor did Meres himself claim such a distinction. In his dedication to Thomas Eliot of the Middle Temple he acknowledges in somewhat bombastic similes that his book is the second part of a triad of commonplace books under the generic name *Wit's Commonwealth*:

"And now I have my wished desire. Wherefore I may rejoice for three things, as *Philip* King of *Macedonia* rejoiced. He rejoiced that he had won the Games at *Olympus* by the running of his chariots; that his captain *Parmenio* had overthrown the Dardarians; and that his wife *Olympia* had born him a son, called Alexander: So I exceedingly rejoice, and am glad at my heart, that the first part of *Wit's Common-*

wealth, containing sentences, hath like a brave champion gloriously marched and got such renowned fame by swift running, equivalent with *Philip*'s chariots, that thrice within one year it hath run through the press. If this second part of mine, called *Wit's Treasury* containing similitudes, being a stalk of the same stem, shall have the like footmanship, and find the same success, then with *Parmenio* I shall be the second in *Philip*'s joy. And then *Philip*'s joy will eftsoon be full, for his *Alexander*, whom not *Olympia*, but a worthy scholar is conceiving, who will fill the third part of *Wit's Commonwealth* with more glorious examples than great Alexander did the world with valiant and heroical exploits."

Though Meres places the gathering of commonplaces above the historical feats of Alexander the Great he did not, in fact, think higher of his task than that of John Bodenham's, the gatherer of the commonplaces for parts 1 and 3 of *Wit's Commonwealth*. In 1904 Gregory Smith qualified Meres' "Comparative Discourse" within *Palladis Tamia* as a "directory of writers" and his method as "absolute scissors and paste".[98] It is not much of an exaggeration.

Don C. Allen probably came closest to the mark when he spoke of one who "had a contracted obligation to fulfill". Though Meres was without doubt more than a "hack," his "Comparative Discourse" is no less a compilation than the rest of his book, or than the other two books of the *Wit's Commonwealth* series are. The above verbatim borrowing from another work is the rule, not the exception. Hardly any textual passage in "Comparative Discourse" is not borrowed from existing works. Meres has therefore occasionally been accused of plagiarism.

What might we expect as we inch along in a jam of fifty-eight paragraphs, all of them shaped according to the same monotonous formula? The first paragraph reads:

As Greece had three Poets of great antiquity *Orpheus, Linus, Musoeus* and Italy, other three auncient Poets, *Livius Andronicus, Ennius, Plautus*: So hath England three auncient Poets, *Chaucer, Gower, Lydgate.*

Few begin differently. They all take the form of an equation with the AS-side listing ancient authors (in a few cases an Italian and in even fewer cases a French or Spanish author), and an equal number of English authors listed on the SO-side. The message is a simple one: the symmetry asserts that English literature can stand the comparison with ancient literature. Were it not for the symmetric structure, Meres' "Comparative Discourse" would be an amorphous succession of names. It is still a monotonous one. But:

Sometimes in a heap of mud,
A piece of gold is shut.

Wit's Commonwealth: *a publishing project*

The commonplace book series *Wit's Commonwealth* presents all the features of a project of one or more publishers. Who could have ordered *Palladis Tamia*, the second part of *Wit's Commonwealth*? It is reasonable to search Meres' employers among the publishers of *Wit's Commonwealth*, the whole of the series. We meet two old acquaintances: the publisher of the first and third part was Nicholas Ling, the printer of both was James Roberts. *Palladis Tamia* was published by Cuthbert Burby and printed by Peter Short. But Cuthbert Burby stood in some partnership relation with Nicholas Ling. In 1607, shortly before his death, he transferred some of his copies to the latter. On the publishing side, then, we have two men who were occcasional partners. Cuthbert Burby published the two amended second issues of *Love's Labour's Lost* (1598) and *Romeo and Juliet* (1599). He also published Meres' translation of the second book of Luis de Granada's *A Sinner's Guide*. Ling and Burby may have been Meres' employers.

Was Meres a "plagiarist"?

In his *Discourse of English Poetry* (1585) William Webbe writes: "And *Cicero* in his *Tusculane* questions is of that minde, that a Poet cannot expresse verses aboundantly...".[99] Meres repeats this phrase *verbatim*, and, likewise, does not scruple to borrow almost literally from other authors, most heavily from Puttenham's *The Arte of English Poesie*. A list is prefixed to his book naming the authors from whom he **quotes**; among them Philip Sidney and John Harington in the section "Poetry" preceding the two sections "Poets" and "A comparative discourse." But authors from whom he **borrows** in these two latter sections are not listed: William Webbe, Puttenham, Roger Ascham, and others. Should Meres, therefore, be accused of plagiarism?

Actually, we do not think so. After all, the "Comparative Discourse" was part of his commonplace book. A commonplace book by definition is a collection of citations. Hence, Meres continued to practise what he did in the rest of his book, where he translates quotes ordered according to subjects, though here, in the "Comparative Discourse," without listing the sources. Given that few of his comments are his own and that not a single work is mentioned for the majority of listed authors, calling Meres a "literary critic," and his "Comparative Discourse" an "extremely valuable survey of English literature," seems very wide of the mark indeed.

Meres´s "expertise"

Nonetheless, two mentions seem to indicate that Meres was keeping his ear to the literary ground. He knew that Michael Drayton was busy writing his *Poly-Olbion*. "Michael Drayton is now in penning in English verse a Poem called *Poly-olbion* Geographical and Hydrographicall of all the forests, woods, mountaines, fountaines, rivers, lakes, flouds, bathes and springs that be in England." The work was not published until 1612/13. He also includes Evrard Guilpin´s satire *Skialetheia*, registered as late as 15 September 1598, a full week after the registration of Meres´ *Palladis Tamia*.

But one man would have known better than anyone, even Francis Meres, about Guilpin´s forthcoming satire: Nicholas Ling. It was entered to him and he published it. The printer was again James Roberts. Possibly, the work was still in the process of being printed when Meres´ *Palladis Tamia* was published. Ling must also have known that Drayton was composing his *Poly-Olbion*. Had he not died in 1607 he is likely to have published that work. He published nearly all the works of Drayton before 1607, always with James Roberts as printer (see list in Appendix IV). Nicholas Ling thus appears as the driving force behind the whole *Wit's Commonwealth* project. He signed the dedication and the epistle to the reader of the first part and it is likely that the unsigned dedication and epistle of the third part are also his work.

Meres' method

In paragraph 36 on iambic poets or hexametrists, Meres clearly describes his method:

"Among the Greeks I will name but two for Iambics, *Archilochus Parius* and *Hipponax Ephesius*: So amongst us I name but two iambical poets, *Gabriel Harvey*, and *Richard Stanyhurst*, because I have seene no more in this kind."

Don C. Allen[100] was probably the first to discover the main source from which Meres had taken the names of the ancient authors, Ravisius Textor's *Officina*, a then widely used encyclopedy.[101] Textor, of course, lists many more ancient authors of alexandrines (iambic hexameters). But as Meres can only find two English hexametrists, he selects only two from Textor. In the same way he chooses only as many ancient authors of tragedy as he can find English ones (14), the same for comedy (16), and so on.

In one case, however, Meres commits a blunder serious enough to have his scholarship called into question by Allen. "It should be apparent from this account that Meres's statements about Greek and Latin poets were at second hand. However, Meres commits a greater sin than ignorance, since he gives definite evidence on one occasion that he was stupid. In his section on satirists, Meres records among the Latin writers of this sort Lucullus and Lucilius. The latter name falls within the definition, but the former, Lucullus, was at best a historian."[102] The paragraph in question reads [the numbering is ours]:

As 1. *Horace*, 2. *Lucilius*, 3. *Iuvenall*, 4. *Persius* & 5. *Lucullus* are the best for Satire among the Latins: So with us in the same faculty these are chiefe 1. *Piers Plowman*, 2. *Lodge*, 3. *Hall* of Imanuel Colledge in Cambridge, 4. the Authour of *Pigmalions Image, and certaine Satyrs*, 5. *the Author of Skialetheia*.

The author of *Pygmalion's Image and certain satires*, published in 1598 by E. Mattes and printed by James Roberts, was Kinsayder, the pseudonym of John Marston. Meres knew Kinsayder to be a pseudonym and thus omitted the name. Of course James Roberts and Nicholas Ling must also have known it. Evrard Guilpin's *Skialetheia* had been published anonymously by Nicholas Ling and printed by James Roberts. How was Meres "stupid"? "The error in the case of Lucullus is Textor's, not Meres', since the tenth paragraph in Textor's list begins: "Lucullus Satyrographus, ex Arunca urbe Italiae." This clearly explains Meres' error and provides a very tangible proof of his use of the *Officina*. However, if this is accepted, how can Lucilius, who is not found in Textor's catalogue (but whom Meres places correctly among the Latin satirists), be accounted for? The *Officina* gives the explanation of this and also indicates Meres' method of compiling data."[103] Immediately after the heading "De poetis Graecis et Latinis" Textor refers to Petrus Crinitus, an author of the biographies of ninety-five poets. "These biographies were exceedingly popular in the first half of the century and were used for the *vitae* of most editions of classical authors published at that time. In this small book there is no mention of Lucullus, but in the same order as that of the *Officina* is noticed: "C. Lucilius Satyrarum scriptor... Ex Arunca urbe Ausoniae fuit."[104]

Our own hypothesis is that Meres was less stupid than tricky. The only difference between Crinitus and Textor is that the former uses the ancient name of Italy: Ausonia. As the name of the author differs only by three letters and the name of the town is identical, this can hardly have been the cause of the error. But Meres was facing a difficulty. In all other cases he could find names in overplus in Textor's *Officina* to select as many authors in the genre as there were English authors. Here, for satirists, the situation was reversed. Textor mentions only four satirists but there were many more English satirists at hand. Disregarding the printing error in Textor allowed Meres to add one name more. It was not a scholarly procedure, but he could keep to his symmetric structure. Still, the paragraph conspiciously lacks one name. Though separately mentioned, Thomas Nashe, the outstanding satirist of the 1590s, is left out in favour of two newcomers, John Marston and

Evrard Guilpin. This decision seems to have rested more on commercial rather than on scholarly considerations. Guilpin was published by Ling and printed by Roberts, Marston was printed by Roberts.

Infatuated with numerology

Meres' dedication begins with the words "Tria sunt omnia" (all good things come in threes). Apart from the last sentence, every other line in the euphuistic dedication is a variation on this motto. It returns in his "Comparative Discourse." In numerology three, and its multiples six and twelve, are perfect numbers. Four poets are given special mention in the "Comparative Discourse": Edmund Spenser, William Shakespeare, Samuel Daniel, and Michael Drayton. Spenser and Daniel are given three paragraphs, Shakespeare four, Drayton six.

Spenser published his *Fairie Queene* in two parts, books I-III in 1590, books IV-VI in 1596, each of them is mentioned in a paragraph. The third paragraph is for *The Shepherd's Calendar.* None of his other publications; the collected poems in *Complaints* (1591), *Daphnaida* (1591), *Colin Clouts come home againe* (1595), the sonnet cycle *Amoretti* and *Epithalamion* (1595), are mentioned.

Samuel Daniel is mentioned with three works: *Delia* , *Rosamond* and *Civil Wars*. His tragedy *Cleopatra* (1594) is omitted.

Michael Drayton is mentioned with six works : *The civil wars of Edward the second, and the Barons* (*Mortimeriados, or the Baron's Wars*); *England's Heroical Epistles*; *Robert of Normandy*; *Matilda*; *Peirs Gaveston*; *Poly-Olbion. Idea* (1593) and *Endimion and Phoebe* (1595) are omitted.

Symmetry and homespun numerology are thus favored over completeness, and this holds true in Shakespeare's case. Of four paragraphs, two contain general statements without mention of works. One paragraph cites his poems, honoring the "all good things come in threes" principle by mentioning *Venus and Adonis, The Rape of Lucrece*, and the *Sonnets*, subsuming the rest under "&c." Twelve plays are mentioned, six comedies and six tragedies.

Balancing and counter-balancing is another quirk exhibited by Meres. Among the comedies, *Love's Labour's Lost* is counterbalanced by

Love's Labour's Won, a title which hitherto, as far as we know, has never been convincingly traced[105] and has triggered much speculation about which play could actually be meant. Though *Much Ado About Nothing* and *All's Well that Ends Well* seem plausible candidates, it cannot be entirely ruled out that the title simply derives from Meres's fondness of antithesis, a figure which looms large in euphuistic style. He practises the same in his paragraphs on tragedy and comedy, mentioning for tragedy first an author of the University of Cambridge, then one of Oxford, following the reverse order in the paragraph on comedy.

Meres's arithmetic "errors".

From the paragraph on satirists we have seen how tenaciously Meres adhered to symmetry. He was even prepared to use a cheap trick, profiting from a printing error to get one ancient satirist more than he had found in his source, the *Officina* of Ravisius Textor, and willing to deny the true standing of the foremost contemporary satirist Thomas Nashe. To control whether Meres always counted correctly seems as senseful as counting sheep to fall asleep. However, a letter of 29 September 1996 from Derran Charlton informed us that one person had not thought it beneath his scientific dignity to do exactly that. The man in question was the late Enoch Powell. In a speech delivered to the De Vere Society in England, he had communicated his finding that Meres did not list the same number of ancient and English authors of comedy. There were sixteen ancient and seventeen English authors, Powell pointed out. This paragraph was unbalanced! He concluded: "It would be a natural assumption that one name was added without corresponding adjustment of the symmetry. It also happens to be the one place where there is a reference to Edward Earl of Oxford."[106]

Other inferences are possible. Orthodox scholars could argue that this proves "beyond doubt" that Oxford and Shakespeare were two different persons. Oxfordians, however, could argue that the asymmetry is a deliberate imbalance, and that it points to the identity of Oxford as Shakespeare; the asymmetry would thus be illusory, the paragraph *looks* asymmetrical but is not. Powell's observation on the unequality between the number of ancient and English authors is correct, but to test the validity of his interpretation it would be necessary to examine whether the rule of symmetry had been broken in other paragraphs. Suddenly, a dreadfully tedious occupation looked, if not exciting, much less tedious and at any rate, worth the counting. Certainly, if this were the only paragraph where Meres missed his numbers, the supernumerary might be significant.

Results

Meres always observes some kind of symmetry, which is achieved in four ways:

1) Same number of Greek, Latin, and English poets.
   As seen above, in the first paragraph three Greek (*Orpheus, Linus, Musoeus*) and three Latin authors (*Livius Andronicus, Ennius, Plautus*) are set against three English authors (*Chaucer, Gower, Lydgate*).
   In the second paragraph we have one Greek (*Homer*) and one Italian (*Petrarch*) against one English (*Chaucer*). Also para. 8: eight Greek and eight Latin against eight English. Para. 12, one Greek (*Theocritus*) and one Latin (*Virgil*) against one English (*Spenser*). To this can be added the rather odd para. 52: "As *Achilles* tortured the dead body of *Hector,* and as *Antonius,* and his *Fulvia* tormented the liveless corps of *Cicero*: So *Gabriel Harvey* hath shewed the same inhumanity to *Greene* that lies full low in his grave."

2) One poet is set off against each of two poets
   In Para. 9, *Xenophon* & *Heliodorus,* both Greek authors, are likened to *Sir Philip Sidney,* in para. 12, *Lucan* to *Daniel* & *Drayton.* The proportion 2:1 counterbalances the proportion 1:2.

3) A difference in the **number of poets** is made up for by **adding works:**
   In para. 18, *Drayton* is mentioned with three works:
   As *Accius, M. Attilius* and *Milithus* were called Tragoediographi, because they writ Tragedies: So may we truly term *Michael Drayton*

Tragoediographus, for his passionate penning the downfals of valiant *Robert of Normandy*, chast *Matilda*, and great *Gaveston*.
Paragraph 38 on pastoral poetry contains another example.
4) In all other paragraphs there is always the same number on the **AS-side** (Greek, Latin, Italian, French (1), Spanish (1), and the **SO-side** (English).
However, four paragraphs must be excepted. Here there is clearly asymmetry not balanced out by any devices. In these four cases there is a supernumerary. To restore symmetry we would have to posit the phrase from Shakespeare's sonnet 136: "Among a number one is reckoned none."
The paragraphs are:
Para. 7: [numbering is ours]:
As these Neoterickes [1] *Iovianus Pontanus* [2] *Politianus* [3] *Marullus Tarchaniota* [4] the two *Strozæ*, the father and the son, [5] *Palingenius* [6] *Mantuanus*, [7] *Philelphus* [8} *Quintianus Stoa* [9} *Germanus Brixius* have obtained renown and good place among the ancient Latin Poets: so also these English men being Latine Poets [1} *Gualter Haddon* [2} *Nicholas Car* [3] *Gabriel Harvey* [4] *Christopher Ocland* [5] *Thomas Newton* with his *Leyland* [6] *Thomas Watson* [7] *Thomas Campion* [8] *Brunswerd* & [9] *Willey*, have attained good report and honorable advancement in the Latin Empyre.
The two Strozzi are the Latin writing Florentines, Vespasiano Strozzi (1424-1505), the father, and Ercole Strozzi (1473-1508), the son. Is there really asymmetry? The answer is yes, and no. There is **asymmetry of persons** (10: 9), but **symmetry of names**, as only **one name** is given for the **two** Strozzi. One name thus stands for two persons.

Paragraph 39:
These and many other *Epigrammatists* the Latin tongue hath [1] *Q. Catulus* [2] *Porcius Licinius* [3] *Quintus Cornificius* [4} *Martial* [5} *Cn. Getulicus*, and [6] wittie sir *Thomas Moore*: so in English we have these, So [1] *Heywood* [2] *Drante* [3} *Kendal* [4} *Bastard* [5} *Davies*.
We have six Latin epigrammatists, including Sir Thomas More, who wrote in Latin, and only five English epigrammatists. There is undenia-

bly asymmetry of names, but the asymmetry of persons is only apparent. The name **Davies** stands for **two contemporeanous epigrammatists**, Sir John Davies (1569-1626) and John Davies of Hereford (ca. 1565-1618). So we have the reverse relation of para. 7, asymmetry of names but symmetry of persons operated by the same means: one name stands for two persons.

Writing it schematically:

Para. 7 : N, P+1 (on AS-side) : N, P (on SO-side);

Para. 39 : N+1, P (on AS-side) : N, P (on SO-side).

Counterbalancing requires this to be mirrored on the SO-side. What we have to find are two paragraphs of this structure:

Para. X: N, P (on AS-side) : N, P+1 (on SO-side)

Para. Y: N, P (on AS-side) : N+1, P (on SO-side).

Para. X is par. 46 :

As [1] *Terence* for his translations out of *Appolodorus & Menander*, and [2] *Aquilus* for his translation out of *Menander*, and [3] *C. Germanicus Augustus* for his out of *Aratus*, and [4] *Ausonius* for his translated *Epigrams* out of Greeke, and [5] Doctor *Johnson* for his *Froggefight* out of *Homer*, and [6] *Watson* for his *Antigone* out of *Sophocles*, have good commendations: So these versifiers fot their learned translations are of good note among us, [1] *Phaere* for *Virgils Aeneads*, [2] *Golding* for *Ovids Metamorphosis* [3] *Harington* for his *Orlando Furioso* [4] the translators of *Seneca's Tragedies* [5] *Barnabe Googe* for *Palingenius* [6] *Turbervile* for *Ovids Epistles* and *Mantuan* and [7] *Chapman* for his inchoate *Homer*.

The translators of Seneca are given as a nameless entity, as a one-ness. We have an equal number of names but not of persons. A nameless collectivity stands for several persons.

Para. Y is 34, the one on comedy:

The best Poets for Comedy among the Greeks are these [1] *Menander* [2] *Aristophanes* [3] *Eupolis Atheniensis* [4} *Alexius Terius* [5] *Nicostratus* [6] *Amipsias Atheniensis* [7} *Anaxandrides Rhodius* [8] Aristonymus [9] Archippus Atheniensis and [10} Callias Atheniensis and among the Latines [11} *Plautus* [12} *Terence* [13] *Naevius* [14] *Sext. Turpilius* [15] *Licinius Imbrex* and [16] *Virgilius Romanus*: so the best for Comedy amongst us bee [1] *Edward* Earl of Oxford [2] Doctor *Gager* of Oxford [3] Master *Rowley*, once a rare Scholler of learned Pembroke Hall in Cambridge [4] Master *Edwardes* one of her Majesty's Chapel, [5] eloquent and witty *John Lily* [6] *Lodge* [7] *Gascoigne* [8] *Greene* [9] *Shakespeare* [10] *Thomas Nashe* [11] *Thomas Heywood* [12] *Anthony Munday*, our best plotter [13] *Chapman* [14] *Porter* [15] *Wilson* [16] *Hathway* [17] *Henry Chettle*.

We have $N + 1$ names. To be balanced as group, it is necessary that P, the number of persons, should be the same (as in the case of the two epigrammatists John Davies). Which means that two names must stand for one and the same person.

Theoretically there are as many possibilities as combinations: 17!/15! 2! = 17x16 : 2 = 136. It is not necessary to check each of them. In conjunction with what was found at the end of the preceding chapter the answer is clear. At the end of the analysis of the entry *of Merchant of Venice* only two candidates remained: George Carey, 2nd Baron Hunsdon, Lord Chamberlain of the Royal Household, and Edward de Vere, 17th Earl of Oxford, Lord Great Chamberlain of England. The former does not even show up on Meres' list. This would be sufficient. Oxford is the Lord Chamberlain who as author reserved the decision on the date of printing. Independently, Meres' arithmetical arrangements confirm the finding. Edward, Earl of Oxford, and Shakespeare are one and the same person.

Can this pattern of deviations from symmetry, in itself balanced, be ascribed to mere chance? We do not think this a reasonable assumption, the less so because the square of departures carries a meaning, a contrapuntal composition on the theme "What's in a name"? In one case the crucial name indicates the relation from father to son; in the second case the name stands for two unrelated namesakes; in the third case, the item causing the asymmetry of person is an anonymous entity; in the fourth case the relationship is pseudonymous.

It seems as if we are encountering one of the phenomena historians have observed in courtly society: something is concealed and at the same time revealed. Here de Vere is concealed and at the same time, by a fugue-like textural procedure, revealed, as Shakespeare. Which 16th- and 17th-century reader would have seen it? Kent A. Hieatt may give us a hint.[107] The work analyzes Edmund Spenser's poem *Epithalamion*. He points out that, as in other works of the Renaissance, the poem follows a symbolic structure. "Understanding of this symbolism requires at least some knowledge of the geography and values of a particular medieval-Renaissance world-view... This method requires that beneath a simple literal surface profound symbolic communication of an integrated continuity should take place covertly..."

Elizabethan readers were better exercised in allegorical, multi-layer reading, especially those persons to whom court rituals were familiar. Ultimately, Meres' list of the "best for Comedy" is not so very different from Spenser's arrangement in the fourth Book of *The Fairie Queene.* Alistair Fowler explains that the eighteen knights symbolize concord.[108] But "concord is repeatedly impaired by significant departures from the pattern." The departure from the pattern consists in the inclusion of a mock-knight named Braggadocchio. And he adds: "Although several features of the tournament episode remain obscure, we can at least be sure that it is not intended merely as a portrayal of physical conflict... It is meant rather as a poetic imitation of a *balletic* tournament, of a kind which actually took place in the sixteenth century. Miss Frances Yates' recent account of tournaments at the Valois court has indicated some of the ways in which ideals of political and cosmic order were set forth by means of symbolic arrangements. The symbolism of place and number in Spenser's tournament is in a similar mode."[109] Thus, to understand what "actually took place in the sixteeenth century," we would do well to learn this courtly language again.

"Comparative discourse" does not operate quite in the manner of Spenser's tournament, but the device is analogous. The symmetry is broken and at the same time preserved, through the ambivalent use of names.

Part II
Narrative And Legal Fictions

Chapter I
A Tale Of A Tub

In 1592 a tale, *Greene's Groatsworth of Wit*, provoked some turmoil in the London literary world. Robert Greene, who died on 2 or 3 September 1592, would have written it while dying. The small book contained a letter (Appendix I to this chapter) in which Greene warned three unnamed playwrights against the unscrupulous theatre companies. One actor was singled out. He was nicknamed "Shake-scene." This would be the first and for several years the only reference to the actor William Shakespeare. The allusion to Shakespeare seems impervious to doubt. The pun on the name Shakespeare and the line quoted from one of his plays are believed to be entirely reliable, indeed unequivocal, marks of identification. The first playwright was called a "gracer of Tragedians" but denounced as a follower of Machiavelli and his "diabolical Atheism." The general consensus is that this must be Christopher Marlowe. The second playwright was admonished for taking "too much liberties" with scholars; he was addressed as "young Juvenal, that biting satirist." Opinion as to his identity has for some time been divided between Thomas Lodge and Thomas Nashe, but the general consensus now favors Nashe. He was called "Juvenal" by Francis Meres in 1598; also in 1598 or some time before, the character Moth in Shakespeare's play *Love's Labour's Lost* is nicknamed Juvenal; Thomas Nashe is thought to have informed to some extent that personage. The third playwright is thought to be George Peele. Exactly what this third playwright was charged with has thus far eluded commentators.

Robert Greene, if we are to believe the publisher, penned another work on his deathbed, *The Repentance of Robert Greene*, published a few weeks after *Greene's Groatsworth of Wit*. But according to the publisher of *Greene's Vision*, also published the same year, **this** was unquestionably his ultimate work, written as it was, "at the moment of his death." This publisher erred. One work certainly came later: *Greene's News both from Heaven and Hell*, published the following year. Contemporaries, of course, did not believe that. Nor did they all believe that Robert Greene was the author of the first of these works capitalizing on the death of the popular author. Henry Chettle, a compositor and playwright, was suspected to have written *Greene's Groatsworth of Wit*. In due course a public apology was required of him. Chettle followed suit in a preface (Appendix II to the present chapter) to a pamphlet, *Kindheart's Dream*. In this apology he states that "one or two" of the three playwrights had taken offense and that he had been compelled to publicly apologize. One of the offended authors was the first playwright, Christopher Marlowe. The other was in all likelihood the third playwright, who did not request this apology personally. "Divers of worship" visited Henry Chettle and required a recantation, witnessing to the third playwright's "facetious grace in writing" and to his "honesty". Here the orthodox identification of Peele as the third playwright founders, for an excuse would not have been required by the "divers of worship" for George Peele, playwright and "university wit," but rather for 'Shake-scene' (presumed to be Shakespeare), the actor whom the three playwrights should especially fear. Such is the camel which the mainstream of orthodox theory, whilst straining at gnats, has been swallowing for a long time: Shakespeare would have been warned against himself. *Prima facie* this is a crude illogicism, at least if put forth in what can perhaps be called the unsophisticated orthodox version of which Brian Vickers, in **Shakespeare, Co-Author,** writes: "From Malone to Schoenbaum biographers of Shakespeare have happily identified him as the writer so soothingly conciliated. But Lukas Erne has recently read these texts more carefully, showing that Chettle's pamphlet is addressed to one of the three 'Gentlemen' writers..." Erne is correct in his conclusion that it is the third playwright who is "conciliated," but as will be seen in the next chapter, Erne does not grasp the contemporaneous meaning of the terms of 'honesty' and 'civility' and thus fails to identify the third playwright correctly.[110]

However, there exists a more sophisticated version identifying the person to whose "facetious grace in writing" the "divers of worship" testify, but it still contains many riddles.

Unsolved problems

The first question to be asked is: what exactly was the nature of the offense implied in the address to the third playwright, and in what terms did Chettle apologize for it? Only a few lines were written to this third playwright:

> "And thou no less deserving than the other two, in some things rarer, in nothing inferior; driven (as myself) to ex-treme shifts, a little have I to say to thee: and were it not an idolatrous oath, I would swear by sweet S. George, thou art unworthy better hap, since thou depend on so mean a stay."

Does Chettle *negate* any of these statements? Does he say, 'no, he is **not driven** to extreme shifts and **does not depend** on so mean a stay'? Or, 'yes, **he does depend** on so mean a stay but he has assuredly **deserved better**'? No, on the contrary, Chettle apologizes in a manner apparently **wholly unrelated to those lines in the letter**. His demeanor (the playwright's), Chettle writes, is "civil", as excellent as he is in "the quality he professes." Now, seemingly, the "divers of worship" (who extracted the apology from Chettle) were satisfied. Chettle must then have affirmed what they wanted publicly said of this man. We observe that Chettle dutifully reports what they told him:

> "Besides, divers of worship have reported his uprightness of dealing, which argues his honesty, and his facetious grace in writing, that approves his Art."

"Facetious grace in writing" evidently evokes Shakespeare. But how does this correlate to the reproach in the letter? Orthodox scholars have unceremoniously dispensed with these difficulties. They tell us that there was **nothing offensive** in the lines to the third playwright and that therefore the divers of worship must have intervened **on behalf of the vilified actor** 'Shake-scene,' the only party, besides Marlowe, who had reason to feel offended. But Chettle tells us that he was **not certain** whether this other party felt personally offended. Some worshipful persons held he was. And Chettle also clearly states that **one or two of the playwrights addressed in the letter were offended**:

> "About three months since died M. *Robert Greene*, leaving many pa-

pers in sundry booksellers' hands, among other his Groatsworth of
Wit, in which a letter written to divers play-makers, is offensively
by one or two of them taken..."
Chettle is speaking of the **third** playwright when he says, "one or two
of them." It was E.K. Chambers who coined the legerdemain (or at least
gave it the necessary currency) which seemed to resolve the difficulty.
Chettle would have meant 'Shake-scene,' alias Shakespeare. "It is possible that the first play-maker here referred to is Marlowe and the second Shakespeare, although this implies some looseness in Chettle's
language." But, Chambers goes on, "there is nothing in the letter as we
have it which could be offensive to any play-maker except Marlowe,
who is spoken of as an atheist and Machiavellian, and Shakespeare,
who is openly attacked."[111] Let us repeat: Chettle then, for some reason,
would not have been able to adequately express what he meant. The
same position is adopted by D. Allen Carroll: "All anti-Stratfordians, I
should think, and some Stratfordians, assume that the apology is directed elsewhere – to George Peele, perhaps — and that Chettle's apology therefore cannot be read as evidence that Shakespeare was a playwright, let alone an accomplished one." He continues: "Stratfordians
should by no means easily concede the point. No evidence suggests
that either Nashe or Peele were ever actors. Moreover, the criticism leveled at these two playwrights does not match, either in degree or kind,
that directed to Marlowe and Shakespeare. Why would Nashe or Peele
have expected an apology at all?"[112] Carroll fails to explain to us what
would have amounted to a charge of "dishonesty" or "uncivility" in
the invective against 'Shake-scene.'

At least this much seems clear: Chettle possibly referred to an actor.
In Elizabethan and Stuart times the phrase "quality he professes" often
denotes a player. Thomas Heywood, himself a playwright and actor,
uses the term "quality they profess" (to describe an actor's profession)
several times in his *Apology for Actors*, published in 1611.[113]

If Chettle meant Shake-scene/Shakespeare, then he certified his civility, whereas the "divers of worship" certified his honesty. If Chettle,
when he verified that the man in question showed a civil demeanour,
employed "loose language," then so did the divers of worship in af-

firming that he was "honest." As will be seen in the next chapter, "civility" and "honesty" were interchangeable terms in the 16th and 17th centuries. The failure to consider what the terms "civility" and "honesty" actually denoted in the early modern era is a particularly egregious omission in the discourse of the meaning of the letter in *Greene's Groatsworth of Wit*. For all the ink spilled in hopes of illuminating the mysteries of this letter, scant attention has been given to what these terms would have contemporaneously signified in the invective (either against the third playwright or 'Shake-scene'), that would have caused Chettle and the "divers of worship" to negate the charge by witnessing to "his civility" and "honesty," respectively.

The difficulties do not end there. Chettle seems uncertain whether the third playwright, or Shake-scene/Shakespeare was offended, or "one or two" took offense. And "why," Carroll asks, "'one or two'? That Chettle intended to comment on 'two' of those alluded to in the attack must have been as clear to Chettle as it is to us, and if the 'two' were Marlowe and Peele, the scholar playwrights to whom the letter was addressed, why not simply say 'two'? I am not sure. Certainly Marlowe and Peele were both gentleman scholars, but there was motive for saying 'one *or* two' if Shakespeare was the one praised."[114]

At this juncture Carroll does not appear to grasp the significance of the fact that Peele, Shakespeare or Mr. Whosoever did not **personally** intervene with Chettle, thus Chettle was unsure if he was personally offended. The divers of worship apparently told him nothing of the third playwright's or Shake-scene's personal feelings about the injury; they simply have urged Chettle to revoke it publicly, and Chettle has done so, despite the fact that he doesn't know whether Shake-scene or the third playwright was himself bothered about it. Carroll's interpretation is that Chettle would have been laying "flattering unction" to Shakespeare's soul by assimilating him as a gentleman, in the hope that he might pen comedies for the "upstart Crow's" company in the future: "By blurring the social distinction and lumping together two playwrights, one a gentleman (Marlowe) and one not (the actor Shakespeare) — he can flatter Shakespeare, allowing the reader to suppose that Shakespeare was a gentleman, elevating him in rank to compensate for the attack and perhaps to recognize Shakespeare's growing importance in the theatrical scene. If such was indeed Chettle's motive, then the apology does not seem to have succeeded. Chettle went on to write, wholly or in part, forty-eight plays, and not one for Shakespeare's company. Chettle attempts with a sleight of pen ('one or two'), along with an apology, to protect himself from the potential consequence for his part in the attack."[115]

This explanation smells of the tale-of-the-tub-thrown-to-the-whale to prevent the beast from swallowing what Carroll considers "a key piece of evidence." Would every reader have known who the "one or two" were? Neither is named, either in the letter in *Greene's Groatsworth of Wit* or in Chettle's apology. Insiders of the literary world, those who knew Marlowe and/or Shakespeare anyway, would have known both the man and his status. Further, it is not known when Henry Chettle started writing plays. Even fragments of his plays are not known before 1598, though he most probably had written some by that time, as Francis Meres lists him under "best for comedy" in 1598. Yet all Chettle's known or presumed plays were written for the rival company, the Admiral's Men. Thus, three key questions have arisen:

1) Is there really nothing in the lines addressed to the third playwright constituting or implying a charge of "uncivility" or "dishonesty," making sense of Chettle's revocation?

2) If the third offended person was not the third playwright but Shakescene/Shakespeare, what in the lines about him could be construed as a charge of uncivility or dishonesty?

3) Why was Chettle not certain whether one of the two was personally offended?

Before addressing these issues, another perplexing question that has received little or no attention will be examined.

The strange case of Thomas Nashe – Odd man in

Nashe, according to the more sophisticated orthodox version of the *GGW* affair, would have had no reason to require an apology. In fact, Chettle did apologize to Nashe. In his apology Chettle writes: "for I protest it was all *Greenes*, not mine nor Maister *Nashes*, as some unjustly have affirmed." Obviously, rumours had been spread that Nashe himself was the author of *Greene's Groatsworth of Wit*. We do not know by whom. In October 1592 Nashe had returned from the country to London. In a preface to the second edition of his *Pierce Penniless His Supplication* to *the Devil* Nashe emphatically rejects the charge. "Other news I am advertised of, that a scald trivial lying pamphlet, called *Greene's Groatsworth of Wit* is given out to be of my doing. God never have care of my soul, but utterly renounce me, if the least word or syllable in it proceeded from my pen, or if I were anyway privy to the printing of it."[116] Again, Nashe gives us no names. Those unknown persons who thought Nashe to be the author can hardly at the same time have thought him to be the playwright warned in the letter. And, as Shakespeare would have warned himself against his own presumptuousness in writing plays, Nashe, though a scholar (albeit a young one), would have warned himself not to speak bitter words against scholars. But who would have spread the rumour of Nashe's authorship of *Groatsworth*? We might find the answer within some textual allusion, veiled in the kind of dark language at which Elizabethans were so skilled.

Gabriel Harvey, in his third pamphlet against Nashe, *Pierce's Supererogation*, would seem to insinuate that Nashe was the author: "He may declare his dear affection to his paramour [Greene]: or his pure honesty to the world; or his constant zeal to play the Devil's orator: but no Apology of Greene, like *Greene's Groatsworth of Wit*: and when Nashe will indeed accomplish a work of supererogation, let him publish Nashe's *Penniworth of Discretion*."[117] That Harvey considers *Greene's Groatsworth of Wit* an apology for Robert Greene is also clear from the sentence immediately preceding, in which he derisively compares Nashe's alleged apology for Greene with Plato's apology for Socrates: "It is the least of his famous adventures, that he undertakes to be *Greene's advocate*: as divine Plato assayed to defend Socrates at the Bar: and I know not whether it be the least of his doughty exploits, that he salved his friend's credit, as that excellent disciple saved his master's life."[118] Keeping in mind that Harvey wrote these lines in 1593, less than a year after Nashe's denial and Chettle's public exculpation of Nashe in the apology, we find no other explanation than that Harvey took Nashe to be the author of *Greene's Groatsworth of Wit*.

Chettle, as we have seen, also denied his own authorship of GGW: "I had only in the copy this share: it was ill written, as sometimes *Greene's* hand was none of the best; licensed it must be, ere it could be printed, which could never be if it might not be read." Which license did Chettle mean?

At the peril of Henry Chettle

Generally a publisher had to obtain the license of the authorities before presenting a book for entrance in the Stationers' Register to the wardens of the Stationers' Company, which regulated the printing, publishing and bookselling trade. As seen in Chapter 2, since the Star Chamber Decree of 23 June 1586, the Elizabethan Press Act, this licensing power lay with the Archbishop of Canterbury and the Bishop of London or their deputies, who in most cases were members of the clergy. The second kind of license, entirely independent of the episcopal license, was that of the wardens, the right to publish. *Greene's Groatsworth of Wit* was entered without previous submission to an episcopal censor but no "further" or "sufficient authority" was requested by Richard Watkins. With the name Watkins we have steered our plough into the next hard furrow. Watkins' licensing activities in the Stationers' Company confront us with an irregularity. It is absolutely clear that the license of the company, the copyright, was assigned by the two wardens or either of them; that was one of the functions for which they were elected each year about the end of June, commencing their term in the first half of July. For the term from July 1592 to July 1593 the master was George Bishop, the upper warden Henry Con(ne)way, the under warden Thomas Stirrop. Watkins was no warden and, therefore, had no official power of licensing! Why did he license *Greene's Groatsworth of Wit*? A historian of the Stationers' Company remarks that "from 1591 Richard Watkins began to act as a fairly regular licenser in place of the Wardens whoever they might be."[119] This statement is not wholly borne out by the facts. The under warden did license books in that period, but not the upper warden Conway, who had been elected for two consecutive terms from July 1591 to July 1593.[120] Watkins acted in his stead. And beyond that, he also exerted censorial functions. Most entries are "under the hand" of either Watkins or the under warden or both, which means that Watkins effectively granted the license of the Stationers' Company. But in several cases the license is granted by the under warden "by warrant" of master Watkins; in one case a proviso is added to the entry, "Provided that this book must be perused by master Watkins before it be printed."[121] In these cases Watkins did not substitute himself for the wardens but probably took the place of an episcopal censor. The question is of some importance in order to assess who caused the clause "upon the peril of Henry Chettle" to be included in the entry and why. Was it the publisher William Wright or the licenser Richard Watkins? Carroll seems to take it for granted that it was William Wright, for fear of troubles which could have arisen from the presence of the fable of Lamilia, in which the fox might have been understood as a quip at Lord Burghley, Elizabeth's powerful Lord Treasurer. "The risk involved in printing this fable may account for the warning and possible attribution of responsibility carried in the allowance 'uppon the perill of *Henry Chettle*,' by which peculiar entry Wright, the publisher, protected himself... Two features of this fable seem certain. First, after the public reaction to Spenser's *Mother Hubbard's Tale* in the *Complaints* volume (ent. 29 December 1590), any such fable would be taken to allude to serious matters involving those in high places... Second, the fox in the fable would be taken for Burghley."[122]

As a matter of fact, though, Chettle did not have to apologize for the fable. Moreover, it is difficult to see why a fox in a fable would have been inevitably associated with Lord Burghley. The fox is a figure in many fables, for instance in Nashe's tale of the bear in *Pierce Penniless*, a story with a much more clear-cut political thrust than Lamilia's fable. *Pierce Penniless* was entered in the Stationers' Register six weeks before *Greene's Groatsworth of Wit*. It had been licensed by the same Richard Watkins and authorized by none other than the Archbishop of Canterbury. The Archbishop did not associate Nashe's fox with Lord Burghley. And would Wright have been so imprudent to publish the book had he suspected it contained some matter offensive to the mighty Lord Treasurer Burghley? Would Watkins under these circumstances have been so daring to encroach upon the powers of the lawful censors? Would he not have preferred to require from Wright "lawful or sufficient authority"? And, as will be seen below, it is highly unlikely that John Wolf, a client of the Cecils, would have printed this part of *GGW*.

Now the possibility that Watkins expected some trouble from the letter cannot be rejected and must be given equal weight. After all, Watkins had witnessed a similar case during his first term as upper warden in 1580. The trouble then befell the living author of a letter, namely Gabriel Harvey, but in 1592 the declared author Robert Greene was dead. In cases of slander the law made not only the originator responsible but, if the originator was unanswerable, being dead or unknown, also the propagator. It is not likely that Watkins would have licensed the book had he suspected it to contain some slanderous matter on Lord Burghley. But if he or the publisher William Wright suspected some slander on private persons or some other troubles it would have been prudent to make Henry Chettle, the editor and suspected author, liable.

Another possibility, however, has never been considered. It could well be the one which best explains the clause "at the peril of Henry Chettle". As mentioned, soon after *Greene's Groatsworth of Wit* Cuthbert Burby published a similar work, *The Repentance of Robert Greene*. Both Wright and Watkins might have anticipated a conflict of interest with Burby over rights in the copy caused by the use of identical papers of Greene. If Chettle had partly used the same papers as Burby (see below) this might be considered an infringement of Burby's rights. "The owner of a copy had not only the exclusive right to reprint the text, but also the right for a fair chance to recover his costs. He could therefore seek the Company's protection if *any* book — not necessarily a reprint or plagiarism of his own copy — threatened his ability to dispose of unsold copies of an existing edition... George Thomason tried to block the publication of Dugdale's *History of St. Paul's Cathedral* (1658) on the grounds that Daniel King ´hath written upon yᵉ same subject´ in his *Cathedral... Churches of England and Wales* (1656)."[123] The records of the Stationers´ Company do mention a controversy between John Danter (the printer) and Chettle and between Danter and Burby on 5 March 1593, but, unfortunately, it is not stated what the litigious matter was.[124] At least two other entries in the Stationers´ Register suggest that if the wardens expected "perils" or "troubles" it was in connection with copy ownership.

On 7 May 1582 a book was entered to Edward White with the proviso "And the said **Edward** hathe undertaken to beare and discharge all troubles that maie arise for the printinge thereof."[125] The book in question, *The Pathway to Health for the Poor,* was a relatively popular book. It was printed eight times between 1587 and 1664. The wardens probably expected that some other stationer could have the right either to it or to a work on a similar subject. The other entry is to William Jaggard on 5 December 1608 of Thomas Heywood´s *Britain´s Troy.* The proviso reads "PROVIDED that yf any question or trouble growe hereof. Then he shall answere and discharge yt at his owne Losse and costes."[126] From Thomas Heywood´s epistle to the printer in his *Apology for Actors* we know there were troubles. Heywood complained on the one hand about the very bad printing and Jaggard´s refusal to correct the errors on the ground that he would rather charge the author with errors than publicly to disavow his own workmanship; on the other hand, Jaggard had added several pieces from that work to an edition of *The Passionate Pilgrim.* The work was allowed by the episcopal censor Etkins, therefore failing authority cannot have been the cause. Heywood´s two epistles having probably been added to the *The Passionate Pilgrim* in 1612, three years later, this cannot have been the cause either. Perhaps Jaggard had printed the work without Heywood´s consent. In the case of Chettle in 1592, William Wright might have expected similar troubles from Cuthbert Burby. Such clauses in entries were generally inserted when the wardens foresaw possible conflicts of copy ownership. On the contrary, when they expected trouble from the authorities, they were used to requiring that the work be submitted to the censors. In this view, neither Richard Watkins´ activity nor the clause "at the peril of

Henry Chettle" need incite us to look for some "dangerous matter" in the contents of *Greene's Groatsworth of Wit*.

Strictures for young Juvenal

Another aspect which has not received due consideration is the possible role Gabriel Harvey might have played in the events leading up to the publication of *Greene's Groatsworth of Wit*. The lines to "young Juvenal" exude the same attitude toward Nashe as Harvey's *Four Letters* written at about the same time, September 1592:

"With thee I join young *Juvenal,* that biting Satirist, that lastly with me together wrote a Comedy. Sweet boy, might I advise thee, be advised, and get not many enemies by bitter words: inveigh against vain men, for thou canst do it, no man better, no man so well: thou hast a liberty to reprove all, and name none; for one being spoken to, all are offended; none being blamed no man is injured. Stop shallow water still run-ning, it will rage, or tread on a worm and it will turn: then blame not Scholars vexed with sharpe lines, if they reprove thy too much liberty of reproof."

Harvey's admonitions to Nashe percolate the same mixture of patronizing well-wishing and threat as those in the letter in *GGW*. It is surprising that these parallels have only been referred to in passing. In his edition of *GGW* Carroll points to only one of them.[127] "Alas, even his fellow-writer, a proper young man if advised in time..."[128]. But a whole set of phrases in Harvey's *Four Letters* more than just savour of the warning to "young Juvenal" in the letter in *GGW*:

"Now, good sweet Muse, I beseech thee by thy delicate wit, and by the quaintest inventions of thy deviseful brain... and either advance thy vertuous self, maugre Fortune... or mightily enchant some magnificent Mæcenas, for thou canst do it..."[129], and "Good sweet Orator, be a divine Poet indeed: and use heavenly eloquence indeed: and employ thy golden talent indeed...as noble Sir Philip Sidney and gentle Maister Spenser have done... and I will bestow more compliments of rare amplifications upon thee then ever any bestowed upon them",[130] and "I speak generally to every springing wit; but more specifically to a few; and at this instant singularly to one: whom I salute with a hundred blessings...I protest, it was not thy person that I anyway disliked; but thy rash, and desperate proceeding against thy well-willers..."[131] Praise, advice, menace. "Wronged men are seldom tongue-tied: the patientest creature wants not blood in his heart, or ink in his pen: and although his blood be not wildfire, yet it is blood: that will not be cooled with a card or daunted with bugswords,"[132] or "There is a certain thing called modesty. If they could light upon it: and by my young Master's leave, some pretty smack or discretion would relish well"[133] and "May it please gentle Pierce, in the divine fury of his ravished spirit, to be graciously good unto his poor friends, who would be somewhat loath to be silly sheep for the wolf or other sheep-biter: I dare undertake, that abused Author of the Astrological Discourse... shall unfainedly pray for him..."[134]

Despite the extensive comments on *Greene's Groatsworth of Wit* and more particularly on the letter, other critical questions have received scant attention, e.g.: 1) Which comedy could Nashe have written together with Greene? 2) Why was Nashe addressed as "young Juvenal"? 3) Who are the scholars against whom Nashe is known to have written "bitter" words by 1592?

Which scholars had Nashe vexed?

The only scholars Nashe is known to have vexed are Gabriel Harvey's younger brothers: John and, more massively, his brother Richard. In 1583 Richard Harvey published An Astrological Discourse upon the great and notable Conjunction of the two superior Planetes, SATURNE & IUPITER, which shall happen the 28. day of April, 1583. The work was complemented in the same year by John Harvey's Astrological Addition or supplement to be annexed to the late Discourse upon the great conjunction of Saturne and Iupiter. Likely, also in 1583, John Harvey published an almanac of prognostications, with another following in 1588. In 1589 a 22-year-old fresh academic, bursting with self-confidence, rushed into print as a critic with a survey of English literature entitled "To the Gentlemen Students of Both Universities," published as preface to Robert Greene's romance Menaphon. Young Nashe's boldness seems to have stirred up gall in Richard Harvey, who in the preface to one of his sermons, A Theological Discourse of the Lamb of God and his Enemies, published early in 1590, set out to crop the young man's feathers. Richard Harvey first complained of the tactics used by the bishops in the embittered contention between the Anglican Church and the radical pamphleteer(s) Martin Marprelate. Professional writers, among them Nashe and John Lyly, had been hired by the bishops to lampoon Martin Marprelate in anti-Martinist pamphlets and on the stage. Richard Harvey wrote: "God help the Church when it must be reformed by such men and such means."[135] Later in the preface he abruptly lashes out against Nashe personally:

"... but it becomes me not to play that part in Divinity, that one Thomas Nash has lately done in humanity, who takes upon him in civil learning as Martin does in religion, peremptorily censuring his betters at pleasure, Poets, Orators, Polyhistors, Lawyers, and whom not?.. I wis this Thomas Nash, one whom I never heard of before (for I cannot imagine him to be Thomas Nash our butler of Pembroke Hall, albeit peradventure not much better learned) showed himself none of the meanest men, to censure Sir Thomas Moore, Sir John Cheke, Doctor Watson, Doctor Haddon, Maister Ascham, Doctor Car, my brother Doctor Harvey, and such like; yet the jolly man will needs be playing the doughty Martin in his kind... Yet let not Martin, or Nash, or any such famous obscure man, or any other piperly makeplay or makebate, presume overmuch of my patience as of simplicity, but of choice. As I am easily ruled by reason, so no fierce or proud passion can overrule; no carping censor, or vain Papphatchet, or madbrain Scoggin or gay companion, any thing move me."[136]

'Papphatchet' is the pseudonym under which John Lyly had written an anti-Martinist pamphlet in which he had also hurled some darts at Gabriel Harvey. As for Nashe, it is true that he had mentioned Gabriel Harvey in his preface to Greene's romance, though by no means scoffingly, possibly not as extollingly as Gabriel and his brother Richard believed themselves to merit: "I know not almost any of late days that has shown himself singular in any special Latin poem... I will not say but we had a Haddon, whose pen would have challenged the laurel from Homer, together with Car, that came as near him as Virgil to Theocritus. But Thomas Newton with his Leiland, and Gabriel Harvey with two or three other is almost all the store that is left us at this hour."[137] Richard Harvey judged Nashe, "young Juvenal," too young and cocksure. Nashe retaliated in Pierce Penniless.

"On the contrary side, if I be euil entreated, or sent away with a flea in my ear, let him look that I will rail on him soundly... I haue terms (if I be vexed) laid steep in Aquafortis, & Gunpowder, that shall rattle through the skies and make an earthquake in a peasant's ears. Put case (since I am not yet out of the theme of wrath) that some tired jade belonging to the Press, whom I neuer wronged in my life, has named me expressly in print (as I will not do him) and accuse me of want of learning, upbraiding me for reviving in an epistle of mine the reverent memory of Sir Thomas Moore, Sir Iohn Cheeke, Doctor Watson, Doctor Haddon, Doctor Carre, Maister Ascham, as if they were no meat but for his Mastership's mouth, or none but some such as the son of a ropemaker were worthy to mention them... Thou hast a brother, hast thou not, student in Almanackes?, Go to, I'll stand to it, he fathered one of thy bastards (a book I mean) which being one of thy begetting was set forth under his name. Gentlemen, I am sure you haue heard of a ridiculous Ass that many years since sold lies by the great, and wrote an absurd Astrologicall Discourse of the terrible Conjunction of Saturn and Iupiter, wherein (as if he had lately cast the Heauens' water, or beene at the anatomizing of the Skies entrails in Surgeon's hall) he prophesied of such strange wonders to ensue from stars distemperature, and the unusual adultery of planets, as none but he that is bawd to those celestial bodies, could ever discry. What expectation there was of it both in town and country, the amazement of those times may testify: and the rather because he pawned his credit upon it, in these express terms; If these things fall not out in every point as I haue written, let me for euer hereafter loose the credit of my Astronomy. Well so it

happened, that he happened not to be a man of his word; his Astronomy broke his day with his creditors and Saturn and Iupiter
proved honester men then all the World took them for: whereupon,
the poor Prognosticator was ready to run himself through with his
Iacob´s Staff, and cast himselfe headlong from the top of a Globe (as
a mountaine) and break his neck. The whole Uniuersity hissed at
him, Tarlton at the Theatre made jests of him, and Elderton con-
sumed his ale-crummed nose to nothing, in bearbaiting him with
whole bundles of ballads."[138]

The passage contains a quip for John Harvey, whose addition to his
brother´s Astrological Discourse Nashe suggests was in truth Rich-
ard´s. There might have been a stealthy quip for Gabriel Harvey, too, in
the word "earthquake." An earthquake was the subject of one of
Gabriel Harvey´s Three Familiar Letters in which he libeled the Earl of
Oxford in 1580. Some of the ingredients of Nashe´s invective in Pierce
Penniless had also appeared in the original version of Robert Greene´s
A Quip for an Upstart Courtier: ´maker of almanacs, astrological discourse,´ and above all, ´son of a ropemaker.´ Greene´s book is likely to
have appeared in print only weeks before Nashe´s Pierce Penniless (it
was entered in the Stationers´s Register on July 21, 1592, Pierce Penniless on August 8, 1592). The passage on the Harvey brothers was excised from the second edition of a Quip, and for a long time the edition
was thought lost, till a copy resurfaced in 1919. It reads:

"The ropemaker replied, that honestly journeying by the way, he
acquainted himself with the Collier, & for no other cause pretended.
And whether are you a going quoted I? Marry sir quoted he, first to
absolve your question, I dwell in Saffron Walden, and am going to
Cambridge to three sons that I keep there at school, such apt children, sir, as few women have groaned for, and yet they have ill luck.
The one [Richard] sir is a divine to comfort my soul, & he indeed,
though he be a vainglorious ass, as divers youths of his age be, is
well given to the show of the world, and wrote of late the Lamb of
God, and yet his parishioners say he is the limb of the devil, and
kisses their wives with holy kisses, but they had rather he should
keep his lips for madge his mare[139]. The second, sir, is a Physician

[John] or a fool, but indeed a physician, & had proved a proper man if he had not spoiled himself with his Astrological discourse of the terrible conjunction of Saturn and Jupiter. For the eldest [Gabriel], he is a Civilian [doctor of civil law], a wondrous witted fellow, sir reverence sir, he is a Doctor, and as Tubalcain was the first inventor of music, so he, God's benison light upon him, was the first that invented English Hexameter: but see how in these days learning is little esteemed, for that and other familiar letters and proper treatises he was orderly clapped in the Fleet, but sir a hawk and a kite may bring forth a coystrel, and honest parents may have bad children. Honest with the devil, quoted the Collier..."[140]

Which comedy could Nashe and Greene have written together?

The above passage has been quoted in full because it may lead us to the answer to another question still puzzling scholars: which comedy did Greene and "young Juvenal" write together? Several plays have been put forward but the one that would seem the most obvious candidate has been overlooked. This is Greene's *Quip*, in which we believe Nashe had a hand, first of all because the quoted passage is written in a light-hearted, satirical vein much more typical of Nashe than of Greene. In particular, the name Tubalcain suggests Nashe's quick-witted coinage. This intentional 'malapropism' disturbed Gabriel Harvey. The biblical inventor of music is Jubal, "the father of all who play the harp and the flute" (Gen. 4:20). Tubal-Cain is the father of the blacksmiths who "forged all kinds of tools out of bronze and iron" (Gen. 4:22). On the one hand, Tubalcain was a craftsman, a "mechanic", as a ropemaker was. On the other hand, the substitution of Jubal with Tubalcain would hammer home the message that the English hexameters of the pedantic scholar Harvey clanged like metal beaten with a hammer. Which is, we think, pure Nashe, not Greene. Nashe returns to this conflation four years later when he presents one of his interlocutors under the name of Don Carneades de boone Compagniola, "a busy Country Justice, [who] sits on the Bench and preaches to thieves out of their own confessions: or rather, like a Quarter-master or Treasurer of Bride-well, whose office is to give so many strokes with the hammer... and by the same Tubal's music to warn the blue-coat Corrector..."[141] **As for Harvey**; the allusion hit its intended target but was apparently repressed in his subconscious, only to surface in a *Freudian slip*. Harvey later wrote:"It goes somewhat hard in my harsh legend, when the father of music must be mocked, not Tubalcain, as he mistermed him, but Tubal, whom Genesis vouchsafes honourable mention."[142] Harvey corrects the author of the incriminated passage but then commits an error himself by not naming **Jubal** for Tubal-Cain, but instead **Tubal**, the name of the Rabelaisian pedantic (the full name being Tubal Holofernes, and Holofernes, it should be remembered, is the name Shakespeare gives to the pedantic classicist in *Love's Labour's Lost*).

Secondly, Nashe was fond of the passage. Refuting Harvey's contention that it was expunged by Greene for fear of legal action being taken against him, he writes: "Marry, this I must say, there was a learned doctor of physic, to whom Greene in his sickness sent for counsel, that having read over the book of Velvetbreeches and Clothbreeches, and laughing merrily at the three brothers' legend, willed Greene in any case either to mitigate it, or leave it out: Not for any extraordinary account he made of the fraternity of fools, but for one of them was proceeded in the same faculty of physic he professed, and willingly he would have none of that excellent calling ill spoken of."[143]

Thirdly, this physician had read "the book of Velvet-breeches and Cloth-breeches." What was this "book"? "On the outside of prompt-books used in an Elizabethan theatre, the title of the play was usually preceded by the words 'The Book of'."[144] In one instance Nashe speaks of the *Quip*, in two others simply of *Velvet-breeches and Cloth-breeches*. Thus while it is possible that the physician read a prompt-book of the play *Velvet-breeches and Cloth-breeches*, the single word "book" is too tenuous a clue to rely too strongly on.

But, fourthly, the subtitle of Greene's *Quip* was "A quaint dispute between Velvet breeches and Cloth breeches." As seen in chapter 2 of part I, on 27 May 1600 James Roberts registered a play called *A Moral of Cloth Breeches and Velvet Hoses*."[145] The play is no longer extant. It is even not known whether it was ever printed. But there can be no doubt that this was either Greene's work or based upon Greene's work; in either case it is the most plausible candidate for the comedy Nashe and Greene are said to have written together.

Finally, Nashe seems to obliquely acknowledge the authorship of the lines in the *Quip*.

Greene's Insult

The puzzling question of the passage in the *Quip* and the declared motive of Gabriel Harvey's anger at it, is that it contains little that could have been construed as slander of the father of the Harvey brothers. He is merely said to be a ropemaker; the whole blame is laid upon his sons. The trade of ropemaker was an honorable one, or, as Elizabethans more often termed it, an 'honest' one. Nashe himself, in his dedication to *Strange News*, the pamphlet in response to Harvey's *Four Letters*, writes that "An honest man of Saffron-Walden kept three sons at the University together a long time,"[146] and that "no man denied or impaired" his honesty.[147] The incriminated passage reads "and honest parents may have bad children." In reply to Nashe, and by implication also in response to the lines in the *Quip*, Gabriel Harvey reciprocates that phrase by writing that a "saint" might sometimes have a "reprobate" father.[148] By contrast, Nashe's passage contains several slanderous remarks on the three sons, especially on Richard and Gabriel. Richard is said to be a "a vainglorious ass," a womanizer, "the limb of the devil", Gabriel to have been "orderly clapped" in the Fleet prison.

Actually, it was not the alleged dishonorable mention of his father which infuriated Harvey but, far exceeding any other conceivable injury, the mention of his own low descent from a man who by occupation was a "mechanic," not a practiser of the "liberal" arts which Gabriel Harvey was proud to be. However, this is not what he emphatically protests in his first letter dated 29 August 1592. The foe in this and in his next letter is Robert Greene; Nashe is mentioned only in passing and on the whole rather favourably. Harvey states that Greene has abused his father. The words were supposedly those of 'M. Christopher

Bird,´ who apparently wrote a letter (also printed), recommending Harvey to a well-known Antwerp merchant, Emmanuel van Meeteren (Demetrius). There follows a text referring to a sonnet, said to be Bird´s, but unmistakably no less Harvey´s own than the text following Bird´s letter, the style matching that in the rest of Harvey´s pamphlets like two peas in a pod. Harvey, writing in Bird´s person, declares: " I send you my opinion in a plain but true Sonnet upon the famous new work intituled *A Quip for an upstart Courtier*; ...: as fantastical and fond a Dialogue as I have seen: and for some particulars one of the most licentious and intolerable invectives that I ever read. Wherein the lewd fellow and impudent railer, in an odious and desperate mood, without any cause or reason, amongst sundry other persons notoriously defamed, most spitefully and villanously abuses an ancient neighbor of mine, one M. *Harvey*, a right honest man of good reckoning; and one that above twenty years since bore the chiefest office in Walden with good credit. And hath maintained four sons, in Cambridge and elsewhere, with great charges, all sufficiently able to answer for themselves, and three (in spite of some few *Greenes*) universally well reputed in both Universities and through the Realm."[149]

In the second letter dated 5 September, two or three days after Greene´s death, all his fury is levelled at Greene, whose death he regrets for the sole reason that "I was deprived of that remedy in law, that I intended against him in the behalf of my father, whose honest reputation I was in many duties to tender."[150]

Here is Harvey´s red herring again, for nothing disparaging was said of his father, it was the man´s sons, Harvey and his brothers, who had been taunted in a manner nothing short of calumny. Of course, the possibility should be contemplated that the play *Cloth breeches and velvet hoses* had already been staged, possibly containing slanders of Harvey´s father. This seems far from likely, however. Gabriel Harvey would not have failed to explicitly comment on the play in his letters, and he only refers to the *Quip*. Finally, given that the play was perhaps never printed, this hypothesis must remain purely theoretical.

Nashe´s Insult

What made Gabriel Harvey fire off these letters? In the third, dated 8 and 9 September, he writes that he had been very loath to come into print "these twelve or thirteen years." "Yet partly the vehement importunity of some affectionate friends and partly my own tender regard of my father´s and my brothers´ good reputation have so forcibly overruled me that I have finally condescended to their passionate motion."[151]

Something new had happened between 5 and 8 September: the first edition of Nashe´s *Pierce Penniless* had been published. Without question, Harvey had read it. Suddenly, the target of his attacks is no longer Greene, now his principal target is Nashe. Nashe had also harped upon the trade of ropemaker. Young Juvenal´s "sharp lines vexing scholars" — in all probability we have them here:

"The Lambe of God make thee a wiser Bellweather then thou art, for else I doubt thou wilt be driven to leaue all and fall to thy father´s occupation, which is, to go and make a rope to hang thyself."[152]

It may be that Gabriel Harvey had come to wonder whether the passage in the *Quip* was perhaps not Greene´s, but rather Nashe´s.

Syntactic contrivance or contraption?

Nashe broaches the subject in the section where he confutes Harvey´s first letter. At one place this passage seems gramatically defective.

"´...thou will object thy father was abused, & that made thee write.´ What, by me, or Greene, or both? If by Greene and not me, thou shouldst have written against Greene and not me. If by both, I will answer for both. But not by both, therefore I will answer but for one."[153]

The first of the last two sentences is unproblematic: if, according to Nashe, Harvey thinks his father was abused by Greene alone, he should have written against Greene, not against Nashe, as Harvey did, in his third letter. Taken separately, the first part of the next sentence presents no difficulties either: if Harvey thinks his father was abused by both Greene and Nashe for calling the Harvey brothers "sons of a ropemaker" in the *Quip* and in *Pierce Penniless* respectively, then Nashe will answer for both. However, the second part of this sentence has its antecedent in the first part. It is not clear to which part the phrase "but not by both" should be semantically connected.

After the consideration of two of three possibilities, one would rather have expected the remaining third possibility: after by "Greene alone" and "by both Greene and me," would logically follow "by me (alone)". This might have been expressed by the slightly circumlocutory phrase 'if not by both, I will answer for myself alone.' And would imply that Nashe was assuming responsibility for the passage hitherto ascribed to Greene. The passage in the *Quip* did infuriate Harvey. If Nashe implied that Harvey's anger might not have been due to Greene, he would be intimating that Greene was not the author of the passage in the *Quip*. But no such conditional "if not" appears. Besides, Nashe would have made an erroneous use of the result conjunction, "therefore."

If we relate the phrase "but not by both" to "answer," we obtain: "I will answer for both; but not answer by both, therefore I will answer but for one." By "but for one" Nashe clearly means himself. Immediately thereafter he challenges Harvey to indicate one passage where he has reason to feel himself or his father injured:

"Give an instance ... wherein in any leaf of *Pierce Penniless* I had so much as half a syllable relation to thee or offered one jot of indignity to thy father, more than naming the greatest dignity he hath, when for variety of epithets I called thy brother *the son of a ropemaker*."

The "variety of epithets" should of course not be taken seriously. What we obtain if we relate the last clause to "answer" is a nonsensical statement: 'I will answer for both, but not by both, therefore I will not answer for both, but only for one.' On the top of this absurdity it follows that Harvey cannot be answered by Greene, who is now dead.

It seems that we have to understand "but not by both" as an elliptic affirmative clause, the consequence of the affirmation being that Nashe will only answer for himself. "Therefore" makes sense, if we read "but not by both" as an ellipsis for "but your father was not abused by both, he was so by me alone, therefore I will answer but for one." In other words, if Nashe concludes that as a result of "not by both" he will answer only for one, he is the only one whom Harvey can make responsible for the grievance he resents at the passage in the *Quip*. If, however, Nashe is responsible for both the passage in the *Quip* and the one in *Pierce Penniless*, he only answers for the latter. Hence, the ellipsis "but not by both" telescopes two related but different statements: Nashe affirms that the passage in the *Quip* was not Greene's but his, and he declares that he will only answer for one of them, that which was published under his own name: "under my name in *Pierce Penniless*."

Why Juvenal?

The name "Juvenal" for a young satirist around 1590 cannot surprise us in a time when comparisons with Cicero, Homer et al, were daily bread. One need not be a dyed-in-the-wool classicist like Harvey to apply the name to Nashe. But nevertheless the namegiving might point more to Harvey than to anybody else. Harvey more than once addresses Nashe as "sweet youth" and, as seen, "tender Juvenal" is how in *Love's Labour's Lost* Don Armado, whom Shakespeare has given so many touches of Harvey, nicknames the page Moth, whose quick wit evokes Nashe. Harvey aspired to the role of Nashe's mentor. He exhorts him to write "... not according to the fantastical mode of *Aretine* or *Rabelais*, but according to the fine model of *Orpheus, Homer, Pindarus,* & the excellent wits of Greece."[154] Here Juvenal is not named but from his not being named in another context in the same *Four Letters* we may infer that in Harvey's eyes Juvenal was an acceptable model for a satirist. In this passage Harvey inveighs against railers and drops some unexpected names:

"Invectives by favour have been too bold: and Satires by usurpation too presumptuous: I overpasse *Archilochus, Aristophanes, Lucian, Julian, Aretine,* and that whole venomous and viperous brood of old & new railers : even *Tully* and *Horace,* otherwhiles overreached: and I must needs say, Mother Hubbard, in heat of choler, forgetting the

pure sanguine of her sweet Fairy Queen, wilfully overshot her mal-contented self."[155]
Cicero, Horace, his friend Edmund Spenser are not names which one would expect Harvey to allude to in this context, even if they are placed on the railing fringe. But Juvenal is not mentioned among the reprehensible railers. Writing of Nashe in his *New Letter of Notable Contents* (1593) he confirms he wanted to play the mentor to Nashe:

"Though *Greene* were a *Julian*, and *Marlowe* a *Lucian*: yet I would be loath, *He* should be an *Aretin*."[156] In his pamphlets Aretine and Rabelais appear as the two most dangerous railers. "When the sweet youth haunted *Aretine*, and *Rabelais*, the two monstrous wits of their languages..." But an Aretine was what Nashe himself meant to be and how he was seen by fellow-authors like Thomas Lodge in *Wit's Misery and the World's Madness: Discovering the Devil's Incarnate of this Age* : "LILLY, the famous for facility: SPENSER, best read in ancient Poetry: DANIEL, choice in word and invention: DRAYTON: diligent and formal: TH. NASH, true English Aretine."[157]

Nashe, however, explicitly states that he does not want to follow Juvenal's example: "*Horace, Perseus, Juvenal,* my poor judgment lends you plentiful allowance of applause; yet had you, with the *Phrygian* melody that stirs men up to battle and fury, mixed the Dorian tune that favoureth mirth and pleasure, your unsugared pills (however excellently medicinable) would not have been so harsh in the swallowing."[158]

A quondam acquaintance

The letter is addressed to "quondam acquaintances." However, Chettle declares he was not acquainted with either of the two offended playwrights. He was certainly acquainted with Nashe at the time he wrote his apology, and probably before. According to Chettle, Nashe was not a "quondam" acquaintance, the other two weren't acquaintances of any kind. Chettle is likely to have tailored the tale of Roberto in *Greene's Groatsworth of Wit* after Greene's fashion in *Francesco's Fortunes*. Chettle also borrowed a line from Nashe's preface to Greene's *Menaphon*. Nashe had written: "...if our Poets had not peecte [tricked up] with the supply of their periwigs, they might have anticked it until this time up and down the country with the King of Fairies, and dined every day at the peas porredge ordinary with *Delfrigus.*"[159] *Groatsworth* has: "Nay, then, said the Player, I mislike your judgement: why, I am as famous for Delphrigus, and the King of Fairies, as ever was any of time." We also find "Up and down the country," a phrase which Chettle altered slightly by letting the player add he was a country player.

Another reason which makes it unlikely that Chettle wrote the passage about "young Juvenal" is his professed respect for scholars, a statement which we think can be believed. But of course Chettle was writing under the name of Robert Greene. Even then the term "quondam" is inappropriate, at least for Nashe who had lately written a comedy with Greene and caroused with him in August, less than a month before. The juxtaposition of "quondam" and "lastly wrote a comedy with me together" gives rise to suspicion. One who is "quondam" is no longer an acquaintance, and for this to be true, a certain time must have elapsed (surely more than a month, keeping in mind that the acquaintance would have "lately" collaborated on a comedy). And so we come back to Harvey, not for the last time.

If Harvey wrote the letter or at least the passage to Nashe, it could account for the presence of the out-of-phase word "quondam." The word makes very good sense as applied to Harvey and, as far as we can see, it is only applicable to him. It would mean that in writing "quondam," Harvey, as is common with forgers, would have (consciously or unconsciously) left behind an identification mark, a certain clue, the equivalent, so to speak, of the chewing-gum used to fill up the teeth of the "pre-historic" Piltdown man.[160] Harvey had known Nashe and Greene at Cambridge in the 1580s. He had also known John Lyly, whom he greets in the second part of *Pierce's Supererogation*, a work published in 1593, the first and third part having been written that same year, although the second part had actually been written in November 1589:

"Pap-Hatchett (for the name of thy good nature is pitifully grown out of request), thy old acquaintance in the Savoy, when young Euphues hatched the eggs, that his elder friends laid, (surely Euphues

was someway a pretty fellow: would God Lyly had always been
Euphues and never Pap-Hatchet;) that old acquaintance, now somewhat straungely saluted with a new remembrance, is neither lubba-
bied with sweete Papp, nor scarre-crowed with thy sower
hatchet."[161] In the same *Pierce's Supererogation* and also in *Foure Letters* Harvey more than once refers to his former acquaintances. In his
third letter he writes: "Who cannot return home a quip, or requite
one libel with another? Nothing more common in books, or more
ready in mouths then the invective vein and the whole art of railing.
Some scholars have choice of nimble pens & smooth tongues at
commandement. And there was a time when peradventure I could
speak with them that talked with me."[162]

Marlowe, Nashe and Greene, were former, "quondam" Cambridge acquaintances to Harvey, Lyly was a former Oxford acquaintance. And
would Greene blame Nashe for having written caustically against the
Harvey brothers? *Pierce Penniless* was not yet in print when he died.
Though he could have seen it in manuscript, it was unpublished. What
is even more, Greene would have reprimanded Nashe for the same reason and in the same way as Harvey did in his *Four Letters*, providing
Harvey with a mighty weapon in his subsequent quarrel with Nashe. If
even his friend Greene thought Nashe's dealings with scholars (the
Harvey brothers), presumptuous, what an opportunity there would
have been for Harvey to seize upon. Yet neither in his *Four Letters* nor
in his two pamphlets of the next year, *Pierce's Supererogation* and *A New
Letter of Notable Contents*, did Harvey once use this argument.

Timing of events

It is useful at this juncture to recall the dates of the key events in order
to shed more light upon what happened or could have happened between July/August 1592 and January of the following year.

Greene's *Quip for an Upstart Courtier* is entered in the Stationers'
Register on 21 July 1592. A second edition must have quickly followed.
Nashe knew that the incriminating passage on the Harveys had been
excised. At some time in August, probably early in the month, Nashe
and "Will. Monox" met Greene for a "banquet of Rhenish wine and

pickle-herring," and Nashe reports that he and 'his Lord' left London for the province because of the plague. Their departure from London took place shortly after the "banquett," maybe immediately following it. *Pierce Penniless* was then entered in the Stationer's Register on 8 August. At the end of the month Gabriel Harvey arrived in London, and shortly thereafter Robert Greene died, on 2 or 3 September. Harvey wrote his *Four Letters, and certain Sonnets.* His letters were entered in the Stationers' Register on 4 December, but the first two (the second being his narration of Greene's death and funeral) had already been issued in print separately, to **this** edition he subsequently added his third letter and published the whole as *Three Letters, and certain Sonnets.*[163] *Greene's Groatsworth of Wit* was registered on 20 September, *The Repentance* on 6 October, Chettle's *Kindheart's Dream* on 8 December, finally Nashe's *Strange News* on 12 January 1593 (1592 old style) and printed in the year 1592 (1593, new style), which means that it must have been in print before 25 March 1593. When Nashe is back in London he learns of the publication of *Greene's Groatsworth of Wit* and of the rumours that he is the author. However, when **does** Nashe arrive back in London?

Even in the event *Groatsworth* was printed soon after registration on September 20, three weeks seems rather a short interval until Nashe would return. But it is not impossible. McKerrow conjectures 7 October as the earliest possible date, "but Oct. 15 seems more likely."[164] If Harvey wrote the letter in *GGW* or part of it, it must have been between 8/9 and 20 September. And somehow this letter would have to come into Chettle's possession.

At this stage, our hypothesis that Gabriel Harvey was the author of at least part of the letter in *Groatsworth* has still several difficulties to overcome. If Harvey did pen the letter in whole or in part, and Chettle wrote it over, they would have to have accomplished their task within the exiguous time interval of at most ten days.

What kind of papers did Greene leave with certain booksellers?

In *Greene's Groatsworth of Wit* we can easily discern two distinct parts. Within the tale proper, about two thirds of the small volume, Greene is spoken of as 'Roberto.' The tale is an imitation of Greene's own *Francesco's Fortunes,* forming the *Second part of Never too Late,* by Chettle. It seems to us that the tale could have been elegantly ended with Roberto's lethal dropsy now "comfortlessly languishing, having but one groat left (the just proportion of his father's legacy) which looking on, he cried: O now it is too late, too late to buy wit with thee." It would have been a suitable dramatic conclusion, tuned to the title and an apt continuation of Francesco's adventures, for whom it was "never too late." And so it was probably conceived by Chettle: as the third part of "Never too Late." Another phrase serves as transition to the beginning of the last part: "and therefore will I see if I can sell to careless youth what I negligently forgot to buy." Immediately after that, the third person is replaced by the first:

> "Here, Gentlemen, break I off *Roberto's* speech; whose life in most parts agreeing with mine... Hereafter suppose me the said *Roberto,* and I will go on with that he promised: *Greene* will send you his groats-worth of wit..."

It sounds like the prelude to a second narration; in fact, it is the stroke of a gong announcing the start of a complete breakdown of the narrative. What follows is merely a medley of loose pieces.

First there is a poem, "Deceiving world, that with alluring toys," in which the author complains of having squandered his wit and life. Then comes a list of 10 maxims, mainly gathered from the Bible. Such lists of maxims occur in other works of Greene. In *Greene's Mourning Garment* (1590) an old rabbi quotes 12 maxims by way of farewell to his son. *Greene's Never too Late,* first part, (1590) contains a similar list of 12 maxims at the farewell of a friend. It is likely that Greene, like Nashe,[165] kept a notebook of maxims and quotations to employ in his tales. But in Greene's other works such discrete units are woven into the tale, whereas in *Greene's Groatsworth of Wit* and in *The Repentance of Robert Greene* alike they are simply assembled in what looks like an "appendix of posthumous papers."

Third comes the famous (or infamous) letter and, finally, the tale of the ant and the grasshopper. And after this tale we find something remarkable that to our knowledge has gone unnoticed by any other commentator. The tale closes with a Latin motto, the same one as appears on the title-page: "Fœlicem fuisse infaustum" (to be happy one must have been unhappy). It appears that the tale should have ended with the story of the ant and the grasshopper. However, after the tale and the motto comes Greene's letter to his wife "found with his book after his death." Beneath this letter re-appears the same Latin motto: "Fœlicem fuisse infaustum." We think it safe to conclude from the curious double appearance of the motto that *Greene's Groatsworth of Wit* was already in print before the letter came into the possession or even the notice of Chettle and the printer John Danter. The letter was also reprinted in a less romanticized form in *The Repentance*. Possibly the letter did not exist in either form but only in the form first related by Gabriel Harvey in his second letter, dated 5 September, which might have been published soon afterwards, as a note to a bond:

> "... as appeared by his own bond of ten pounds, which the good woman kindly shewed me, and beseeched me to read the writing beneath. Which was a letter to his abandoned wife in the behalf of his gentle host, not so short as persuasible in the beginning and pittyful in the ending.
>
> *Doll, I charge thee by the love of our youth, & by my soul's rest, that thou will see this man paid, for if he, and his wife had not succoured me, I had died in the streets.*

The same letter is quoted in *The Repentance*, which structurally bears a resemblance to *Groatsworth*. After a brief account of Greene's life, then of his death (which parallels the tale proper in *Groatsworth*), there follows another list of 12 maxims "sent by Robert Greene to a friend of his (as a farewell) written with his own hand." This is likely true, his "commonest chattels," to use Nashe's expression, would be one kind of papers Greene would have retained for future use. And finally, followed by another very short piece, "Greene's prayer in the time of his sickness," the letter:

> "Sweet Wife, as ever there was any good will or friendship betweene thee and me, see this bearer (my Host) satisfied of his debt: I owe him ten pounds, and but for him I had perished in the streets. Forget and forgive my wrongs done unto thee, and Almighty God

have mercy with my soul. Farewell till we meet in heaven, for on earth you shall never see me more.

This 2 of September.   1592.
> *Written by thy dying husband.*
> *Robert Greene."*

The version in *Groatsworth* is much longer and embellished. Chettle must have heard of the letter or read it in Harvey's two letters at the time the printing of *Groatsworth* had just been finished, whence the double presence of the Latin motto. Both the appending of what look like Greene's materials, his "commonest chattels", and the letter seem to have been done in a hurry. Ten days could have been sufficient.

The next consideration again leads us back to Gabriel Harvey. In his apology Chettle speaks of "many papers in sundry booksellers' hands, among other his *Groatsworth of wit.*" The truth is, Roberto's tale contains so many passages echoing Greene's former works Chettle would have had no need of other papers to compose his imitation. Thus we are inclined to relate Chettle's words not to Roberto's tale but only to the last part of *Groatsworth*, which is indeed a sequence of papers. It is out of question that Greene himself would have dispatched such a sequence of raw materials to a printer. The question is, then, how these papers could have come into the possession of the booksellers. And of which booksellers?

The printers and publishers

It is easy to see how it might have happened through Gabriel Harvey. In fact, only through him. From his second letter it appears that he was in attendance at Greene's funeral. So, Harvey accompanies Greene's hostess, Mrs Isam, to her house. He worms his way into her confidence. She reveals to him a few salient details of Greene's last days. She wonders what she should do with Greene's papers? She cannot read. She shows Harvey the bond with Greene's message for his wife, asking him to read what was written beneath.

The publisher of *Groatsworth* was William Wright, who also published Chettle's *Kindheart's Dream*. The publisher of *Repentance* was

Cuthbert Burby, who had recently ended his apprenticeship under William Wright. John Danter printed *The Repentance*. It was he who entered it in the Stationers' Register and probably retained some right in it. But the publisher named on the title-page is Cuthbert Burby. The two others, *Groatsworth* and *Kindheart*, were printed in shared arrangement between John Wolfe and John Danter.[166] Wolfe printed the first, Danter the second half. Henry Chettle was associated with Danter, but not with John Wolfe. How did John Wolfe become involved in the printing of these two books? And how William Wright? For Cuthbert Burby the answer seems clear, provided we can answer the two other questions.

John Wolfe

In the 1580s John Wolfe printed "five works of Machiavelli in Italian with false imprints."[167] He was himself a Machiavellian figure. When early in the 1580s the battle against the monopolies raged, the owners of such monopolies (privileges to print best-selling books such as the *Latin Grammar*, the *A.B.C. and the little Catechism*, etc.) petitioned Secretary of State Sir Francis Walsingham (the exact date is not indicated, the year is 1582):

> "We your poor Orators, the Ancients of the Company of the Stationers are not ignorant, Right Honorable, that your honors are already overburdened with the most weighty affairs of the kingdom, and therefore being unwilling to add any more business... but that through the too importunate and unjust exclamations, and insolent behaviour of some wilful and troublesome persons we are urged and compelled to."[168]

Two enclosures were joined to the petition. In the first we read:

> "But now WOLFE finding himself of more ability then before, printed divers men's copies without exception and thereupon hath grown much trouble. Notwithstanding all this upon the 14th of May last past **Barker** [the Queen's printer] sent for the said WOLFE and demanded of him why he printed the Copies belonging to his office: he answered, 'Because I will live.'... **Barker** replied saying, 'WOLFE leave your Machiavellian devices, and conceit of your foreign wit, which you have gained by gadding from country to country...'"[169]

The second enclosure contains 13 items of which 12 begin with the name "WOLFE". Wolfe was not just a Machiavellian, he also felt himself the Martin Luther of the printing trade reformation:

"WOLFE being admonished that he being but one so mean should not presume to contrary her Highness government: 'Tush', said he, 'LUTHER was but one man, and reformed all the world for religion, and I am that one man that must and will reform the government in this trade', meaning printing and bookselling."[170]

He had, of course, fellow-combatants. Eight of them are named in the petition, one of them is William Wright.

Wolfe was finally translated from the company of fishmongers, to which he originally belonged, to the company of stationers where the wolf proved one of the most influential and zealous guardians of the flock. In particular, he seems to have been a client of Lord Burghley and his son Robert Cecil. When on 24 October 1588 Lord Burghley decided to divulgue in print "The Pope's bull in Dutch with the answer thereto, to be translated," it was Wolfe he chose as publisher[171]; four days later Walsingham entrusted him with the printing of a letter to the former Spanish ambassador Mendoza, who had been expelled from England in 1584[172]; on 23 October 1590 the Privy Council authorized him to print certain maps in connection with a pretended Spanish invasion; on 27 December of the same year to print some reports on the wars in France authorized by the French ambassador; on 5 July 1591 by order of the Privy Council to print a report of the battles of the English forces in Britany.[173] In 1591 it was Wolfe who carried out Lord Burghley's order to call in a surreptitious edition of Sidney's *Astrophel and Stella*.

He also played an astounding role in the publication of the first part of John Hayward's *The Life and Reign of King Henry IV* in 1599. It caused the author to be sentenced to imprisonment, essentially because of the fulsome dedication to the Earl of Essex. The dedication provided ammunition for any who suspected or wanted others to suspect Essex aspired to play the role of Bolingbroke, later Henry IV. One of these was Essex's main foe, then Secretary of State Sir Robert Cecil, who in the aftermath of Essex's execution, claimed "that for years the earl had been devising ways of emulating Bolingbroke".[174] Even the censor who had authorized the work, Samuel Harsnett, chaplain to Richard Bancroft, Bishop of London, was threatened with imprisonment. Harsnett had authorized the book on advice of a good acquaintance and seems to have been unaware of the dedication. It is not clear whether the author himself was entirely privy to the dedication. One man certainly knew it, the publisher John Wolfe (he had become printer of the City of London and from about 1594 on restricted himself to publishing books printed by others).

On 13 July 1599 Wolfe was examined by General-Attorney Edward Coke. It turned out that when Hayward asked Wolfe to publish the book it had no dedication at all. After some conversation between Wolfe and Hayward "it was dedicated to the Earl of Essex, he being a martial man."[175] It looks as if the dedication was Wolfe's idea. Or perhaps Robert Cecil's, for despite his active part in the publication, Wolfe was let off scot-free. Wolfe's involvement and his relationship with the Cecils make it still more unlikely that the fable of Lamilia might have contained anything offensive to Lord Burghley, as Carroll surmises. The fable is the last section of A-C, and it is the part printed by Wolfe.

John Wolfe was a personality aiming at leadership. It is no rash conclusion to place him at the center of the printing history of *Groatsworth, Repentance* and *Kindheart*. Twice the publisher was his old comrade William Wright, in the case of *Repentance* it was the latter's former apprentice Cuthbert Burby, Danter being the printer. Wolfe and Danter shared the printing of *Groatsworth* and *Kindheart*. If Harvey had gotten hold of Greene's papers he would naturally take them to John Wolfe, as he was his printer. It was Wolfe who published and also printed Harvey's *Foure Letters* in 1592, his *New Letter of Notable Contents*, dedicated to "My loving friend John Wolfe, printer in the City", and *Pierce's Supererogation* in 1593. Wolfe and Danter were profiting commercially from the Nashe-Harvey quarrel. It was also Wolfe who printed Greene's *Quip*. Danter printed both Nashe's replies, *Strange News* (1593) and *Have With You to Saffron-Walden* (1596). The following scenario seems likely, and explains all the known facts:

At Mrs. Isam's house Gabriel Harvey lays hold of Greene's papers: lists of maxims, maybe some quotations, poems, fables. He offers them to his printer, John Wolfe. At the same time Chettle, Danter's associate, is writing the tale of 'Roberto.' Wolfe informs Danter that he is in possession of some of Greene's papers. They strike a deal: in exchange for Chettle's use of some of Greene's papers, Wolfe will print half of *Groatsworth* (Wolfe's printing of half of *Kindheart's Dream* may be a sequel to the deal in September). Now Chettle must somehow fit Greene's papers into his own tale. Lacking time, he simply appends them. When Harvey's second of *Foure Letters* is published in the second half of September, there is a need of incorporating it in *Groatsworth*, the printing of which is done (with the Latin motto both opening the work on the title page and closing it). Chettle restyles Greene's lines to his wife as reported by Harvey and closes anew with the Latin motto.

As seen, Harvey falsely ascribed a letter and a sonnet to Mr. Bird at the end of August 1592. In September 1593 he will fake a sonnet by the scholar John Thorius to Nashe's detriment.[176] Could Harvey have written the letter? Certainly the lines to Nashe are typical of Harvey's rhetoric style and echoed in his *Foure Letters*, especially the third and fourth ones. But then this would lead us to believe that Harvey also wrote the lines to the third playwright. They might have been edited by Chettle, yet still retain hints of Harvey's rhetorical style, "in some things rarer, in nothing inferiour," a frequent antithetical construction typical of the writings of the rhetorician Harvey. On the other hand, these rhetorical turns of phrase are noticeably absent in the lines concerning Marlowe, which unmistakeably invoke Greene's invective against Marlowe in his preface to *Perimedes, the Blacksmith,* (published in 1588), while the invective against Shake-scene recalls the diatribe against "Roscius" in *Francesco's Fortunes*.

Now if Gabriel Harvey had a hand in the letter in *Greene's Groatsworth of Wit*, he would also have had an interest in spreading the rumour that Nashe was the author, particularly if Harvey had also foisted the lines to the third playwright into Greene's papers.

Appendix I

The Letter From *Greene's Groatsworth Of Wit Bought With A Million Of Repentance*

[...] But now, though to my selfe I give *Consilium post facta;* yet to others they may serve for timely precepts. And therefore (while life gives leave) I will send warning to my olde consorts, which have lived as loosely as my selfe, albeit weaknesse will scarse suffer me to write, yet to my fellow Schollers about this Cittie, will I direct these few insuing lines.

To those Gentlemen his Quondam acquaintance, that spend their wits in making plaies, R. G. wisheth a better exercise, and wisdome to prevent his extremities.

If wofull experience may move you (Gentlemen) to beware, or unheard of wretchednes intreate you to take heed: I doubt not but you wil looke backe with sorrow on your time past, and indevour with repentance to spend that which is to come. Wonder not, (for with thee wil I first begin) thou famous gracer of Tragedians, that *Greene,* who hath said with thee (like the foole in his heart) There is no God, shoulde now give glorie unto his greatnes: for penetrating is his power, his hand lyes heavie upon me, hee hath spoken unto mee with a voice of thunder, and I have felt he is a God that can punish enemies. Why should thy excellent wit, his gift, bee so blinded, that thou shouldst give no glorie to the giver? Is it pestilent Machivilian pollicy that thou hast studied? O peevish follie! What are his rules but meere confused mockeries, able to extirpate in small time the generation of mankind. For if *Sic volo, sic iubeo,* hold in those that are able to commaund: and if it be lawfull *Fas et nefas* to do any thing that is beneficiall; onely Tyrants should possesse the earth, and they striving to exceed in tyrannie, should each to other be a slaughter man; till the mightiest outliving all, one stroke were lefte for Death, that in one age mans life should end. The brocher of this Diabolicall Atheisme is dead, and in his life had never the felicitie hee aymed at: but as he began in craft; lived in feare, and ended in despaire. *Quam inscrutabilia sunt Dei iudicia!* This murderer of many brethren, had his conscience seared like *Caine:* this betrayer of him that gave his life for him, inherited the portion of *Judas:* this Apostata perished as ill as *Julian:* and wilt thou my friend be his disciple? Looke but to me, by him perswaded to that libertie, and thou shalt find it an infernall bondage. I knowe the least of my demerits merit this miserable death, but wilfull striving against knowne truth, exceedeth all the terrors of my soule. Defer not (with me) till this last point of extremitie; for litle knowst thou how in the end thou shalt be visited.

With thee I joyne yong *Juvenall,* that byting Satyrist, that lastly with mee together writ a Comedie. Sweet boy, might I advise thee, be advisde, and get not many enemies by bitter wordes: inveigh against vaine men, for thou canst do it, no man better, no man so well: thou hast a libertie to reproove all, and name none; for one being spoken to, all are offended; none being blamed no man is injured. Stop shallow water still run-ning, it will rage, or tread on a worme and it will turne: then blame not Schollers vexed with sharpe lines, if they reprove thy too much liberty of reproofe.

And thou no lesse deserving than the other two, in some things rarer, in nothing inferiour; driven (as my selfe) to ex-treme shifts, a litle have I to say to thee: and were it not an idolatrous oth, I would sweare by sweet S. George, thou art unworthy better hap, sith thou dependest on so meane a stay. Base minded men all three of you, if by my miserie you be not warnd: for unto none of you (like mee) sought those burres to cleave: those Puppets (I meane) that spake from our mouths, those Anticks garnisht in our colours. Is it not strange, that I, to whom they all have beene beholding: is it not like that you, to whome they all have beene beholding, shall (were yee in that case as I am now) bee both at once of them forsaken? Yes trust them not: for there is an upstart Crow, beautified with our feathers, that with his *Tygers hart wrapt in a Players hyde,* supposes he is as well able to bombast out a blanke verse as the best of you: and beeing an absolute *Johannes fac totum,* is in his owne conceit the onely Shake-scene in a countrey. O that I might intreat your rare wits to be imploied in more profitable courses: and let those Apes imitate your past excellence, and never more acquaint them with your admired inventions. I knowe the best husband of you all will never prove an Usurer, and the kindest of them all will never prove a kind nurse: yet whilest you may, seeke you better Maisters; for it is pittie men of such rare wits, should be subject to the pleasure of such rude groomes.

In this I might insert two more, that both have writ against these buckram Gentlemen: but lette their own workes serve to witnesse against their owne wickednesse, if they persevere to maintaine any more such peasants. For other new-commers, I leave them to the mercie of these painted monsters, who (I doubt not) will drive the best minded to despise them: for the rest, it skils not though they make a jeast at them.

But now returne I againe to you three, knowing my miserie is to you no newes: and let mee hartily intreat you to be warned by my harms. Delight not (as I have done) in irreligious oathes; for from the blasphemers house, a curse shall not depart. Despise drunkennes, which wasteth the wit, and maketh men all equall unto beasts. Flie lust, as the deathsman of the soule, and defile not the Temple of the holy Ghost. Abhorre those Epicures, whose loose life hath made religion lothsome to your eares: and when they sooth you with tearms of Maistership, remember *Robert Greene,* whome they have often so flattered, perishes now for want of comfort. Remember Gentlemen, your lives are like so many lighted Tapers, that are with care deliv-ered to all of you to maintaine: these with wind-puft wrath may be extinguisht, which drunkennes put out, which negligence let fall: for mans time is not of it selfe so short, but it is more shortned by sinne. The fire of my light is now at the last snuffe, and for want of wherewith to sustaine it, there is no substance lefte for life to feede on. Trust not then (I beseech ye) to such weake staies: for they are as changeable in minde, as in many attyres. Wel, my hand is tyrde, and I am forst to leave where I would begin: for a whole booke cannot containe their wrongs, which I am forst to knit up in some fewe lines of words.

Desirous that you should live, though himselfe be dying:

Robert Greene.

Appendix II

Chettle´s Apology In The Preface Of *Kind-Heart´s Dreame.*

To the Gentlemen Readers.

It hath beene a custome Gentlemen (in my mind commendable) among former Authors (whose workes are no lesse beautified with eloquente phrase, than garnished with excellent example) to begin an exordium to the Readers of their time, much more convenient I take it, should the writers in these daies (wherein that gravitie of enditing by the elder excercised, is not observ´d, nor that modest decorum kept, which they continued) submit their labours to the favourable censures of their learned overseers. For seeing nothing can be said, that hath not been before said, the singularitie of some mens conceits, (otherwayes exellent well deserving) are no more to be soothed, than the peremptorie posies of two very sufficient Translators commended. To come in print is not to seeke praise, but to crave pardon: I am urgd to the one; and bold to begge the other, he that offendes being forst, is more excusable than the wilfull faultie, though both be guilty, there is difference in the guilt. To observe custome, and avoid as I may cavill, opposing your favors against my feare, Ile shew reason for my present writing, and after proceed to sue for pardon. About three moneths since died M. *Robert Greene*, leaving many papers in sundry Booke sellers hands, among other his Groatsworth of wit, in which a letter written to divers play-makers, is offensively by one or two of them taken, and because on the dead they cannot be avenged, they wilfully forge in their conceites a living Author: and after tossing it two and fro, no remedy, but it must light on me. How I have all the time of my conversing in printing hindred the bitter inveying against schollers, it hath been very well knowne, and how in that I dealt I can sufficiently proove. With neither of them they take offence was I acquainted, and with one of them I care not if I never be: The other, whome at that time I did not so much spare as since I wish I had, for that as I have moderated the heate of living writers, and might have usde my owne discretion (especially in such a case) the Author beeing dead, that I did not, I am as sory, as if the originall fault had beene my fault, that I did not, I am as sory as if the original fault had beene my fault, because my selfe have seene his demeanor no lesse civill, than he exelent in the qualitie he professes: Besides, divers of worship have reported his uprightnes of dealing, which argues his honesty, and his facetious grace in writing, that aprooves his Art. For the first, whose learning I reverence, and at the perusing of *Greenes* Booke, stroke out what then in conscience I thought he in some displeasure writ: or had it beene true, yet to publish it, was intollerable: him I would wish to use me no worse than I deserve. I had onely in the copy this share, it was il written, as sometime *Greenes* hand was none of the best, licensd it must be, ere it could bee printed which could never be if it might not be read. To be breife I writ it over, and as neare as I could, followed the copy, onely in that letter I put something out, but in the whole booke not a worde in, for I protest it was all *Greenes*, not mine nor Maister *Nashes*, as some uniustly have affirmed. Neither was he the writer of an Epistle to the second part of Gerileon, though by the workemans error T. N. were set to the end: that I confesse to be mine, and repent it not. Thus Gentlemen, having noted the private causes, that made me nominate my selfe in print; being as well to purge Master *Nashe* of that he did not, as to iustifie what I did, and withall to confirme what M. *Greene* did: I beseech yee accept the publike cause, which is both the desire of your delight, and common benefite: for though the toye bee shadowed under the Title of *Kind-hearts Dreame*, it discovers the false hearts of divers that wake to commit mischiefe. Had not the former reasons been, it had come forth without a father: and then shuld I have had no cause to feare offending, or reasone to sue for favour. Now am I in doubt of the one, though I hope of the other; which if I obtaine, you shall bind me hereafter to bee silent, till I can present yee with some thing more acceptable.

Henrie Chettle.

Chapter II
Honest Or Civil Conversation

The identification of Shake-scene as a playwright on whose behalf some worshipful persons required an apology from Chettle is based on an assumption of the innocuity of the reproaches addressed to the other two, an assumption based upon a naïve, patently unhistorical view of early modern society. The offense given by Shake-scene would be that of pride, one of the seven deadly sins. Shake-scene would have transcended the charge of hubris Robert Greene had levelled at actors four years before in his *Francesco's Fortunes*: "... for it grew to a general vice among the actors to excel in pride as they did exceed in excellence, and to brave it in the streets as they brag it on the stage: so that they reveled it in *Rome*, in such costly robes that they seemed rather men of great patrimony than such as lived by the favour of the people."[177] Shake-scene, however, thought himself as able to "bombast out a blank verse" as the best of the three others. In *Francesco's Fortunes,* Greene names no actors, but he is nonetheless plain enough about whom he is writing : the actors of the Queen's Men, officially servants to the queen, "grooms of the Queen's chamber": "…disdain no thy tutor, because thou pratest in a King's chamber".[178]

In 1590, the year *Francesco's Fortunes* was published, these men could have been John Laneham, Lawrence Dutton, John Singer, or others. None of them is known to have taken offense. Nor is anyone known to have required an apology from Thomas Nashe, when in the epistle to Greene's *Menaphon* (1589) he scolded actors and some authors alike: "I am not ignorant how eloquent our gowned age is grown of late; so that every mechanical mate abhors the English he was born to... But herein I cannot so fully bequeath them to folly as their idiot art-masters, that intrude themselves to our ears as the alchemists of eloquence: who, mounted on the stage of arrogance, think to outbrave better pens with the swelling bombast of a bragging blank verse."[179] Nashe and Greene had accused them of pride, yet nothing is heard of a scandal in 1589 or 1590. In 1592, in *Groatsworth,* it was the charge of atheism laid against Marlowe that made the difference, not. the reproach of pride levelled at Shake-scene. But was it in fact the accusation of pride that Chettle rescinded, and that the "divers of worship" denied? No, clearly it was the charge of "dishonesty" and "uncivility" which was repealed.

Chettle recants by saying that the demeanor of the man in question (either the third playwright or, as most orthodox scholars have it, 'Shake-scene') was "civil," whereas the "divers of worship" testify to his "honesty." Take both witnesses together and you have more or less the same testimony as that of Francis Meres' about Michael Drayton: "a man of virtuous disposition, honest conversation, and well-governed carriage, which is almost miraculous among good wits in these declining and corrupt times." Here we obtain a glimpse of the nature of the charge that had been made by the author of *Groatsworth* against the third playwright: that he was not, as was his fellow-author Michael Drayton, "of honest conversation, and well-governed carriage." The orthodox assumption that there was nothing offensive in this rests on another 'tale of a tub.'

The vital importance of being honest

In *Euphues and His England* John Lyly (universally regarded as having had a profound influence on Shakespeare) defined what contemporaries understood by 'honesty':

> "Honesty, my old grandfather called that when men lived by law not list [lust]; observing in all things the mean which we name virtue; and virtue we account nothing else but to deal justly."[180]

If we compare this definition with the reproach to the third playwright, we can see that something in it amounted to a charge of "dishonesty." He who is "driven to extreme shifts" does not observe the mean. The mean can be nothing else than virtue and virtue nothing else than dealing justly or "dealing uprightly," another term the "divers of worship" used. Nothing of the kind was levelled at Shake-scene. The "divers of worship" were not using "loose language"; if both Chettle and they did, all Elizabethans, Meres, Lyly, and others were doing; and what is more, they intervened on the behalf of the third playwright, not of Shake-scene. Now, Lyly offers an alternative definition of honesty. Elsewhere he writes that "late watching in the night" is "unhonest" while a wife's honesty is essentially her honour.[181] Again the word "honest" refers in a general way to a lifestyle. Lyly also uses the word "honest" in the sense of a man's "honour."[182] Again, did Chettle use "loose language"? Lyly remarks: "There belongs more to a courtier than bravery... It is sober and discrete behaviour, civil and gentle demeanour."[183] Alternatively we find "uprightness of life." Speaking of behavior at court Lyly remarks: "But in things which come on the sudden one cannot be too wary to prevent or too curious to mistrust. For thou art in a place either to make thee hated for vice or loved for virtue, and as thou reverencest the one before the other, so in uprightness of life show it."[184]

Thus we see that in both Lyly's and Meres' usage these terms do not carry the meaning modern commentators of the letter in *Groatsworth* and Chettle's apology, have assigned them. A courtier should affect a "civil demeanour," Lyly writes. Is this not what Chettle affirms, that he knew the man (for whom the "divers of worship" demanded an apology) to be of "civil demeanour"? Let us ask: what does Francis Meres mean when he lauds Drayton's "honest conversation"? Was this not the same as the "civil conversation" Stefano Guazzo wrote of in *Civil Conversatione?* "The phrase was not invented by Guazzo, but beyond all doubt, his use gave the expression its European currency during the sixteenth and seventeenth centuries. Neither of the constituent words, conveys to the modern reader what would have been its normal meaning for an Elizabethan. The phrase, therefore, must be glossed if it is to be properly understood. In Guazzo's day the meaning was so patent that the expression could be transferred literally from the Italian into Latin, French, Spanish, or English without the slightest confusion. The German translation (1599) of the *Civil conversatione* equated the title page Latin, *civilis conversatio*, with *bürgerlich Wandel*, and the Dutch (1603) rendered it as *burgerlyck Ommegangh*."[185] The German translation can be rendered in English as "civil way of life," the Dutch one as "civil intercourse" or "civil social dealing". "Civil conversation" is "civil behaviour." Stefano Guazzo himself gives the following definition of "civil behaviour," equating civility to honesty:

"You see then that we give a large sense and signification to this word for that we would have understood, that to live civilly, is not said in respect to the City, but of the quality of the mind. To be short, my meaning is, that civil conversation is an honest, commendable, and virtuous kind of living in the world."[186] It is the way Shakespeare's contemporaries understood it. In the 1580s Lodowick Bryskett wrote his *Discourse of Civil Life*, published in 1606. Bryskett was a friend of Spenser's and Sidney's; he accompanied Sidney on his journey to Italy. The purpose of his dialogue is "to frame a gentleman fit for *civil conversation*."[187] Cotgrave's French-English dictionary (1611) lists the following meanings for the French adjective *honneste*: honest, good, vertuous; just, upright, sincere; gentle, civill, courteous, worthy, noble, honorable, of good reputation, comelic, seemelic, handsome, wellbefitting. What an author on *honnêteté* and *civilité* in 17th-century France observes, also holds for 16th- and 17th-century England and Italy. "The gobal unit of significance in the discourse of sociability – what we traditionally call courtly behavior – was *civilité*, an unmotivated sign which drew its meaning from conventions rationalized through time. In Nicole's view, *civilité*, is one of those 'simple laws of decorum, whose authority originates in a consensus among people who have agreed to condemn those who do not obey them... This is why we owe to those around us the civilities laid down by the *honnêtes gens*, even though they may not be governed by clearly stated laws."[188] Despite the centrality of these notions in contemporary works on education, Shakespeare scholars have not understood it so, not like Guazzo, Lyly, and a multitude of others. But Elizabethans understood it so. "Honesty" and "civility" are broad behavioral categories, meaning, as Guazzo stresses, largely the same. And let us remember, it is the third playwright's **behaviour** to which Chettle refers, his "demeanour," **not to his play-writing.**

In 1951, the eminent Shakespearean scholar John Dover Wilson challenged the orthodox interpretation. He reasoned that something graver must have happened to trigger the intervention of the worshipful persons:

"And this brings me back to my argument. Why should men of rank in that age of rigid class distinctions go out of their way to make representations to an obscure printer on behalf of a player-poet? Such things are not done without good cause and a definite end in view, and Chettle's words themselves strongly suggest that the extraction of a complete and public apology was what was aimed at, possibly even peremptorily required. But an apology for what? What was the nature of the charge which had moved these gentry of worship to intervene in defence of their protégé? Here Chettle is plain enough. They have assured him, he tells us, and we may guess have bidden him assure the world at large, that Shakespeare is both an excellent dramatic poet and honourable man. Moreover, these two assurances were, we need not hesitate to assume, directly related to the attack made upon him. Greene's sneers about 'bombast' and 'an absolute *Iohannes fac totum*' are for example countered by the testimony to a 'facetious grace in writing', that is to say, a polished and witty poetic and dramatic style. But why drag in that pointed reference to 'honesty' and 'uprightness of dealing'? One does not publicly certify a friend is no thief unless someone else has previously asserted the contrary as publicly."[189]
However, given the wide range of meanings the words "honest" and "civil" could denote it is by no means a foregone conclusion that "honesty" and "uprightness of dealing" must be the opposite of **theft**. It is, in the light of Lievsay's clarifications, even unlikely they could have meant what Wilson understands by them. Somewhere in her memoirs Marguerite de Valois reports an encounter with Don John of Austria, whom she qualifies as "fort honnête homme," "a very honest man. " Clearly it is ludicrous to imagine that she would have meant that Don John of Austria would never steal something. She praised his "decorum," his "very refined manners."

Thus if we apply the meanings defined by Lyly, the cause for the intervention of the worshipful persons points to the third playwright. Being "driven to extreme shifts" and earning a living not in accordance with his social status was living "dishonestly" or "uncivilly." The concepts go back to Cicero:

"The ideal expressed in Cicero´s book ´On Duties´ (*De officiis*), a work of moral education addressed to his son and presumably intended for upper-class readers, is rather more flexible. The emphasis falls on what the author calls *decorum*, in other words the adaptation of social behaviour, including posture and gesture, to circumstances and style of life, *genus vitae*. Decorum implies self-control, the control of reason over the passions, and it also implies self-consciousness, especially the conscious avoidance of extremes..."[190] But did the invective against Shake-scene contain a charge which could be interpreted as "dishonesty" or "uncivility" in the wide contemporary sense? As a lack of self-control? Hardly, but the words written to the third playwright clearly did.

Lyly and Stefano Guazzo were not the only authors of their time to understand "honesty" and "civility" as broad behavioral categories. In Italy Torquato Tasso wrote a long dialogue on "honest pleasure."[191] In another dialogue on nobility between two gentlemen, Antonio Forno (whose name the dialogue is given), and Agostino Bucci, he too links honesty to virtue. Antonio asks: "What shall therefore be the difference between the vice of incontinence and the heroical virtue?" Agostino answers: "It is the object which distinguishes the heroical virtue from this vice, because the object of virtue is honesty, and true honesty; whereas the object of vice, and also of incontinence, will be profit or lust."[192] Here honesty is set off against incontinency or intemperance. And this is what the reproach to the third playwright seems to mean, that he is"driven to extreme shifts." This idea is even more emphatically expressed in the counselling the French aristocrat Henri de la Tour d´Auvergne (Vicomte de Turenne, later Duke of Bouillon) gives to his son in his *Mémoires,* written between 1565-1586: "Take heed not to act as I did and always to honour those who will recommend you to have your acts guided by reason and to subject your passions to honesty."[193] That he should subject his passions to reason was the very observation made by Lord Burghley which the earl of Leicester took in high dudgeon. In an undated letter which must have been written in the run-up to Leicester´s expedition in the Low Countries in 1585, Leicester addresses Burghley irately: "... what was it but to leave me, in her majesty's opinion, to be a man either affectionate, or opiniative in my own conceits... That I like so ill, that I would and could find way to anger you as well. I can hardly dissemble, or bear the unkind dealing of them: but rather to deal as I am dealt withal... And that I said was to your Lordship's self and before none other; but moved, as your Lordship said, in passion."[194]

Why was Leicester so incensed? Commentators on the Groatsworth affair would likely aver that there was nothing in Burghley's criticism to justify the intensity of the earl's response, yet Leicester's ire is perfectly understandable. By reproaching him for being led by opinion, not reason, and for not controlling his own passions, in fact, accusing him of not behaving honestly, Burghley denied Leicester the qualities of a "governor."

The words "honest" and "honesty" abound in Thomas Elyot's *The Boke of the Governor* (1531), dedicated to Henry VIII. In his dedication Elyot explains why he has chosen this title: "And for as much as this present book treats of the education of them that hereafter may be deemed worthy to be governors of the public weal under your highness... I therefore have named it The Governor."[195] A "governor" is a member of the ruling elite, in Elyot's political philosophy a member of the aristocracy. Gentle birth, military prowess, sportly skill, however, were no longer the only criteria for political leadership, learning and good manners were equally, if not more, essential. Elyot echoes Castiglione's *Book of the Courtier* which had only appeared two years before. Elyot "knew Thomas Cromwell and may well have learned of the *Courtier* through him as early as 1530." The "most striking parallel between the two texts is Elyot's suggestion that a young nobleman should study not only music but the visual arts, 'if nature do thereto induce him,' though without turning into a common painter or carver."[196] As the egregious negative example of an aristocrat turning player and singer Elyot holds up the Roman emperor Nero. "But in this commendation of music I would not be thought to allure noblemen to have such delectation therein, that in playing and singing they should put their whole study and felicity: as did the emperor Nero, which all along summersdays would sit in the Theatre (an open place where all the people of Rome beheld solemn acts and plays) and in the presence of all the noblemen and senators would play on his harp and sing without cessing."[197]

On the other hand, a striking difference between Castiglione and Elyot lies in the terms used to describe seemly behaviour. Whereas Castiglione uses rather aesthetic qualities such as *sprezzatura* (artful nonchalance), "elegance," "grace," Elyot's key notions are "honest" and "honesty," derived from Cicero's "honestum" and "honour." In Cicero one can see that "he did not lack the knowledge of geometry, nor music, nor grammar, finally of no manner of art that was honest."[198]

Learning had to be combined with "some honest and moderate"[199] disport: hawking, dancing, music, etc. A generation after Elyot, Ascham's *Scholemaster* (1570) strikes the same cord *prestissimo*. He also underscores the need of self-discipline. The city of Athens, Ascham argues, did not only care "to bring up their youth in honest company and virtuous discipline... the City was not more careful to see their children well taught than to see their youth men well-governed: which they brought to pass not so much by common law as by private discipline."[200] Honesty mattered. It mattered for all men but it mattered more for the aristocracy than for any other group of the society, it was one of the qualities required to rule the realm. Ascham, like Elyot, assigns to the aristocracy the role of being the living model of honesty as a basic legitimation to govern society. Shakespeare has Henry V echo Ascham: "Dear Kate, you and I cannot be confined within the weak list of country's fashion; we are the makers of a manners." (V.ii.287). Either the "makers of manners" or the "marrers of manners," Ascham wrote. To charge an aristocrat with dishonest living unequivocally degraded him from a "maker" to a "marrer" of manners, and was dishonouring to him. This aspect of the role of the aristocracy is dramatically highlighted in the trial of the Earl of Castlehaven in 1631. Being accused of having compelled his own wife, a daughter of Ferdinando Stanley, 5th Earl of Derby, to engage in sexual intercourse with a servant and other crimes, the earl was indicted of felony. "A peer was less likely than anyone else to find himself a defendant, but indicted of felony, the aristocrat probably had less chance of acquittal,"[201] precisely because of the aristocracy's social function as the "makers of manners." Behavioral exemplarity was one legitimatory pillar of their rule, or of their right to being "governors." As the judge condemning the Earl of Castlehaven declared: "The earl's position gave him greater than normal obligations, not greater than normal latitude. 'As he is great in his birth, so should he have been good in his example.'" Or as a moralist put it: "... a debauched son of a noble family is one of the intolerable burdens of the earth, and as hateful a thing as hell."[202]

What at first remains mysterious is that the "divers of worship" should refer to the third playwright's "facetious grace in writing, which approves his art," to bear witness to his "honest way of living". We must recall that Castiglione had defined the ideal courtier's behavior by criteria borrowed from the aesthetic sphere: painting, music and dancing. In Puttenham's *The Arte of English Poesie* the standard-setting is sometimes inverted. It is the courtier's behavior which in some cases serves as stylistic criterion. When, for instance, Puttenham explains allegory, he refers to the courtier's art of dissembling. "... and first by the Courtly figure *Allegoria*, which is when we speak one thing and think another, and that our words and our meanings meet not. The use of this figure is so large, and his virtue of so great efficacy as it is supposed no man can pleasantly utter and persuade without it... insomuch as not only every common courtier, but also the gravest councillor, yea an the most noble and wisest prince of them all are many times enforced to use it...And you shall know that we may dissemble, I mean speak otherwise than we think, in earnest as well as in sport..."[203] One other example: "And there is a decency to be observed in every man's action & behaviour as well as in his speech & writing which some peradventure would think impertinent to be treated of in this book, where we do but inform the commendable language & style: but that is otherwise, for the good maker who is in decent speech & good terms to describe all things and with praise or dispraise to report every man's behaviour, ought to know the comeliness of an action as well as of a word..."[204]

Courtly behaviour and good poetry had become interchangeable, an aspect of Puttenham's theory which has escaped most commentators of his work. "While critics have shown that many of its theoretical pre-scriptions reflect and anticipate English poetic practice, hardly anyone has observed that courtly manners determine the viability of these pre-scriptions. Yet one of the controlling assumptions in the work is that to be a good poet entails being a proper courtier."[205]

And this is what the "divers of worship" testified to by insisting on the third playwright's "facetious grace in writing": he was a good poet and a proper courtier.

The Italianate gentleman : a marrer of manners

In 1592, Gabriel Harvey had grown more sober. As seen, he published his *Four Letters, and certain sonnets*, one letter more than twelve years earlier but with a considerably shorter title. The full title of his 1580 publication is *Three proper wittie familiar Letters, lately passed betweene two Universitie men, touching the Earthquake in April last, and our English re-formed versifying*. He refers to these three letters in 1592. Not unlike Chettle, he regrets not having used more discretion. Harvey tells us why he had been somewhat indiscreet, "I was then young in years, fresh in courage, green in experience, and as the manner is, somewhat overwhelming in conceit."[206] Harvey had libeled someone, clearly a 'special' person. Chettle may have meant the same when he wrote in his apology, "The other whom at that time I did not so much spare, as since I wish I had, for that as I have moderated the heat of living writ-ers, and might have used my own discretion (especially in such a case), the author being dead." It is possible to read Chettle as saying that he has moderated the heat of living writers and could have done the more so in this special case because the author was dead and, to use his own words, "because they cannot be avenged, they wilfully forge in their conceits a living author." However, if Chettle had moderated "the heat of living writers" how much easier could he have done so in the case of a dead author — as he had indeed done in the case of the other of-fended playwright: "For the first, whose learning I reverence, and at the perusing of Greene's book, stroke out what then in conscience I thought he in some displeasure wrote: or had it been true, yet to publish it, was intolerable." It is possible, and probably correct, to understand Chettle as referring to the particularity of the third playwright.

Like Chettle twelve years later, Harvey had been compelled to apologize for something he had published, also by persons "of worship." He explains that "the sharpest part of those unlucky letters had been overread at the Council Table; I was advised by certain honourable and divers worshipful persons to interpret my intention in more express terms."[207] It is even likely that he **was** sent to the Fleet prison for slander or at least threatenened with it, though he expressly denies that he was "orderly clapped in the Fleet for the foresaid letters: where he saw me, saw me in Constantinople."[208] McKerrow found the meaning of the last phrase in Stow's *London*: "where it is said that for a bribe the Marshall will allow prisoners in the King's Bench to go where they please insomuch, that when anyone asks the rules, or limits of this prison, answer is made, at Constantinople; and indeed anywhere."[209] This may mean that Harvey was formally committed to the Fleet but could come and go freely. We need not speculate about the "Council Table" and the identity or function of the "some honourable and divers worshipful persons," **they** are privy councillors. Two of them Harvey identifies: second secretary of state Thomas Wilson and Sir Walter Mildmay, Chancellor of the Exchequer.

What had been Harvey's offense? In 1592 (we should by now realize) the charge laid against the third playwright was a "lack of honesty" or "civility." So it had been in 1580, partly. The third of the *Three familiar letters* (the one on English versifying) contained a lampoon on the 17th Earl of Oxford. De Vere, though not named, was the recognizable target. In a poem entitled "Speculum Tuscanismi" (the mirror of Tuscanism or Italianism), the earl was depicted as one with effeminate Italianate manners, a smear not as grave as the atheism with which Marlowe was charged in 1592, but a defamation of character nonetheless. Only ten years before Ascham's *The Scholemaster* had branded Italy in general as "the court of Circe" and the Italianate Englishman in particular as an "incarnated devil." "If you think we judge amiss... hear what the Italian says of the Englishman... Inglese Italianato è un *diabolo incarnato*, that is to say, you remain men in shape and action, but become devils in life."[210] Only bad manners could be learnt in Italy. "He that by living and traveling Italy brings home into England out of Italy the religion, the learning, the policy, the experience, the manners of Italy... for manners, variety of vanities, and change of filthy living. These be the enchantments of Circe, brought out of Italy to mar men's manners in England, much by example of ill life, but more by precepts of fond books, of late translated out of Italian into English, sold in every shop in London, commended by honest titles the sooner to corrupt honest manners."[211] And in unmistakable allusion to Machiavelli, "they make Christ and his Gospel only serve civil policy".[212] The reproach of the Italianate was not too far from that of atheism. Lord Burghley held similar opinions. In instructions to his son Robert Cecil he gives this advice: "And suffer not thy sons to pass the Alps: for they shall learn nothing there but pride, blasphemy, and atheism."[213] Some of Ascham's characterizations occur in Harvey's libel: "Vanity above all," "Indeed most frivolous, not a look but Tuscanish always," "None do I name, but some do I know, that a piece of twelvemonth,/ Hath so perfected outly and inly." Twelve months was about the time Oxford had passed in Italy. There could be no doubt that Oxford was aimed at, the more because "Speculum Tuscanismi" was immediately followed by the comment, "Tell me in good sooth, does it not too evidently appear that this English poet wanted but *a good* pattern before his eyes, as it might be some delicate and choice elegant Poesie of good M. Sidney's and M. Dyer's."[214] Finally, any hypothetical residual doubt is dissolved by Harvey's *Letter-book* (not printed until 1884) where a slightly different version of "Speculum Tuscanismi" appears, followed by the comment "Now tell me, I beseech you, if this be not a noble verse and politic lesson... in effect containing the argument of his courageous and warlike apostrophe to my Lord of Oxenforde in his fourth book Gratulationum Valdinensium."[215]

Besides, Harvey had been spewing dragonish flames of insult at Dr. Andrew Perne, his "old controller... A busy and dizzy head, a leaden brain, a wooden wit, a copper face; a stony breast, a factious and elvish heart... a morning bookworm, an afternoon maltworm, full of his sleights... odd shifts,and knavish practices, as his skin can hold. He often tells me he loves me as himself, but out liar out, you lie in your throat."[216] Ironically, twelve years later Harvey would call Thomas Nashe a "Thundersmith of terms" using "rattling terms... to rail his patrons, to bite his pen, to rend his papers, to rage in all points."[217] Perne was vice-chancellor of the University of Cambridge, the highest permanent official, Lord Burghley's chancellorship being in fact virtually an honorary office. Four years after Perne's death (1589) Harvey's rancour was still haunting him; over no less than sixteen pages (pp. 295 -311) in *Pierce's Supererogation*), oscillating between admiration and hatred, he describes Perne as a sly fox. Harvey had hoped to be appointed public orator of the university, and egocentric as he was, he might have thought himself the only one suitable for the office. It may well have been his overweening that caused the cautious Dr. Perne to oppose his candidature. Unfortunately for Harvey, old Sir James Croft, controller of the royal household, believed the insults were levelled at him. It is hard to see how Croft could have drawn this conclusion; apart from the word "controller," it lay on the surface that Harvey's insults were directed against some high-ranking official at the university of Cambridge. But at that time Harvey was a client of the earl of Leicester with whom Croft had recently run afoul over politics with Spain. Leicester led the war party, Croft belonged to the Spanish faction, being an ardent advocate of peace negotiations. At some time before 1581 he had received a pension from the Spanish crown. He might have wanted to give the servant 'a punch to pinch the lord.'

According to Harvey's own account, which must be taken with a grain of salt, it all ended well. "Indeed Sir James Croft, whom I never touched with the least tittle of detractions, was cunningly incensed and reincensed against me. But at last pacified by the voluntary mediation of my honorable favourers, M. Secretary Wilson and Sir Walter Mildmay, unrequested by any line of my hand or any word."[218] After that Harvey was informed that Sir James Croft was satisfied. But at no time did Sir James Croft approach Harvey personally. And Perne? "Only he wished me to proceed lovingly with the University, howsoever I dealt with that doctor."[219] In other words, as foremost representative of the university of Cambridge Dr Perne had to be respected. But it does not seem that Dr Perne ever approached Harvey to ask for **personal** satisfaction. It is almost certain he never did. No more than Sir James Croft. Instead, some "worshipful persons" intervened on their behalf, at least two of which were privy councillors.

Dr. Perne and Sir James Croft, even if they felt personally slandered (which Perne certainly was) could not intervene personally. It was more than their personal affair. It was an affair of state.

Scandalum Magnatum

Dr. Perne and Sir James Croft were protected against slander by several statutes.

First, by Statute 3ºEdward I. (1275) c.34: "Forasmuch as there have been oftentimes found in the Country Devisors of Tales, whereby discord or occasion of discord, hath many times arisen between the King and the People, or Great Men of this Realm... It is commanded, That from henceforth none be so hardy to tell or publish any false News or Tales, whereby discord, or occasion of discord or slander may grow between the King and his People, or the Great Men of the Realm." The chapter was re-enacted in 2º Richard II. (1378) as chapter 5. The "Great Men of the Realm", the class of "magnates" was more detailedly specified: "Prelates, Dukes, Earls, Barons, and other Nobles and Great Men of the Realm, and also of the Chancellor, Treasurer, Clerk of the Privy Seal, Steward of the King's House, Justices of the one Bench or the other, and of other Great Officers of the Realm." Dr Perne's rank as vice-chancellor and dean of Ely qualified him as a prelate, Croft's office of controller of the royal household as one of the "other Great Officers of the Realm". The chapter was again re-enacted as chapter 11 of 12º Richard II. (1388). A significant addition was made to the last phrase of the previous statute, "to be punished by the Advice of the Council, notwithstanding the said Statutes."

"Notwithstanding the said Statutes", those of 1275 and 1378, means that the common law courts were no longer the sole venues for cases of slander of "Great Men." They still retained part of the jurisdiction but in the course of time restricted their cognizance ever more to the civil aspect of the matter, the tort, that is material damages resulting from slander, and concerned themselves much less with the immaterial consequences, injury of reputation. Hence, "it was held that a charge of unchastity made against a duke's chaplain, whereby he lost his office, was actionable. If, on the other hand, the office was an honorary office, such as the office of a justice of peace, though a charge of corruption is, a charge of want of ability is not, actionable."[220] Only if slander could be construed as a tort did common law courts, mainly the King's Bench and the Common Pleas, usually take cognizance of actions in defamation, be it in written or spoken form, that is libel or slander. But this distinction between libel, written defamation, and slander, spoken defamation, was not introduced till after the Restoration.[221] Slander as a criminal offence, be it slander of peers, legally termed "scandalum magnatum" or defamation of private persons, became more and more the jurisdictional precinct of the Privy Council or, what makes no great difference, the Court of the Star Chamber. Something must be said on the relation between the Privy Council and the Star Chamber and the way they dealt with slander. It may assist us in better understanding one passage in Chettle's apology. The passage runs:

"For the first, whose learning I reverence, and at the perusing of Greene's book, stroke out what then in conscience I thought he in some displeasure wrote: or had it been true, yet to publish it, was intolerable: him I would wish to use me no worse than I deserve."

It is noteworthy that these words not only point to Marlowe, they address him directly and personally. Nothing equivalent is contained in Chettle's apology regarding the other offended person. But how much worse could Marlowe have treated Chettle? The most cogent assumption is that Marlowe would have sued Chettle. As the charge of Machiavellism amounted to a charge of atheism, Marlowe's reputation was at stake, not any material loss. This kind of slander constituted a criminal law case. The proper venue would have been the Privy Council, either directly or indirectly. 'Indirectly' meant the Court of the Star Chamber. The Privy Council had not only executive but also judicial powers, it was both court and council. The Star Chamber was the judicial branch of the Privy Council; the Privy Council exerted its jurisdiction partly through the Star Chamber. It has been held that the Star Chamber was nothing less than the "King's Council in the Star Chamber" or the "Council at Westminster," assisted by the two Chief Justices. A.F. Pollard strongly objects to this view:

"This was approximately true for 1629… but emphatically it is not true that at any time in the sixteenth century the personnel of the star chamber was limited to the privy council and the two chief justices; and the antedating of the practical identity of the judicial star chamber with the executive privy council obscures one of the effective reasons why Stuart Government provoked so much more ill feeling than that of the Tudors."[222]

Indeed it seems that the close tie-up of the executive and the judiciary functions of the Privy Council was a Carolinian evolution; in Elizabethan times the Star Chamber had not acquired the notorious reputation it was to have by 1642. However, the narrow relation between Privy Council and Star Chamber also existed throughout the reign of the Tudors, and basically the Star Chamber served the same purpose under Tudors and Stuarts, to establish and strengthen the royal prerogative and the public order and, reciprocally, to suppress seditious and private slander alike. Slander of "magnates" was considered seditious, private slander was a breach of the peace. "The Council and the Star Chamber had, in the interests of the peace and security of the State, assumed a strict control over the Press. Naturally the Star Chamber assumed jurisdiction in all cases in which its rules on this matter had been infringed; and this led it to regard defamation as a crime. Borrowing perhaps from the Roman law *Libella Famosa*, it treated libels both upon officials and private persons as crimes. The former were seditious libels, and **directly affected the security of the State** [our emphasis] and the latter obviously led to breaches of the peace. On the same principle it dealt with seditious words."[223] Thus, in the case of the controller Sir James Croft and Dr Perne the slander constituted not just a breach of peace and an affair between private people, it was regarded as a "scandalum magnatum" for which the statute of 12º Richard II., c. 11 provided the possibility of an intervention of the Privy Council. This was not the case for Chettle's slander of Marlowe. But Marlowe could have sued Chettle in the Star Chamber and Chettle would have been facing imprisonment.

The notion that this statute might only have been effective in the 'dark reign' of Richard II or that of his more immediate successors, but with time unfolding toward 'enlightenment' that it would have faded into insignificance, is erroneous. The opposite is true: "There is very little evidence of the working of these statutes during the middle ages, but cases begin to appear in the common law courts under Elizabeth. This is perhaps connected with the fact that the statutes on *scandalum magnatum* were once more re-enacted in 1554 and again in 1559, but with additional clauses on "seditious words"; justices of peace were given the jurisdiction, and the punishment was loss of ears for words, and of the right hand for writing."[224] Thus we see that far from leveling social distinctions and mitigating the punishment for their transgression, both Mary and Elizabeth reinforced the statutory basis for enforcing their respect. On the one hand, the respect of degree was a rationale of the political order. Shakespeare's words are well known:

"Take but degree away, untune that string,
And hark what discord follows, "
--*Troilus & Cressida*, I.iii.109-10).

Queen Elizabeth's words, as related by Fulke Greville, are not nearly so famous. In 1579 she forbade a duel between Philip Sidney and the earl of Oxford. " The Queen... presently undertakes Sir Philip... and lays before him the difference in degree between earls and gentlemen; the respect inferiors owed to their superiors: and the necessity in princes to maintain their own creations, as degrees descending between the people's licentiousness and the anointed sovereignty of crowns: how the gentleman's neglect of the nobility taught the peasant to insult upon both."[225]

On the other hand, neither Mary's claim nor Elizabeth's was firmly established in the wake of the tribulations around the succession in the last years of Henry VIII's reign. Under these circumstances the "scandalum magnatum," the affirmation of "degree," was more and more drained into the jurisdictional sphere of the prerogative courts: the Privy Council in its judicial quality and its prolonged judicial arm, the Court of the Star Chamber. The matter became "pre-eminently the province of the council, and it is unlikely that the justices of peace would be allowed much scope for the independent exercise of their statutory powers under the act of 1559. The throne of Elizabeth was too unsteady, and the political situation much too dangerous for the council to resign the trial of political offences into the hand of the country justices."[226] Violations of the statute of "scandalum magnatum" were nevertheless handled with caution. There was one John Stubbs in the 45 years of the reign of Elizabeth I, there were Alexander Leighton and William Prynne in the 17 years of the reign of Charles I. Not many cases of "slander of peers" are known for the Elizabethan era. There were certainly more than are known today, partly due to the loss of documents, partly because they did not make their way into the public eye, but probably most often because the authorities were cautious not to over-react and simply ignored them.

1580 and 1592 – to and fro

John Lyly was not wallowing in poetic license when in 1589 in his anti-Martinist pamphlet *Pappe with a Hatchet* he announced Gabriel Harvey's entrance into the theatre of the "civil war of wits" and recalled the latter's libeling of Oxford in 1580: "And one will we conjure up, that writing a familiar Epistle about the natural causes of an earthquake, fell into the bowels of libelling, which made his ears quake for fear of clipping... If he join with us, *periisti Martin*, thy wit will be massacred; if the toy take him to close with thee, then have I my wish, for this ten years have I looked to lamback him."[227]

Clipping of the ears was the penalty determined, in the statute of 1559, for slander of peers. In theory Harvey could have been sent into the pillory and had his ears clipped, in practice the only real harm Harvey seems to have suffered was the definitive clipping of his much longed-for academic career. By publicly exposing the earl of Oxford's Italianate manners he had slandered a peer. To be Italianate was to be dishonest, and *noblesse oblige*, it was one of the obligations of the aristocracy to be "makers of manners," honest manners; to deny that an aristocrat had been living honestly was to dishonour him. In 1592 Harvey denies the intent, confirming at the same time the effect: "...whose noble Lordship I protest I never meant to dishonour with the least prejudicial word of my tongue or pen: but ever kept a mindful reckoning of many bound duties to the same: since in the prime of his gallantest youth he bestowed angels upon me in Christ College in Cambridge..."[228] Harvey further writes that Oxford was not put out with him over "Speculum Tuscanismi." "But the noble Earl, not disposed to trouble his jovial mind with such Saturnine paltry still continued like his magnificent self."[229] This is most likely true, but it did not profit Harvey much. Oxford's subjective feelings lost any bearing upon the case the moment John Lyly publicized the libel, drawing the Privy Council's attention to it. Once public, it became a "scandalum magnatum", and the Privy Council could not remain inactive. Had Harvey never met Oxford again he would not have known whether the earl were offended or not. Equally, in 1592, the charge against the third playwright was one of "dishonest" living, of not controlling his passions, and, to boot, living below his status. Chettle did not know whether the third person was offended or not. As Oxford had been silent in 1580, so the third playwright failed to voice his personal displeasure. In 1592, Chettle, though he does not name him, addresses Christopher Marlowe personally. **No such apology was addressed to the third playwright.** So who was this third playwright who did not receive a **personal** apology?

Was it in fact George Peele? The evidence for this identification seems extremely weak. Certainly he was a playwright, a gentleman-scholar, his first name was George, so was the name of England's patron-saint the author of the letter in GGW says, "were it not an idolatrous oath" he would swear by. Chettle's reference to swearing by 'sweet St. George' could be understood to a person bearing this first name, but the oath itself was common, even after the Reformation when it had become "idolatrous." This reduces the onomastic argument almost to insignificance. Above all, according to the social order,

Peele, like Marlowe, would have been addressed personally in Chettle's apology. To slander him was a private matter , not an affair touching the security of the state requiring the intervention of privy councillors, of "divers worshipful persons" or "divers of worship."

Perhaps nothing would have happened between Harvey and Oxford in 1580 had not John Lyly publicized the affair. In *Pierces Supererogation* (the part written in 1590) Harvey says: "Papp-hatchet, desirous for his benefit, to curry favour with a noble Earl; and in defect of other means of commendation, labouring to insinuate himself by smooth glosing & counterfeit suggestions..."[230] But further details do not appear. Harvey is more outspoken in his *Four Letters*: "And that was all the Fleeting that I ever felt; saving that an other company of special good fellows, (whereof he was none of the meanest that bravely threatened to conjure up one, which should massacre Martin's wit, or should be lambacked himself with ten years provision) would need forsooth very courtly persuade the Earl of Oxford that something in those letters, and namely the Mirror of Tuscanismo, was palpably intended against him."[231] Then, we learn from the notebook of a contemporary that Lyly drew the Privy Council's attention to it. Once apprised, the Council had to act. Harvey's letters were overread by the Council. And it is likely that Sir James Croft, a privy councillor, thereby learned of Harvey's insults against the "old controller," and thought or wanted to think that he, not Dr. Perne, was the target of Harvey's insults. For his part, Lyly was ultimately disappointed. By denouncing Harvey he had awakened dogs which the council would have preferred to let lie. Oxford himself might have preferred not to take notice of it. If Harvey had reached beyond his station in slandering a peer, Lyly had been overzealous in remonstrating with him. The notebook of the contemporary scholar, William Withie, contains the following doggerel:

Thus to apply, by tattling them
as I think Lyly lets not ofttimes great men.
who troubled perchance with matters of weight
plucks up by the root this Lyly grown straight
him great men & grave men do laugh still to scorn
Thus checked, they bid him go where he was born.[232]

"Matters of (great) weight" were matters of state and the province of privy councillors (see, for instance, the letter above of the printers to Sir Francis Walsingham; the earl of Oxford himself uses the phrase in a letter to Sir Robert Cecil). Simply ignoring the letter in *Groatsworth* would also have been a workable procedure in 1592. But somehow the letter had been broadcast. By whom? Or by which concatenation of events? Was it because it appeared in Robert Greene's alleged last work? And because Harvey's *Four Letters* had highlighted Greene's demise? Another hypothesis looks more likely.

In 1580 it was Lyly who brought the libel into the public sphere, in 1592 it could have been Christopher Marlowe. Marlowe too had been slandered, more seriously than the other two. If, as in 1580, the other author who had been libeled was the same, the Earl of Oxford, or for that matter any other high-ranking person, Marlowe would have been motivated to link his own claim to an apology from Chettle, with Oxford's case. In attracting the Privy Council's attention to the slander of a peer, Marlowe would have prompted the privy councillors, the "divers of worship," into action. This would have lent more threatening power to his own demand. It would have been a skilful move.

But was the third playwright the earl of Oxford? Any other man of rank would, on principle, do as well. But there are not so many possibilities. Of all nobles known to have written plays only four come into consideration. We have besides Oxford, Thomas Sackville, Lord Buckhurst; there is Ferdinando Stanley, Lord Strange, who would succeed to the earldom of Derby in September 1593. In 1592 he was patron of a company of players and without doubt a man of literary culture; and we have his brother William, succeeding him to the earldom in April 1594, and reported to have written plays. But none of the three stands the test like Oxford. Lord Buckhurst can be discarded. He did write some plays but seems to have abandoned his literary activities long before 1592. In 1589 the author of *The Arte of English Poesie* states that Lord Buckhurst is among the "best for tragedy" and to have been a poet when "he was young".[233] Thomas Sackville was a co-author of *Gorboduc* and a contributor of *The Mirror of Magistrates*. Nothing more is known. Those plays were written about 1560, when Sackville "was young," twenty-five years old. But, it might be objected, Edward de Vere, Ferdinando Stanley and William Stanley were peers, not gentlemen. The term "gentleman" was used with more than one meaning, however. A nobleman could be spoken of as "gentleman" which then stressed more his "gentle behaviour" than his "gentle birth".

The address in the heading of the letter in *Groatsworth* is to "quondam acquaintances", not to scholars. But in the introduction Greene is said to be addressing his "fellow-scholars" and in his apology Chettle defends himself by claiming : "How I have all the time of my conversing in printing hindered the bitter inveighing against scholars, it hath been very well known, and how in that I dealt I can sufficiently prove." William Shakespeare was no scholar and, as seen, a somewhat wounded tale has to be produced in order to co-opt him into this category. The same objection cannot be made against Edward de Vere, Ferdinando and William Stanley. Though they were noble gentlemen by birth and not by scholarship, it is possible to vindicate for them the predicate of "scholar" or "university wit." The two Stanley brothers were educated at Oxford, Edward de Vere at Cambridge, and Robert Greene, Christopher Marlowe, and Thomas Nashe were all Cantabrigians; all, including Greene, were quondam, former Cambridge acquaintances of Gabriel Harvey. If Harvey wrote the letter, either partly or wholly, and foisted it into Greene's papers, Chettle, upon receiving it, might have thought it was addressed to fellow-scholars without any distinction of social status (in fact, as will be seen in part III, it was probably Oxford whom Harvey meant when he wrote a "grammar scholar in Art"). This would also help to explain why Harvey labeled Chettle "Lob-Assar-Duck" in *Pierce's Supererogation* (see part III, chapter II).

One difficulty persists. Chettle speaks of the "quality he professes," possibly meaning an actor, which, if so, excludes George Peele, already eliminated for other reasons. Oxford was certainly involved in theatrical life more than any other nobleman, even more than Ferdinando Stanley, patron of the company that would form the core of the Lord Chamberlain's Men in 1594. But no evidence exists of his ever having acted in the public or private theatre. However, John Davies of Hereford, in his famous epigram on Will. Shake-speare, says he could have have been a "companion to a king" if he had not "played some kingly parts in sport."

"companion to a king" had to be near the king and the court, he would have to be a courtier. And if he were not at court it would mean that he had fallen into disgrace for having acted.

Chapter III
Shake-Scene, The Upstart Crow

The identification of Shakespeare as "Shake-scene," the actor who meddles in playwriting by "bombasting out" plays, rests on two assumptions; the first being that 'Shake-scene' is a pun on the name Shakespeare; and the second, that a line from Shakespeare's play *3 Henry VI* (I.iv.137), spoken by the Duke of York to Queen Margaret, "O tiger's heart wrapp'd in a woman's hide," is paraphrased in the letter as "Tiger's heart wrapped in a Player's hide." The full passage reads:
"Yes trust them not: for there is an upstart Crow, beautified with our feathers, that with his *Tygers hart wrapt in a Players hyde,* supposes he is as well able to bombast out a blanke verse as the best of you: and being an absolute *Johannes factotum,* is in his owne conceit the onely Shake-scene in a countrey."

Is "Shake-scene" a pun on the name Shakespeare?

Brian Vickers writes on p. 209 of his book *Shakespeare, Co-Author*: "The italicized English words parody a line in *3 Henry VI…* and make it clear that Shakespeare is being mocked."[234] Before we challenge the veracity of Prof. Vickers' assertion, we must first address the issue of italicized words. Italics are the letter-type used in modern editions of ancient works to distinguish the following: emphases, foreign words or quotations in foreign languages or from other works, personal names and puns on personal names. Generally, italics are not used for aptronyms. These are names "that match its owner's occupation or character," for instance, "Sir Midas Mammon" for a miser or usurer.[235] Actually, the original versions either did not use or made inconsistent use of italics for those elements of the text. What now appears in italics may have been in another letter-type in the original. If the main text was in black-letter, those elements were often written in Roman type. We will nevertheless only use the term 'italics' in reference to those elements of the text that have been set apart. No imprecision can result from this, the replacement in modern editions by italics being wholly isomorphous.

In the passage on Shake-scene the quote from the play and the Latin expression "Johannes fac totum" are printed in italics, but not 'Shake-scene.' It should therefore, like the names "Sir John Lacke-land" and "Mr. Scrape-pennie" that Thomas Lodge uses in *An Alarum against Usurers* (1584) for the gentleman who has lost his lands in the process of borrowing money from a usurer, be considered an aptronym. These names are not printed in italics[236]; nor are "Velvet hoses" and "Clothe breeches" that Robert Greene uses to designate the upstart courtier and the country fellow. Here, 'Shake-scene' denotes an actor, apparently a notorious one.

By contrast, when, in an exchange of verses Sir Fulke Greville and Sir Edward Dyer pun on their own names, a different type signals the pun. Thus, in Sonnet LXXXIV Fulke Greville employs italics:

Let no man aske my name, nor what else I should be;

For *Greive-ill*, paine, forlorne estate, doe best decipher me.

To which Dyer replies, using capitals for his own name:

My Muse if any ask,

Whose grievous case was such

DY ERE thou let his name be known;

His folly shows as much.[237]

However, the pun could be yoked with the aptronym. The compositor of the last half of *Greene's Groatsworth of Wit* was in all likelihood Henry Chettle, who was also the editor and presumed author of the entire work. In this second half, compositor Chettle cannot have ignored the intention of editor and presumed author Chettle. Yet, surprisingly, in the second half of *Groatsworth* the word 'Greene' is used as simple noun, not printed in italics, and nevertheless clearly intended as a pun on the name. The fable of the ant and the grasshopper opens: "An Ant and a Grashopper walking on a Greene..."[238]; a similar allusion occurs in the closing letter to Greene's wife: "I should not send thee a child to bring thee greater charge: but consider he is the fruit of thy wombe... He is yet Greene, and may grow straight, if he be carefully tended: otherwise, apt enough (I fear me) to follow his Father's folly."[239]

Whereas the potential presence of a pun on the name Shakespeare must be left open, the aptronym 'Shake-scene' definitely denotes an actor whose voice and/or presence was so robustious as to make a scene shake. Indeed, the actor must have felt himself incomparable, "in his own conceit" the outstanding actor in all England, or "in a country." In 1592 the qualification would apply to one actor more than to any other.

Edward Alleyn

In 1592 Nashe writes in *Pierce Penniless* (1592): "Not *Roscius* nor *Æsope*, those admired tragedians that have lived ever since before Christ was born, could ever perform more in action than famous *Ned Allen*,"[240] and again in *Strange News* (1593) where he says that "the name of *Ned Allen* on the common stage" was able "to make an ill matter good."[241] In *Skialetheia* (1598) Evrard Guilpin refers to Alleyn in the epigram "On Clodius" (personifying a vainglorious courtier who borrows his attitudes from the theatre):

Clodius me thinks looks passing big of late
  With *Dunston*'s brows, and *Allen*'s *Cutlack* gait.
  What humours have possessed him so, I wonder,
  His eyes are lightning, and his words are thunder.

Of the play *Cutlack* nothing else is known than that it was staged about 11 times between May and September 1594. But the phrase "his words are thunder" probably refers to Alleyn, as "he was apparently a man of exceptional physical stature, with a strong voice to match his size."[242] He acted Tamburlaine and likely also Tamar Can, an imitation of Marlowe's Tamburlaine. Surely, Edward Alleyn could shake a scene.

How does the Stratford Shakespeare match this description? In truth, as a non-descript, for little is known of his acting career. In E.K. Chambers's list of actors the entry on Edward Alleyn covers almost three pages, Richard Burbage's entry takes over three pages, John Heminges nearly three, Augustine Phillips rates one and a half, Thomas Pope has one, and George Bryan thirteeen lines. Bringing up the rear we have John Duke with three lines and finally, William Shakespeare, with two:

"DUKE, JOHN. Strange's (?), 1590-1; Chamberlain's, 1598; Worcester's -Anne's, 1602-9. Four children were baptized at St. Leonard's, where he lived in Holywell Street, from July 1604 to January 1609."
"SHAKESPEARE, WILLIAM. Strange's, 1592; Pembroke's (?) 1593; Sussex's (?) (1594); Chamberlain's-King's (1594-1616); and dramatist."[243]

And even in these two lines we find two uncertain mentions. First, there is no evidence that the player Shakespeare belonged to Sussex's or Pembroke's Men. A question mark that should appear has been omitted, after Strange's Men. Possibly this question mark was misplaced by Duke's name, who definitely **did belong** to Strange's Men. We know that in 1599 John Duke transferred from the Chamberlain's Men to another company, probably Oxford's Men, and from there removed to Worcester's that would become Queen Anne's Men in 1604.[244] For the latter company and its predecessor alike, Duke is documented several times as payee.

Andrew Gurr remarks that Shakespeare's "name does not appear in any of the companies before the Chamberlain's Men some time after 1594, but his plays do... If a company's performance of his plays is anything to go by, they must give clues to his playing allegiances. That puts him in Strange's before 1592..."[245] This last notion adroitly skirts around an inconvenient reality: the two existing documents pertaining to Strange's Men for the years 1592 and 1593 respectively, mention several actors who were to become Lord Chamberlain's Men. But **not Shakespeare**.

Among the several plots preserved among Edward Alleyn's papers at Dulwich College is a plot of the second part of Richard Tarlton's play *Seven Deadly Sins*. The play is no longer extant; it was performed by Strange's Men at the Rose under the title *Four Plays in One* just one day before the second performance of *Harry VI* on 6 March 1592. The names of the actors are mentioned along the plot: Richard Burbage, John Duke, Augustine Phillips, Thomas Pope, George Bryan, Robert Pallant, all of them future Chamberlain's Men. **But no William Shakespeare.**

The other document, dated 6 May, is a license of the Privy Council to travel in the province during the plague epidemic of 1593. The actors mentioned are Edward Alleyn as servant of the Lord Admiral, and five Strange's Men: William Kemp, Thomas Pope, John Heminges, Augustine Phillips and George Bryan. Once again, **no William Shakespeare**.

Furthermore, in which plays might he have acted? The only play recorded by Henslowe before 1594 which could have been thought Shakespeare's is *Harry VI*, but as will be seen later, this play was most likely not written by him. In 1594, there were performances of *Titus Andronicus*, which some scholars think is not Shakespeare's, and *The Taming of A Shrew*, generally thought not to be Shakespeare's, though it might have been a source for his *The Taming of **The** Shrew*. And then? On 8 April 1594 the earl of Sussex's Men act *King Lear*, which according to orthodox chronology is a play Shakespeare would write eleven or twelve years later and therefore this 1594 work is said to be the old *King Leir*, yet is at the same time said not to be his. But the presence of *King Lear* in Henslowe's accounts is possibly the tacit reason Chambers tentatively placed Shakespeare in the company of the Earl of Sussex. This company, however, was most likely the successor of Strange's Men (who with Lord Strange becoming earl of Derby were for a brief spell known as Derby's Men) and which would become soon afterwards (in June 1594) the Lord Chamberlain's Men.

Now from Henslowe's joint accounts for the Chamberlain's and the Admiral's Men, beginning on 3 June 1594, we know which play of Shakespeare's was performed next. It was *Hamlet*, a play he had not on 9 June 1594 (according to orthodox chronology) yet written, wherefore it needs must be the *Ur-Hamlet*, which is said not to be Shakespeare's. Unfortunately, Henslowe's accounts for the Chamberlain's Men come to an end on 13 June, only 10 days after the first of Henslowe's entries for that period. The last performance noted in his accounts is that of *Titus Andronicus* on 12 June. All the plays listed after that date belong to the repertory of the Admiral's Men.

Hence, Gurr's strange notion about Shakespeare's company placement would be more accurately rephrased as: "If a company's performance of his **source plays** is anything to go by, they must give clues to his playing allegiances." Apparently, plays disallowed to identify him as author are restored, that they might lend a chimerical shading to his spooky existence as an actor. Was this the impressive actor who in 1592 thought himself "the only Shake-scene in a country," able to "bombast out a blank verse as well as the best" of the three playwrights? Here, as Carroll justly remarks, 'bombast' does not mean to 'deliver' a line, as an actor would in performance; it means to 'compose' one, and a special kind of line at that. The "actor referred to as 'Shake-scene' had distinguished himself in such a way as to be compared or to compare himself with one of them, apparently with Marlowe in particular...[246] And this is the very thing that Edward Alleyn (the actor who could "shake a scene" and "in his own conceit" as well as in the view of many others, the best actor of his day), was known to have been doing.

Among Alleyn's papers at Dulwich College is "a manuscript of the part of Orlando in Robert Greene's *Orlando Furioso*, probably played by Edward Alleyn... It is written in the hand of some scribe, with corrections and insertions, some of which certainly, and probably all, are by Alleyn... The play which was printed in quarto in 1594, appears to have originally belonged to the Queen's men, and probably passed to Lord Strange's company at the end of 1591. It was played by them at the Rose on 21 (22) Feb. 1591/2."[247]

So this play by Robert Greene, staged in February 1592, only **months before** *Greene's Groatsworth of Wit* was written, had been "bombasted out" by Edward Alleyn, indeed, the actor had had the temerity to add 530 lines of his own. Moreover, Alleyn was the owner of the play *Tamar Can* and likely to have been the author or at the very least a collaborator. Greg comments: "I have little doubt that it [Tamar Can] was written as a rival to *Tamburlain* which belonged to the Admiral's men."[248] Like Marlowe's *Tamburlain* the play consisted of two parts. Only the plot of the first part is extant. The second part was staged by the Lord Admiral's men on 28 April 1592. Thus in the months leading up to the composition of *Groatsworth*, the famous actor Alleyn had manifestly dared to rival both Greene and Marlowe at playwriting.

Alleyn was also a well-known *Johannes factotum*. "From Henslowe's account book of the Rose Playhouse (commonly referred to as his diary) it would appear that he and Alleyn ran the theatre as a shared partnership. Alleyn presumably earned his share of the profits primarily from his work on stage; however, he also co-signed loans to, and for the company, authorized the purchase of playbooks and costumes, witnessed loans for ready money advanced to individual players, and occasionally sold his own copies of playbooks to the company."[249] Another line in the letter in *Groatsworth* points to him (and to his father-in-law Henslowe): "I know the best husband of you all will never prove an Usurer, and the kindest of them all will never prove a kind nurse." Moneylenders, though the taking of ten percent interest was allowed, were considered usurers by Elizabethan public opinion.

The first part of Henry VI: *a thought experiment*

Let us suppose that the author of the letter in *GGW* takes his quotation not from the Duke of York's death scene in *3 Henry VI*, but instead from the death scene (IV.vii) of Lord Talbot, the hero of *1 Henry VI*. It is widely accepted that *Harry VI*, the play recorded by Philip Henslowe with fifteen performances by Lord Strange's men between 3 March 1592 and 31 January 1593, is Shakespeare's *1 Henry VI* and that this is the same play Thomas Nashe praises in *Pierce Penniless* (1592): "How would it have joyed brave *Talbot* (the terror of the French) to think that after he had lain two hundred years in his tomb, he should triumph again on the stage, and have his bones new embalmed with the tears of ten thousand spectators (at several times), who, in the tragedian that represents his person, imagine they behold him fresh bleeding."[250] Now (continuing with our thought experiment), in order to chastise the upstart Crow for his presumptuous conduct, his conceit of imagining himself the "only shake-scene in a country," for bombasting out a blank verse and being a *Johannes Factotem*, the letter in *GGW* would have paraphrased the following lines from Talbot's death-scene:
        And like a hungry lion did commence
        Rough deeds of rage and stern impatience" (ll. 7-8)

as:

> And like a hungry lion did commence
> Rough deeds of stage and stern insolence.

In September 1592 the situation would have been nearly the same for all three parts of *Henry VI*: all three had been staged and all three were unprinted. Would it be possible to confidently state that the paraphrased line (along with 'Shake-scene') unmistakably alluded to Shakespeare? Many a scholar would certainly deny it, because several different hands are recognizable in *1 Henry VI*.

E.K. Chambers, for one, would even deny that the hypothetically paraphrased lines are Shakespeare's: he classifies the different styles from (a) to (f). According to him, only (e), the famous Temple Garden scene in which the earls of Somerset, Suffolk and Warwick, Richard Plantagenet (not yet restored to the title of Duke of York) and two lawyers pluck either a white or a red rose to demonstrate their allegiances, and perhaps (f), might be Shakespeare's. On what grounds does he reject Talbot's death-scenes as authentic? "They [scenes IV.3-7] are often claimed for Shakespeare, but on the whole I think it is more likely that they are by the author of (b), and the duplication of a tasteless comparison of Talbot and his son to Daedalus and Icarus favours this."[251] The sections assigned to (b) are mainly the scenes with Joan of Arc, on which Chambers remarks: "It is in a very inferior style, with many flat and some absurd lines, much tautology, and a tendency to drag in learned allusions."[252] In these scenes, allusions are found to Nero, Hannibal, Rhodope of Memphis, Astraea, etc. The likening of young Talbot (who wants to fly as high as his father) to Icarus and Talbot himself to Daedalus is indeed far-fetched and highfalutin.

Walter W. Greg also recognizes a plurality of authors, "their very disparate styles can only be ascribed to difference of authorship... But disparity of style is not the only ground for suspecting diversity of authorship... For example, the author of V.i, in which Winchester [Henry Beaufort, bishop of] has, it appears, only lately become cardinal, can hardly have read, still less have written, I.iii, in which he already appears in full canonicals."[253]

We can therefore conclude that the plurality of authors and the controversial ascription of scene IV.vii with its un-Shakespearean flaunting of learning would make it hazardous to interpret the quoted lines from *1 Henry VI* as an allusion to him.

But the same problems, though to a much lesser extent, exist for *2* and *3 Henry VI*.

A Tigers´s Heart

3 Henry VI was first printed in 1595 as *The True Tragedy of Richard Duke of York*, also known as *The second part of the Contention betwixt the Houses of Lancaster and York*. The first part of *The Contention* corresponds to *2 Henry VI* and was printed the year before. Both were published anonymously. The paraphrased line " A tiger's heart wrapp´d in a woman's hide" is not only contained in *3 Henry VI*, it is also found in *True Tragedy*. The two versions have much in common, but there are also considerable differences of content and style between them. If *True Tragedy* precedes *3 Henry VI* and is, to boot, by another author, the line paraphrased in the letter in GGW would rather point to the anonymous author of *True Tragedy* than to Shakespeare. An allusion to a largely unknown author would have been but a shot in the dark. Some scholars, most notoriously John Dover Wilson,[254] have identified Greene either as author or main author. If there were different authors, how could this line be associated with a particular author? If the author were Robert Greene and **known** to be him, would the publishers of the two parts of the *Contention* have failed to blazon his name (so heavily capitalized upon after his death) on the title-page? But the play was never assigned to Greene.

Christopher Marlowe has also been named as author. True, some plays of Marlowe had been published anonymously and were only assigned to him some years after his death, but the *Contention* and *True Tragedy* were never ascribed to him. Thus far we neither contest nor affirm Greene's or Marlowe's authorship. But both Greene and Marlowe were household names which a publisher would hardly have failed to put on the title-page in 1594/5, had he known the two plays,

Contention and *True Tragedy*, were written by either of them. As for Shakespeare, in 1598 Francis Meres does not mention *Henry VI* as one of Shakespeare's six tragedies. It was not until 1619, when William Jaggard printed and Thomas Pavier published the two plays in one volume as *The Whole Contention*, that the play was assigned to William Shakespeare. But when *Greene's Groatsworth of Wit* appeared in September 1592, no printed text was available.

What is clear is that the plays performed on the stage were *Contention* and *True Tragedy*, not the versions of 2 and 3 *Henry VI* as printed in the First Folio. No playing company's name is mentioned on the title-page of *Contention*. But a year later, in 1595, the title-page of *True Tragedy* mentions that the play was "sundry times acted by the Right Honourable the Earle of Pembroke his servants." The Earl of Pembroke's Men, though, are unlikely to have performed the play for the first time. "As a matter of fact, there is no mention of Pembroke's before 1592 and no reason to suppose that it had an earlier existence."[255] However, a connection, the nature of which is difficult to retrace with precision, did exist between Strange's and Pembroke's. The title-page of *Titus Andronicus* (1594) mentions performing companies in this order: Derby's, Pembroke's, Sussex's. Lord Strange's became the Earl of Derby's when Ferdinando Stanley, Lord Strange, succeeded as fifth earl to the earldom on 25 September 1593. He died the next year on 16 April. Philip Henslowe's records for Strange's Men commence on 19 February 1592 and end on 1st February 1593. Then there is a large gap due to the closing of the theatres during the Plague epidemic of that year. Henslowe resumes his records in December, but for the Earl of Sussex's Men, not Derby's. These records end on 3 April 1594. From 3 June on the records are for the Lord Admiral's Men and the Lord Chamberlain's Men, but no play of the latter company's repertory appears after 12 June 1594. It seems pretty clear that Strange's, Sussex's and Chamberlain's Men form a continuum. The three companies performed a number of Shakespearean or proto-Shakespearean plays: *1 Henry VI*, *Titus Andronicus*, *King Leare*, *Hamlet*, *The Taming of A Shrew*.

It would have been natural for Strange's Men also to have performed *Contention* and *True Tragedy*, and some circumstantial evidence exists to support this hypothesis. Both in *Contention* and *2 Henry VI*, two Cade rebels are called George Bevis and John Holland, which were also these actors' real names. In plots and prompt-books actors of minor parts such as keeper, captain, attendants were often mentioned by their real names. Another actor of such small roles (probably because of his very low stature),[256] was John Sincler or Sincklo. His name is mentioned in the Folio version of *3 Henry VI*: "Enter Sincklo and Humfrey with cross-bows in their hands."[257] With a brief hiatus Sincler or Sincklo seems to have belonged successively to Strange's, Chamberlain's and the King's Men. In 1604 he is mentioned along with Burbage, Condell, Lowin, and Sly in the induction to John Marston's *The Malcontent*. The names Sincler and Holland also appear in the plot of *The Second Part of Seven Deadly Sins*, acted by Strange's Men as *Four Plays in One* (ie, an induction and a play on the 3 deadly sins Envy, Sloth, and Lechery) on 6 March 1592. As Henslowe subsequently does not record the play again, this performance was probably the last in a series. The plot is among Edward Alleyn's papers, and he is likely to have acted in it, though his name is not mentioned (but no names are given for two leading parts, Henry VI and the monk-poet Lydgate). Sincklo and Holland took several minor roles.

Given that the performance is not recorded by Henslowe and that his records for Strange's Men commence on 19 February 1592, the performance of both *Contention* plays must have taken place early that year or before. Another circumstance corroborates a performance before 1592. *1 Henry VI*, staged early in March 1592, must have been written and performed **after** *Contention* and *True Tragedy* were. Had they been written later, it would be inconceivable that no mention of Lord Talbot, the hero of *1 Henry VI*, is made in them, especially in Humphrey, the Duke of Gloucester's enumeration of the heroes in France (I.ii.75-85). Named are: Henry V, Bedford, Salisbury, Warwick, and York. The last three were still alive, but Henry V and his brother, the Duke of Bedford, were dead. Historically, Lord Talbot was also still alive. But the stage would probably have prevailed over the chronicles. Had *1 Henry VI* already been written, it would not have been possible to omit Lord Talbot from the "hall of fame".

In the absence of a known author, the line in the letter in *GGW* might just as well have referred to the actor who had spoken it on the stage. This actor could have been Edward Alleyn. Richard, Duke of York is the central figure of the *True Tragedy*, though not so much by the number of appearances (he dies in I.iv), but because it is his claim to the throne which dominates the play. However, *Contention* and *True Tragedy* form a diptych. In *Contention* York is one of the leading characters. The case for the line referring to Alleyn must rest there. How, then, could Shakespeare have been associated with the play?

Edmund Malone, the great eighteenth-century scholar seemed to have found a satisfactory answer. *Contention* and *True Tragedy* would have been the source plays for *2 and 3 Henry VI*. One of the authors would have been Robert Greene, and Shakespeare's use of the plays would have provoked Greene's anger, charging Shakespeare with theft. Later, Malone changed his mind in favour of Marlowe as principal author, but the conception that Greene, in his outburst against Shake-scene, was accusing Shakespeare of plagiary, has persisted. One problem was left unaddressed by Malone: when did Shakespeare rewrite the text and why would not his text but the text of the source plays have been staged and printed? The looming consequence of Malone's two theories was that the line probably did not refer to Shakespeare. And Dr. C.F. Tucker Brooke in his 1912 study *The Authorship of 2 and 3 Henry VI* (and fully supported by Dr. Allison Gaw in *The Origin and Development of 1 Henry VI,* written in the early 1920's), argued that the line heard by Greene was by Marlowe, not Shakespeare.[258]

Then, in 1924 another Shakespearean scholar, Peter Alexander, raised the siege of the Shakespeare fortress, but not without letting in a Trojan horse. The relationship between, on the one hand, *Contention* and *True Tragedy* and, on the other, *2 and 3 Henry VI* was reversed. Alexander contended that Shakespeare's versions were the originals, *Contention* and *True Tragedy* corrupt versions of Shakespeare's texts, constructed from the imperfect memory of an actor-reporter. That the reporter was also an actor is thought to have accounted for the presence of both heavily corrupted and more or less genuine parts. The consequence lay at hand: the paraphrased line did refer to the original author. The Trojan horse was that Peter Alexander claimed the same direction of influence for Shakespeare's *King John* and the anonymous *The Troublesome Reign of King John*. But the latter was printed in 1591, whereas the former was placed not earlier than 1595 in the orthodox chronology.

Walter W. Greg duly noted that "it would follow that all the Shakespearian pieces in question would have to be dated considerably earlier than is usually done."[259] Regarding Alexander's new theory, orthodoxy seemed to apply Hamlet's counsel to his mother about the bad and good parts of her heart, "O throw away the worser part of it/And live the purer with the other half." The 'bad part' of the MR (memorial reconstruction) theory was dumped into the barathron. But as in Shakespeare's plays, such corpses tend to reappear as ghosts to their murderers on the eve of the fatal battle.

The MR theory was not yet fully ten years old when its application to *Contention* and *True Tragedy* was vehemently challenged. "So wise so young, they say, do never live long," Richard III muses (III.iii.79). The MR theory **was** young in 1933, however it lived on very long. Because it was unwise, as Clayton Alvis Greer explained in a long article in *PMLA*.[260] Greer's objections, though pertinent, remained without effect, reducing the author to a twenty-four year's silence. In 1957 he made another attempt in a brief note in *Notes and Queries*. The MR theory somehow survived also that, even though the note looked devastating. Greer had pointed to the great number of stage directions shared by, on the one hand, *Contention* and *2 Henry VI* and, on the other, *True Tragedy* and *3 Henry VI*. "Since stage directions were not uttered in a performance and an actor-reporter could not have heard them, how could he have gotten 160 stage directions out of 217 very much the same in word, 38 exactly the same and 122 only slightly altered?"[261] How indeed? The arguments Greer had already advanced in 1933 should have been largely sufficient to subject the MR theory to closer scrutiny. This was not done, perhaps because academia had already embarked on a long publication journey on the topic.

Nevertheless, Greer had also shown that some stage directions in *Contention* and *True Tragedy* were not found in *2 and 3 Henry VI* and instead followed *Holinshed's* and *Hall's Chronicles*. The "actor-reporter" would have reconstructed the texts with Holinshed and Hall at his side; according to general agreement, this was the way Shakespeare had been working himself. Greer further argued that most of the differences cannot be explained by failing memory. Finally, the "actor-reporter" would sometimes have proved an excellent poet. *Contention* and *True Tragedy* each contain some very good poetry not to be found in *2 and 3 Henry VI*.

The *non sequitur* to Greer's cogent arguments might possibly be ascribed to the notion that theories, like myths and customs, die hard, and, like the moon, must run their full course before they can be renewed. Or perhaps the resistance was partly due to the unwieldy solution he proposed. In Greer's view, not only was the author of *Contention* and *True Tragedy* someone other than the author of *2 and 3 Henry VI*, but the author of *The Whole Contention* published in 1619 would have been yet another. It was the more deplorable because he held in his hands the key to what could be the correct answer. Indeed, he listed a number of omissions in *Contention* and *True Tragedy* for each major character, adding that to a certain extent these omissions deprived the characters of their psychological depth. Meditations opening a window to secret thoughts is one of Shakespeare's distinctive marks in comparison with many other playwrights of his time; among them, Christopher Marlowe.

The MR theory rests mainly on the Duke of York's shambolic pedigree in the *Contention*. How this came about is a matter of speculation. Whether or not it is impossible to make the author responsible for this mess, as Greer maintained, it is at any rate difficult to believe that the chaos proceeded from the author, whoever he was. It seems as if someone, perhaps a staunch Yorkist (and anti-Tudor, possibly also a misogynist, and working either in the theatre or in the printing house), was driven by the desire to invest the Duke of York with a male-based and more unequivocal claim to the throne, by making Edmund Langley, first Duke of York, the **second** instead of the fifth son of Edward III.

In *3 Henry VI* Shakespeare, in accordance with history, has the Duke derive his priority claim from the female line of Lionel, Duke of Clarence, the third son of Edward III (John of Gaunt, Duke of Lancaster being the fourth: the second son William of Hatfield had died young, as had the seventh, William of Windsor). The order given in *Contention* is : 1) Edward, the Black Prince, who predeceased Edward III; 2) Edmund of Langley, first Duke of York; 3) Lionel, Duke of Clarence; 4) John of Gaunt, Duke of Lancaster; 5) Roger Mortimer, Earl of Marsh; 6) Thomas of Woodstock, Duke of Gloucester; 7) William of Windsor. According to this pedigree York could claim first through his grandfather Edmund of Langley and secondly through the Duke of Clarence, both elder brothers of John of Gaunt. As Roger Mortimer, Earl of March, also played a major role in York's claim to the succession (he was the son of the Duke of Clarence's daughter Philippe), he was made Edward III's fifth son. From II,ii:

> YORK: Edward the third had seven sons,
> The first was Edward the Black Prince, Prince of Wales.
> The second was Edmund of Langley, Duke of York.
> The third was Lionel, Duke of Clarence.
> The fourth was John of Gaunt, the Duke of Lancaster.
> The fifth was Roger Mortimer, Earl of March.
> The sixth was Sir Thomas of Woodstock.
> William of Windsor was the seventh and last.
> Now Edward, the Black Prince, he died before his father,
> and left behind him Richard, that afterwards was King,
> crowned by the name of Richard the second, and he died
> without an heir. Edmund of Langley, duke of York died,
> and left behind him two daughters, Anne and Eleanor.
> Lionel, duke of Clarence died, and left behind Alice,
> Anne, and Eleanor, that was after married to my father,
> And by her I claim the Crown, as the true heir to Lionel
> Duke of Clarence, the third son to Edward the third.
> Now, sir, in the time of Richard's reign, Henry of
> Bolingbroke, son and heir to John of Gaunt, the Duke of
> Lancaster, fourth son to Edward the third, he claimed
> The crown, deposed the mirthful King, and as both you
> Know, in Pomfret Castle harmless Richard was shamefully

> Murdered, and so by Richard's death came the house of
> Lancaster unto the Crown.

The author of *The Contention* (or the printer of it) would appear to have had trouble imagining a claim to the throne deriving through a woman. It is worth considering what the contemporary audience would have registered of this, or what the response of the reigning monarch would have been; the still unmarried Elizabeth I, now well past child-bearing age and with no declared successor of her own issue, would with her death in a decades time bring to an end the Tudor dynasty. But contrary to *Contention*, it was not as a descendant of Edmund of Langley that Richard, third Duke of York, claimed priority over the Lancasters.

The first Duke of York had two sons. The elder, Edward, inherited the title of Duke of York; the younger, Richard, the third Duke of York's father, inherited Langley's subordinate title of Earl of Cambridge. Richard, Earl of Cambridge, was executed for high treason by the popular King Henry V, something the author of the pedigree in *Contention* apparently wanted to keep hidden from the public. In *Contention* York speaks of him simply as his father, without naming him. The second Duke of York died without issue in 1415, and the title descended upon his nephew Richard; though not immediately, as the attainder of the Earl of Cambridge was still in effect. For a while York simply remained Richard Plantagenet, without title, to which he was restored by Henry VI. The Earl of Cambridge married Anne, sister of Eleanor and daughter of Roger Mortimer, Earl of March, himself son of Edmund Mortimer and Philippe, the Duke of Clarence's daughter. As Shakespeare has York state in 2 Henry VI, II.ii.42-46:

> His eldest sister, Anne,
> My mother, being heir unto the crown,
> Married Richard Earl of Cambridge, who was
> To Edmund Langley, Edward the Third's fifth son, son.
> By her I claim the kingdom: she was heir
> To Roger Earl of March, who was the son
> Of Edmund Mortimer, who married Philippe,

In *Contention* the author of the pedigree seems obsessed with establishing a claim for York that is in every respect superior to that of the Lancasters. Thus Anne and Eleanor are not only the daughters of Roger Mortimer, Earl of March, who is himself made the fifth son of Edward III, they are also made daughters of Lionel, Duke of Clarence, and even of Edmund of Langley, Duke of York. It's as if this author thought: "If there are some women in the succession play, I must them store away somewhere, but I'm not going to rack my brains over this silly question, so I will put them everywhere, one place will at any rate be right." As if all this were not enough, the first or the second Duke of York would have somehow managed to claim the crown in the middle of Henry IV's reign.

A similarly anti-Lancastrian affect seems to lie at the root of another historical error in *True Tragedy*. On the other hand, in *3 Henry VI*, IV.i.47 -58, Shakespeare once again has it right:

> CLARENCE. For this one speech Lord Hastings well deserves
> To have the heir of the Lord Hungerford.
> KING EDWARD. Ay, what of that? it was my will and grant;
> And for this once my will shall stand for law.
> GLOUCESTER. And yet methinks your Grace hath not done well
> To give the heir and daughter of Lord Scales
> Unto the brother of your loving bride.
> She better would have fitted me or Clarence;
> But in your bride you bury brotherhood.
> CLARENCE. Or else you would not have bestow'd the heir
> Of the Lord Bonville on your new wife's son,
> And leave your brothers to go speed elsewhere.

The daughter of Lord Scales married Anthony Woodville, 2nd Earl of Rivers, brother to Queen Elizabeth. Their father was Richard Woodville, 1st Earl of Rivers. The daughter of Lord Bonville was married to Thomas Grey, Marquess of Dorset, son of Elizabeth Woodville, the future queen, and Sir John Grey. Both Richard Woodville and John Grey had been staunch supporters of the House of Lancaster. Sir John Grey was killed at the second battle of St. Albans in 1461; Richard, Earl of Rivers, paid with his head for his Lancastrian allegiances in 1469. Their respective sons are eliminated from *True Tragedy*, by having Lord Scales married to the daughter of Lord Bonville:

CLARENCE: Ay, and for such a thing too the Lord Scales
Did well deserve at your hands, to have the
Daughter of the Lord Bonfield, and left your
Brothers to go seek elsewhere, but in
Your madness, you bury brotherhood.

York's pedigree and, to a lesser degree, the bungled marriages, perhaps support the failing-memory theory. But even here, some system seems at work. In *Contention*, York is given such an outsized claim as to make him appear thoroughly abused by Lancaster; in *True Tragedy* the reminders of the Lancastrian past of the Woodvilles and Greys is avoided. It is, however, hazardous to base a theory on one, at most one and a half, egregious example, for which there is no other comparable instance in *Contention* or *True Tragedy*. How absurd the MR theory thus appears as an explanation for the differences between *True Tragedy* and *3 Henry VI* can be demonstrated by two passages: Gloucester (the future Richard III) in his long monologue in III.ii.124-195, and Henry VI's meditation in II.v.1.54.

In *3 Henry VI* Gloucester's soliloquy has 72 lines, in *True Tragedy* only 30, so according to the MR theory, the "actor-reporter" would have been unable to remember 42. He would have remembered the first ten fairly well, but lines 134-146 would have tumbled straight into dark forgetfulness. From line 147 on his memory would have recovered, but at line 165, and through 190 he would once again have lost his retention. The last five lines he would again have remembered, apart from the phrase "murderous Machiavel" which he would on an apparent creative whim, replace with "the aspiring Catiline." Historically this is perhaps the more appropriate comparison for Richard III, one which sounds as Marlowesque as "murderous Machiavel." Our "actor-reporter" would appear to have been well-versed in Roman history. From his supposedly ragged memory he would, by a happy, nay, a prodigious coincidence, have produced a monologue which is in itself coherent, the sort of result one would expect from a skilled abridger. Or, vice versa, would have been skilfully complemented by Shakespeare.

The cuts, if they are 'cuts' at all, are indeed made with precision, so as not to violate consistency and continuity. In the first 10 lines of the monologue Gloucester reveals his design to seize the crown. In 3 *Henry VI* there follow 13 lines of lyrical meditation. No hiatus in the course of Gloucester's premeditation is caused by leaving these lines out and leaping directly to line 147. But again: did the author of *True Tragedy* abridge Shakespeare's play or did Shakespeare enlarge on a source?

Otherwise put: are these cuts, however apt to give more momentum to the action, from Shakespeare's version, or did Shakespeare aptly insert reflective passages?

In 3 *Henry VI* the lines 1-54 in scene II.v represent the poetical apex of the play. King Henry VI has been sent away from the battlefield by Queen Margaret and Lord Clifford as a hindrance. He weighs up whether it is a better to be a king or a shepherd. He is longing for the monotonous but assuaging cyclic course of a shepherd's existence:

O God! methinks it were a happy life
To be no better than a homely swain;
To sit upon a hill, as I do now,
To carve out dials quaintly, point by point,
Thereby to see the minutes how they run-
How many makes the hour full complete,
How many hours brings about the day,
How many days will finish up the year,
How many years a mortal man may live.
When this is known, then to divide the times-
So many hours must I tend my flock;
So many hours must I take my rest;
So many hours must I contemplate;
So many hours must I sport myself;
So many days my ewes have been with young;
So many weeks ere the poor fools will can;
So many years ere I shall shear the fleece:
So minutes, hours, days, months, and years,
Pass'd over to the end they were created,
Would bring white hairs unto a quiet grave.

> Ah, what a life were this! how sweet! how lovely!

None of this is found in *True Tragedy*. The "actor-reporter"would have remembered nothing, except line 22 shortly before, to which he would have added two lines of his own making:

> Would God that I were dead so all were well
> Or would my crown suffice, I were content
> To yield it them and live a private life.

And the lines he "invented" to make up for his "failing memory" summarize the long meditation in Shakespeare's play. They are far less poetical but they are still good poetry. That the alleged actor-reporter was a good poet was another of Greer's arguments against the MR theory. He would not only have "left 1530 lines out of 5977 unchanged, changed 1711 and omitted 2736 entirely,"[262] he would also have added 620 lines. Greer asks emphatically: "Who was he that added nothing much but poetry? Who was he that could change 1711 lines, mostly poetry and good poetry too? What is this actor-reporter's name? Surely he must have been known in his days as a writer as well as an actor? Surely he must have left to his credit some literary work other than the *Contention* and *The True Tragedy*."[263]

Greer quotes seven lines from *Contention* and 16 lines from *The True Tragedy* **not** contained in 2 and 3 *Henry VI* respectively. Among the lines from *True Tragedy* is the following sequence spoken by the young Prince Edward, King Henry VI's son, in V.iv:

> I will not stand aloof and bid you fight,
> But with my sword press in the thickest throngs,
> And single Edward from his strongest guard,
> And hand to hand enforce him for to yield,
> Or leave my body as witness of my thoughts.

These lines alone bring the unknown poet before our eyes. Compare them with those spoken by another young Prince Edward:

> Think not that I am frighted with thy words.
> My father's murdered through thy treachery;
> And thou shalt die, and on his mournful hearse
> Thy hateful and accursed head shall lie
> To witness to the world that by thy means

His kingly body was too soon interred.

This young prince is of course the young king Edward III in Marlowe's *Edward II*, V.vi.27-32). In the *True Tragedy* prince Edward will "press in the thickest throngs". The phrase occurs twice, once in *True Tragedy*, once in *Contention*. In *Contention*, the future Richard III attests to Warwick, his father's (the Earl of Salisbury) valiancy:

> My Lord, I saw him *in the thickest thronges*
> Charging his lance with his old weary arms. (V.iii.9-10)

In I.i the Earl of Salisbury exhorts his son:

> And thou brave Warwick, *my thrice valiant son*...

In *True Tragedy*, II.iii.15-18, the same Richard reports Salisbury's death:

> Ah, Warwick, why hast thou withdrawn thyself?
> Thy noble father *in the thickest throngs*,
> Cried still for Warwick *his thrice valiant son*,
> Until with thousand swords he was beset,

It is to be noted that the italics are in the original and indicate the cross-reference between the two plays.

Marlowe seems to have had a preference for the phrase "the thickest throngs." He uses it in *Tamburlaine Part II*, III.iii.139-40:

> But then run desperate through the thickest thronges,
> Dreadless of blows, of bloody wounds, and deaths.

Also in *Dido, Queen of Carthage*, II, I, 210-12:

> Yet flung I forth, and desperate of my life,
> Ran in the thickest throngs, and with this sword
> Sent many of their savage ghosts to hell.

However, in the scenes of *2 and 3 Henry VI* (that correspond to the ones cited above from *True Tragedy*) this phrase so favored by Marlowe does not occur:

> Three times to-day I holp him to his horse,
> Three times bestrid him, thrice I led him off,
> Persuaded him from any further act; (*2 HVI*, V.iii)

And in *3 Henry VI*, II.iii.14-19:

> Ah, Warwick, why hast thou withdrawn thyself?
> Thy brother's blood the thirsty earth hath drunk,
> Broach'd with the steely point of Clifford's lance;

And in the very pangs of death he cried,
Like to a dismal clangor heard from far,
'Warwick, revenge! Brother, revenge my death.'

It would seem the phrase "in the thickest throngs" did not please Shakespeare. It occurs nowhere in his works.

Yet there is still evidence of Marlowe in Shakespeare's 2 and 3 *Henry VI*.[264] Display of learning, and the use of Latin quotations and of words of other foreign languages, is atypical of Shakespeare's tragedies, his usage is mostly limited to comic situations. But it is typical for authors like Greene, Nashe, and Marlowe. In *Edward II*, for instance, Mortimer regularly peppers his speeches with Latin phrases. So does the Earl of Leicester, in the same play, in IV.6.53-4:

Too true it is, *quem dies vidit veniens superbum,*
Hunc dies vidit fugiens jacentem.[265]

Further, Marlowe sprinkles his plays with foreign words, mainly from Italian: "diablo" (*Ed. II*, I.iv), "malgrado" (*Ed. II*, II.v), "Corpo di Dio" (*Jew of Malta*, I.ii), etc.

The author of the Duke of Suffolk's death-scene (*2 Henry VI*, IV.ii) seems more likely to be Marlowe than Shakespeare. The lieutenant who is going to behead Suffolk likens him to the Roman dictator Sulla. Suffolk himself likens his murderer to the Illyrian pirate Bargulus mentioned in Cicero's *Officii* (in *Contention* to the Macedonian pirate Abradas), to the murders of Cicero, Caesar, and Pompey. Suffolk uses two Italianisms, "bezonians"(from "bisogno", ie "mechanic", "base") and "banditto". Suffolk also interjects a Latin quotation.

In *3 Henry VI*, I.iii, the young Earl of Rutland, the Duke of York's son, quotes from Ovid just before being killed by Clifford, "Die faciant laudis summa sit ista tuae".[266] That these latin quotations are omitted from *Contention* and *True Tragedy* suggests that the printed plays do not represent Marlowe's full version.

Taking stock: extreme precision would require thoroughly investigating every possibility. Did Marlowe adapt Shakespeare's plays for the stage? Did Shakespeare revise Marlowe's play? Was Marlowe Shakespeare? The most plausible answer would seem to be that *Contention* and *True Tragedy* were originally written by Christopher Marlowe, but that the versions that have come down to us are not in every point true reproductions of his authorial hand. The plays were at one time abridged and adapted for performance by an actor or actors. Later, and **well after** Robert Greene would have been able to witness the scene he quoted in *GGW*, Shakespeare revised Marlowe's authorial texts, and the result was 2 and 3 *Henry VI*.

If so, the "tygers heart wrapt in a player's hide" in the letter in *GGW* would be a paraphrase of Marlowe's "mighty line."

Chapter IV
Legal Fictions And The Clayton Suit

The procedure of the common law, as it emerged at the close of the eighteenth century, consisted of so complicated a mass of rules of all dates, and of so many fictions and dodges to evade inconvenient rules, that the task of erecting upon its foundations a rational system was long and complicated.

William Searles Holdsworth. *A History of English Law*, Vol. IX, p. 262

Was Shakspere a London moneylender? A record from the rolls of the King's (Queen's) Bench seems to lend some credit to this conjecture. In the nineteenth century James Halliwell-Phillipps, one of the most assiduous Shakespeare researchers of the day, held that the Willelmus Shackspere, who during the Easter term 1600 sued one John Clayton of Willington, Bedfordshire, in the Queen's Bench for a debt of £7, was none other than the Bard. Sidney Lee, Edmund Chambers, and other scholars have dismissed this out of hand. What, after all, would the Stratford man have had to do with a man from Willington in the county of Bedford? But the record states that the debt was contracted in 1592 in London, in the parish of St. Mary-le-Bow of the Ward of Cheap. Given the erratic spelling of the time, Willelmus Shackspere could be William Shakspere. The document is in Latin, and Willelmus was one of the Latinized forms of William, while Shackspere is a fairly frequent spelling of the name Shakespeare. And did not a "Willielmus Shackspere" of Stratford sue in 1609 one John Addenbrooke for an amount of £6? Would that not lend credence to the possibility that "gentle Shakespeare," the bard, might have in reality been a hardhearted debtor, a would-be Shylock who had poor Clayton cast into prison not for 3,000 ducats but for seven pounds, and John Addenbrooke for £6?

Indeed, the record tells us that John Clayton was in the custody of the Marshal, a court officer who, together with the steward of the royal household, presided over the court of the Marshal, which body originally dealt with all litigation involving officers and servants of the royal household. To this court was attached a prison, the Marshalcy, as it would have been properly called, and it was so spoken of, though it was written 'Marshalsea.' Obviously, John Clayton was a prisoner in the Marshalsea. And it was Willelmus Shackspere's action which had placed him behind bars. Shackspere had persecuted Clayton, unrelentingly it seems, and had presented to the court two pledges for the prosecution. Their names were John Doe and Richard Roe.

Whenever the names 'John Doe' and 'Richard Roe' or 'John-a-Nokes' and 'John-a-Stiles' show up in a legal record, one should not be too sure-footed and examine the proceedings with particular care. These names represent fictitious instead of real persons, and thus should warn us that the record is perhaps not to be taken as fact throughout. Whenever the **geographical determination** "to wit in the parish of St. Mary-le-Bow in the Ward of cheap" shows up in a record of the King's Bench in the last half of the 16th century or the first half of the 17th century, as it does in the Clayton suit, we may be in for more legal fiction.. The naive empirist may deem legal records a safe-conduct for collecting unassailable empirical evidence. However, in the presence of legal fictions the empirist's new facts often turn out to be the emperor's new clothes.

Legal fictions I – Common recovery

William Searles Holdsworth is the author of the multi-volume *History of English Law*, a classic, arguably **the** classic work on the subject. Holdsworth must have been a man of almost unshakable composure, threading his way through mountains of often cryptic old documents, leaving no stone unturned in search of intellectual justifications of ancient law and jurisdiction, always with a keen eye for changing social conditions, values, attitudes, and on top of all this old law English, and at the very top of that, law French occasionally mixed with shards of Latin, yielding phrases like: "Ove vostre conge, nous voulumus emparler."[267]

In modern French the above reads: "Avec votre congé, nous voulons en parler", (With your allowance, we want to talk about it). This 'talking-about-it' between defendant and plaintiff during a pleading, in law French 'emparler,' was Anglicized as 'to imparl' and 'an imparlance.' As a student of old English law, Holdsworth had become too inured to strange words and phrases to be disturbed by them. Yet the flame of his impatience flares up in the following passage:

"Right down to the nineteenth century, the actual record of the case read as if it had proceeded in strict accordance with the mediæval procedure, and as if entries had been made on the role of the various steps in the cause as it proceeded in court. But long before the nineteenth century, the form in which the record was drawn up was nothing but an elaborate and circumstantial lie."[268]

William Searles Holdsworth is chiding English legal documents for telling "lies." For instance, until well into the 19th century it was always stated that the defendant had been allowed an "imparlance," despite the fact that this part of the procedure had grown into disuse with pleading no longer oral but written. Actually, no "imparlance" could take place when the pleading was in written form, but it was still being recorded as if it had really happened, just to uphold an appearance of continuity with good old, sacred law, the "old field out of which the new corn had to come" according to Sir Edward Coke.

'Don't touch statutes and customs of yore' was one of the unwritten rules guiding English jurisdiction. And, indeed, the judges did not touch statutes and customs, statutes were treated as if they were statues, monuments bowed to with respect but not bent to in earnest, "for the new law of the renaissance period was made, not by flouting the old learning, but by sneaking round it."[269] As a means to keep to the old law and at the same time pace with change, legal fictions were a practical tool. There were sometimes bizarre legal fictions. But even these were still somehow practical.

The serene William Blackstone wrote about the middle of the 18th century, a century and a half before Holdsworth. Even he was not able to suppress a sigh of grief at the fits of fancy to which old English law had to recur in order to reconcile frozen past and boiling change. "To such awkward shifts, such subtile refinements, and such strange reasoning, were our ancestors obliged to get the better of that stubborn statute *de donis*."[270]

Blackstone's comment closes his description of a procedure called "common recovery." Imagine a person, Sir Thomas Black, who wants to sell land to Sir William White. Think of them as enthusiastic participants in mock-trials at the Inns of Court and no less enthusiastic lovers of comedy at the Globe. Business alone being a matter too dull for their vivid spirits, they decide to carry out the transaction in form of a legal comedy. Sir William White (who wants to buy) sues Sir Thomas Black (who wants to sell) on the ground that Black has no legal title in the property. Black demurs and calls to witness George Grey, in the legal terminology of the time: Black vouches Grey. Grey knows neither Black nor White; what is going on is a complete grey area to him. He just happens to be there, he always happens to be there, he is the crier of the court. Grey nonetheless solemnly confirms Black's lawful title to the property. Thereupon White asks the judge to have an imparlance, to talk it over with Grey outside the court room. The judge allows it. After a while White re-enters the court room — alone. Grey has played truant. Black's vouchee having defected, judgment by default is rendered to White. Black, though, will be compensated. Grey is condemned, in absence, to compensate Black with land of equal value, which will always remain a black-out to Black because Grey does not own any land.

Thus functioned a common recovery. The inclusion of additional vouchers, double, treble or multiple, does not change the procedure essentially. Titles other than Black's might have existed in the property. The judgment by default against Black only destroyed his own title, not, for instance, remainders, interests which took effect upon the expiration of that of another. A frequent remainder was when land was conveyed to a son A and the heirs of his body, remainder to B, brother of A. B would become entitled when A died without issue. By a common recovery with single voucher only Black's own title was extinguished, not remainders. Therefore, Black first conveyed, merely fictitiously, the land to Peter Brown. White sued Brown; Brown vouched Black; Black vouched Grey, whose defection annihilated Brown's fictitious and Black's real possession of the land. But as the judgment primarily defeated Brown's title, which was fictitious and, hence, without rights of reversion or remainder, all possible other titles in the land were for ever barred by a court judgment. Grey, here the common vouchee, was always the last link in the chain. The last link had to be "missing in imparlance."[271]

Sir Thomas and Sir William might or might not have been lovers of mock-trial and comedy. It was not what moved them to stage their "legal comedy".

The Statute Quia Emptores

The land Black wanted to sell was an estate tail and therefore unalienable. The alienation had to be disguised as a trial leading to a court judgment which vested the title in the buyer. It was the Statute *De Donis* (1285) which had "turned all fee simple conditional estates in lands of free tenure into estates tail."[272] In fact, it was by this statute that entailed estates came into being. The full title of the statute was *De Donis Conditionalibus* or the "statute on conditional gifts." The Statute *Quia Emptores*, also called 18º Edward I, enacted five years later, is also closely connected with these conditional gifts, which gave the Statute *De Donis* its name.[273]

Before the latter statute only conditional gifts existed. The basic formula of such a gift was "granted to him and/or her and the heirs of his, her or their body." In feudal times the main purpose of such gifts of a lord to a vasall or tenant was probably to create a followership, to have loyal vassals which assisted him in time of war and served him otherwise in time of peace. In the course of time, however, the focus of the lord's interest had shifted.

Such a gift was conditional on the donee's having issue. If he had none, the land returned, "reverted." to the lord. The condition was subject to some variations. Holdsworth distinguishes between three categories: a) The gift was conditional; as long as no heir was born it remained an estate for life only, which returned to the donor when the donee died without an heir; the estate became an estate of inheritance at the birth of an heir but reverted to the donor if the heir predeceased the donee; b) the gift immediately constituted an estate of inheritance but reverted to the donor if no heirs were born or survived the donee;

c) an heir was born to the donee, the condition was fulfilled and regardless of whether the heir survived or not, the donee could freely sell the estate. It seems as if a conditional gift was mostly interpreted in the sense of c).[274] This procedure, besides sub-infeudation, gave the donee the possibility of neutralizing the interest of the lord: he could sell the estate and buy it back. His ownership of the estate no longer rested on the gift but on his purchase. The donating lord lost not only the estate in reversion but a number of other valuable feudal rights. It was this situation which the Statute *Quia Emptores* sought to remedy. The statute opens with the following words: "Forasmuch as purchasers of Lands and Tenements of the Fees of great men and others have many times heretofore entered into their Fees, to the prejudice of the Lords, the Freeholders have sold their Lands and Tenements to be holden in Fee of their Feoffees, and not of the Chief Lord of the Fees, whereby the same Chief Lords have many times lost their Escheats, Marriages and Wardships of Lands and Tenements belonging to their Fees..."

The main rights of the lord are those mentioned in the statute: escheat, marriage, wardship. No material difference existed between escheat and reversion. Whether an estate returned to the donor, escheated to him, because the tenant had died without heirs or because of "felony," which here means a breach of loyalty by the vassal/tenant, made no difference from the purely material point of view. The rights of marriage and wardship proceeded from a feudal logic. As the relationship between lord and vassal was a personal one, defined in terms of loyalty, not of material benefits, it was only logical that the lord took the lands of the tenant at the latter's death as long as the heir had not come of age and could not perform the services for which the land had been granted, and in a time when marriages were alliances, it was important that sons and daughters did not marry into a family inimical to the lord. However, these rights, though derived from a feudal logic, no longer obeyed the same. From personal assurances they had become assets, from security against ill-alliances they were ever more taking on the character of securities in a more modern sense. The rights of wardship and marriage could be sold and, of course, they were the more valuable the greater the value of the collateral land.

But these feudal rights were being hollowed out by another mechanism called sub-infeudation, which was itself, as the word suggests, an intrinsic feudal device. The tenant could sell land to another tenant and become an intermediate lord, a "mesne" lord as opposed to the "chief lord of the fee," and exert the same rights of escheat, wardship and marriage with respect to the land he had donated or "enfeoffed." In the same proportion, as sub-infeudation progressed, the value of the feudal rights of the chief lord regressed.

To put a stop to it, the Statute *Quia Emptores* provided that from then on land was freely alienable, without previous consent of the lord. "That from henceforth it shall be lawful to every Freeman to sell at his own pleasure his Lands and Tenements." This means that the legal ownership of the land was vested in the purchaser. But it was added in paragraph II that the purchaser will hold from the chief lord: "AND if he sell any part of such Lands or Tenements the Feoffee shall immediately hold it of the Chief Lord, and shall be forthwith charged with the Services, for so much as pertaineth, or ought to pertain to the said Chief Lord for the same parcel, according to the Quantity of the Land or Tenement sold."

However, three exceptions to the freedom of selling land remained. First, selling land in mortmain was still subject to a royal license. To sell land in mortmain means to sell it to a corporation, which in the 14th century generally meant a religious corporation, often a monastery. It was a method which tenants had been using for some time before the Magna Carta (1215) in order to evade the feudal burdens of escheat, wardship and marriage. The tenant could sell the land to a monastery and then himself hold from the monastery, whereas the latter held from the Chief Lord. But a corporation never died, it was perpetual: the lord lost his income from escheat; a corporation had no heirs, no son or daughters to marry: the lord lost his rights of wardship and marriage. Therefore statutes made selling in mortmain dependent on a license of the court of chancery. Secondly, land directly held from the Crown could not be alienated without the king's license. In 1256, during the reign of Henry III, an ordinance was issued, prohibiting the alienation of such land on pain of forfeiture. The provision was considerably mitigated by Statute 1º Edward III cc. 12 and 13 (1327); the punishment of forfeiture for the sale of such lands without license of the Crown was substituted by a fine (called "a pardon of alienation").[275] The third exception was the estate tail.

The Statute De Donis

This statute stipulated that the original intent of the grantor that the land was given "to someone and the heirs of his body" ought to be respected and the grantees cannot alienate such an estate. Much emphasis was placed on the concern for the rights of the heir. It is not difficult, though, to see that even more concern about the chief lord's rights of escheat, wardship and marriage had inspired this opening article of the statute. A definitive stop was put to the donee's strategy of selling the land after the birth of the heir and then buying it back, so to defeat not only the reversion to the donor but also his right of wardship and marriage. This provision in itself did not quite give birth to the estate tail, the statute remaining silent on how many generations this prohibition would be effective. It was Chief Justice Bereford who in 1311-12 interpreted the provision as valid to the fourth degree (for three generations). But in 1331 another Chief Justice, Stonore, ruled that it was to last indefinitely.[276] Thus the estate tail was born, which in a time when the economy became ever more monetary, put considerable fetters on the donees' free disposition of their estate. From this point of view the "comedy" of common recovery made good economic sense.

Legal fictions II — The fine

A somewhat similar procedure to bar an entail was the levy of a fine. A fine (*Finalis Concordia*) – not to be confused with a pecuniary penalty – was the solemn conveyance of land in a common law court. A fine "may be described to be an amicable composition or agreement of a suit, either actual or fictitious by leave of the king or his justices."[277] The party who intends to alienate the land first refuses to do so. As long as he refuses he is termed the "deforciant." The refusal merely serves the purpose of establishing a pretext for a suit and so having the conveyance recorded in a court, making it as safe as possible against possible claims by third parties (termed "strangers"). The party to whom the land is to be conveyed brings action for breach of covenant. The deforciant is quick to acknowledge the right of the other party and is from that moment on called the *conusor*; the other party is the *conusee*. Circumvention of the Statute *De Donis*, that is, of an entail, was not the only purpose for which a fine was levied, but it was probably the most frequent one.

Common recovery and fine, both set up as fictitious trials, were the legal devices most frequently employed to get rid of the entailed estate generated by the *Statute De Donis*.

Hamlet and the inheritor

In the gravedigger scene (V.i) there is one long *memento mori*. Hamlet, musing over several skulls, imagining what the people to whom they belonged might have been like in life, walks through a gallery of clever, busy, tricky, wily and successful men: a politician, "one that would circumvent God," a courtier who succeeds at court by skillful flattery, a lawyer, grown rich by diversifying in business but largely by his real estate transactions, then a jester, and lastly the imperious Alexander the Great and Julius Cæsar. On the presumed lawyer Hamlet remarks:

There's another. Why may not that be the skull of a lawyer? Where be his quiddits now, his quillets, his cases, his tenures, and his tricks? Why does he suffer this rude knave now to knock him about the sconce with a dirty shovel, and will not tell him of his action of battery? Hum! This fellow might be in's time a great buyer of land, with his statutes, his recognizances, his fines, his double   vouchers, his recoveries. Is this the fine of his fines, and the recovery of his recoveries, to have his fine pate full of fine dirt? Will his vouchers vouch him no more of his purchases, and double ones too, than the length and breadth of a pair of indentures? The very conveyances of his lands will scarcely lie in this box; and must th' inheritor himself have no more, ha? (V.i.96-110).

Given the contiguous positions of "statutes" and "recognizances", the "statutes" here meant are without doubt the Statute Staple and the Statute Merchant. "A borrower wishing to take up money on Statute Staple applied to a lender and, in return for the loan, gave to him a kind of bond known as *recognizance*, or acknowledgment of obligation already incurred... Originally ... recognizances on Statute Staple had been registered before the Mayor of the Staple in Staple towns, recognizances on Statute Merchant before the chief magistrates of the trading towns concerned. But in the course of time others than merchants found the system convenient and it was abused. It was therefore regulated. By the Statute 23º Hen. VIII, c.6, the local mayors of the Staple were forbidden to register recognizances except for *bona fide* merchants, and a new centralized system was set up in London to provide for those men who, not being merchants, nevertheless wished to lend and borrow money by this convenient method. The obligations contracted under this Act were technically known as 'Recognizances in the nature of Statute Staple', and they were officially registered in the presence of one of the two chief justices or (in vacation) before the Mayor of the Staple in Westminster and the Recorder of London."[278]

But what should be understood by "inheritor"? Obviously, this means "heir." Harold Jenkins, the editor of the Arden *Hamlet*, seems to have doubted that the usual meaning of "inheritor," that is "heir," could make sense. He interprets the meaning as "acquirer," though he indicates that *fines... recoveries* "were procedures for effecting the transfer of estates when an entail or other obstacle prevented simple sale" and a "*voucher* in a recovery suit was the process of summoning a third party to warrant the holder's title, and the customary *double voucher* involved a second warrantor."[279] But we have seen that the fictitious suit, either "fine," or "common recovery," purposed to bar an entail, that is, to defeat the legal title which the heir could claim by virtue of the *Statute De Donis*. A chain of fines and common recoveries would have had the effect of leaving the heir or inheritor with little more land than the space of the grave in which the presumed lawyer himself now lies. Logically, it is also possible to think of the heir of the lawyer himself who in the end would have no more than a grave. But what argues that it was rather the heir that was deprived of his inheritance of land, is the closing interjection "ha" which marks disagreement and disapproval of something which ought not to be and should be ended, recalling Stephano's reply to Caliban in *The Tempest*(II.ii.59): "What's the matter? Have we devils here? Do you put tricks upon's with salvages and men of Ind, ha?" With his common recoveries and fines (and these are the terms Hamlet is punning on), the lawyer has been playing tricks not on his own heir but on the heirs whose entails have been destroyed. Hence, Hamlet's thoughts seem more concentrated upon the inheritor who has been cheated out of his inheritance by the lawyer's tricks (his recognizances and, in the first place, by his common recoveries and fines).

Legal fictions III – Knights of the Post

Another legal device which may partly be considered as a legal fiction and through Thomas Nashe's *Pierce Penniless* has acquired a certain literary notoriety is "the knight of the post." Nashe defines him as "a fellow that will swear you anything for twelve pence."[280]

"Knights of the post" were witnesses for a defendant found guilty by a jury of twelve. In such cases the judge could allow the defendant his wager of law. The wager of law provided a means of defense against false witnesses or a bribed jury. To wage his law the defendant had to bring into court eleven of his neighbors — with himself numbering twelve to counterbalance the twelve men on the jury. His eleven neighbors were called the "compurgators." Then the defendant had to swear an oath that he was innocent. "And thereupon his eleven neighbors or compurgators shall avow upon their oath, that they believe in their consciences that he saith true."[281] Possibly, at some time these compurgators had been honorable men, maybe knights. However, as time went on the procedure seems to have degenerated into what on the surface seems a repulsive legal farce. No longer had the defendant to gather eleven 'neighbors' — though in best English law tradition they continued to be called so — but simply to collect **any** eleven persons who, against a small consideration (twelve pence, according to Nashe), were willing to swear "in their consciences" that the defendant was innocent. The quality of their conscience mattered little to nothing, their reputation might not be the best. They could even have stood in the pillory, at the "post," whence the erstwhile compurgators came to be called "knights of the post."

As in the case of the common recovery, the farce sometimes made good sense. The advantage of maintaining this old procedure was that the judge was given a tool to neutralize the judgment of the twelve jurors when he was convinced they were either misled by false witnesses or themselves corrupt.[282] Thanks to the compurgating knights of the post the judge could play the role of the *deus ex machina,* undoing the machinations of evil witnesses or devilish juries.

The Clayton suit and the King´s Bench´s Bill of Middlesex

In the 16th century another battleground emerged, fatal for facts and fertile for fiction. The contending parties were the common law courts and the equity courts, the former against one another and jointly against the latter. The objective was the annexation of jurisdictional territory. Judicial competency had been regulated partly by statutes, partly by custom. The King´s (Queen´s) Bench was prohibited by statute from taking cognizance of most civil actions; these belonged to the jurisdiction of the Common Pleas. To the Court of Admiralty, an equity court, belonged the jurisdiction of all events happened at sea or overseas. Merchant law was a separate body of the law, outside of both common law and equity, but closer to the latter. As seen in the previous section, it was administered in town courts. But courts of appeal were in most cases equity courts: Chancery, Admiralty, Star Chamber.

However, the King´s Bench had general jurisdiction, criminal and civil, for a limited territory, the county of Middlesex. Francis Bacon writes: "It is the course of the King´s Bench, that they give in charge to a grand jury offences of all natures to be presented, within Middlesex, where the said court is."[283] The King´s Bench was attached to the prison of the Marshalsea, on which Bacon again instructs us: "But the King seeing the realm grow daily more populous and that this one court could not dispatch all, did first ordain that his marshal should keep a court for controversies arising within the verge, which is within twelve miles of the chief tunnel of the court... But this Court did but ease the King's Bench in matters only concerning debts, covenants, and such like, of those of the King's household, never dealing in breaches of the peace or concerning the crown by any other persons, or any pleas of land."[284]

As early as the reign of Edward I (1272-1307) the Court of the Marshalsea had developed a device to extend its jurisdiction. The device consisted in occupying the grey zones around the notion of membership of the royal household. A relationship with the royal household could be stretched into membership and secure the jurisdiction to the Court of the Marshalsea. By a similar device the King's Bench was extending its jurisdiction to civil cases. The master target was the same as in the 14th century for the Court of the Marshal: a debtor had to be brought into the Marshalsea. The device is described by Holdsworth:[285]

"The first step in this process was to get the defendant either actually or constructively into the custody of the Marshal. In one case in Henry VI.'s reign it was held that actual custody was necessary to found the jurisdiction, so that it could not be exercised against a person who was released on bail. This decision was reversed later in the reign; and it was ultimately held that the mere record on the rolls of court that the defendant had given bail would be sufficient evidence of actual custody."[286] This is what the record of the Clayton suit states: John Clayton was in the custody of the Marshal. Actually or 'constructively'? Constructively, that is, fictitiously, as will soon appear.

Holdsworth continues: "To get this evidence on record what was called a bill of Middlesex was filed by the plaintiff against the defendant, stating that he was guilty of trespass vi et armis – an offence falling properly within the jurisdiction of the court. The plaintiff gave pledges for the prosecution, which pledges, even in Coke's day, were the fictitious John Doe and Richard Roe."[287] The record states exactly that: John Doe and Richard Roe were the pledges for the prosecution. As they were fictitious persons, the prosecution itself was a fiction. So they were in the cases *Shexpere v. Rogers* (1604) and *Shackspeare v. Ad-*

denbrooke (1608).[288] Possibly, Willelmus Shackspere of "Somewhere" or Willelmius Shexpere/Shackspeare of Stratford were moneylenders, misers and sharks, but it can 'impossibly' be proven as a fact from a legal fiction.

Holdsworth goes on: "The sheriff of Middlesex was then directed to produce the defendant before the court to answer the plaintiff concerning this plea of trespass. If the sheriff returned to the bill "non est inventus," [not found] a writ of latitat was issued to the sheriff of an adjoining county. The writ recited the bill of Middlesex and the proceedings thereon, stated that the defendant "latitat et discurrit" ["hiding and lurking"] in the county, and ordered the sheriff to catch him. The trespass and the proceedings thereon were fictions invented to give the court jurisdiction."[289] It certainly was so in the case *Shackspere v. Clayton* and likely so in the cases *Shexpere v. Rogers* and *Shackspeare v. Addenbrooke*. On Addenbrooke, Chambers comments that "arrest was also impossible, because the debtor was outside the very limited jurisdiction of the court". But the passage on which this statement is based reads "predictus Johannes [Addenbrooke] non est inventus", precisely the standard formula of the bill of Middlesex. Here, of course, one cannot properly speak of a bill of Middlesex. But the records suggest that the Stratford Court of Record's procedure was an imitation of the King's Bench's Bill of Middlesex.

Finally: "If the defendant appeared and gave sureties for his future appearance he was sufficiently in the custody of the Marshal to give jurisdiction to the court. If he did not appear to the bill or latitat he was liable to be arrested for contempt of the court in not appearing. But as all the proceedings were fictitious, the contempt would seem to share the fictitious character. To arrest a man for a merely fictitious contempt was clearly a hardship. Therefore, in the event of non-appearance, the plaintiff was allowed to enter an appearance for him, and to give as sureties for his appearance his friends John Doe and Richard Roe. This was called giving 'common bail.' In some cases, however, it was desirable that the defendant should be put in substantial bail for his appearance. This was called 'special bail.' The question when special bail could be required was a question depending upon the practice of the court. It was usually required if the plaintiff swore that the cause of action was worth £10 or upwards."[290] This is what Willelmus Shaxspere did. John Clayton was not put in "special bail" for his appearance, but the fictitious John Doe and Richard Roe were the plaintiff's pledges for the appearance of the defendant. The reason is given in the record: the cause of action was worth less than £10.

If Willelmus Shackspere and Willielmus Shexpere or Shackspeare were identical, nothing can be concluded from these records about their merciless character. As a matter of fact, the record of the Clayton suit just tells us that the parties wanted to have the case decided in the Queen's Bench, as so many other litigants did because the procedure in this court was less complicated, speedier and less expensive than in the Common Pleas. But could they have been identical?

Venue

According to statute an action had to be laid in the county in which the litigious event had occurred. But by the end of the 15th century these rigid rules of venue had been relaxed. A difference was made between "local" and "transitory" actions, that is between actions to which the place of the litigious event was material, for instance burglary, and actions to which the place was immaterial, for instance debt. The place where the debt had been contracted was henceforward without any legal importance. "Thus, though by statute the venue must be laid in the proper county, the defendant could not traverse the venue laid by the plaintiff, unless his plea was local in its nature, i.e. depended for its efficacy on the place in which the facts alleged in it happened. If his plea was transitory in its nature he could not object to the venue laid by the plaintiff."[291] In other words, the chosen venue was beyond objection or "untraversable".

But then the question arises as to why the place is mentioned in the Clayton suit: "that he the aforesaid John Clayton on the twenty-second day of May in the thirty-fourth year of the reign of the Lady Elizabeth the present Queen of England, to wit in the parish of St. Mary le Bow in the Ward of Cheap, London, by a certain bond in writing...". The answer is that the place where the debt was contracted still mattered for one class of debts, namely debt wholly contracted and performed abroad, which belonged by statute to the jurisdiction of the Court of Admiralty. At the beginning of the sixteenth century still "no action would lie on a contract made abroad and to be performed abroad, or any other act done wholly outside England. It was during the sixteenth century that this last limitation imposed by the rules of venue was got over by the adoption of the fiction employed by the pleader in the Year Book of 48 Edward III [1374-5]. The plaintiff alleged an act taking place outside the realm, and then asserted that that foreign place was situate at a place in England — 'to wit in the parish of St. Mary le Bow in the Ward of Cheap.' The advantages of this device were obvious. It gave the common law courts jurisdiction in transitory actions over all acts and transactions, even though they happened wholly outside the kingdom; and it was clearly these advantages which led to its adoption."[292] This is exactly the device used in the Clayton suit.

Given that the action of Willelmus Shackspere against John Clayton was about debt, hence transitory, the venue was untraversable. However, **only on condition that it was explicitly stated**. If it were not explicitly stated (which for an action of debt wholly or partly within England had become superfluous), the venue was traversable. "Note that in Dowdale's Case (1606) 6 Co. Rep. 47b, it is said that, 'Where as well the contract and the performance of it is wholly made or to be done beyond sea, *and it so appears*, then it is not triable by our law. [ie. common law].' But by the aid of this fiction it never 'so appeared.'"[293] Had it not been explicitly stated, the venue had been traversable as in the case Robert v. Harnage (1704) "where by the inadvertence of the pleader in omitting to insert the words 'to wit, at London, etc.,' it did so appear, and the writ abated."[294]

To sum up: the place where a debt was contracted was wholly immaterial to the venue, save in cases where it was wholly contracted and performed at sea or overseas. In this case the venue had to be the Court of Admiralty. But common law courts could overcome this statutory barrier by positing a fictitious locality inside England. This legal fiction was untraversable, provided the fictitious place was explicitly mentioned. The fictitious place could be any locality just as the fictitious pledges to the prosecution could be any two names. But as the most common names for the fictitious pledges appeared to be John Doe and Richard Roe, so in the last quarter of the 16th century the most common fictitious locality for cases which had happened outside England was the parish of St. Mary le Bow in the Ward of Cheap. Which proves that the debt of John Clayton to Willelmus Shackspere was contracted and had to be performed abroad, be it in Ireland, France, the Low Countries or elsewhere outside England. **And that neither John Clayton nor Willelmus Shackspere were in London on 22 May 1592.**

The reason that "St. Mary le Bow in the Ward of Cheap" was chosen as fictitious venue is not clear. From the Ellesmere tracts (1611) it appears that other places within the general jurisdiction of the King's Bench were chosen as well. The Lord Chancellor Ellesmere complains of the encroachments by the common law courts on the jurisdiction of the Court of Admiralty. "And so the other side, it were meet, that he that libelleth [ie, lays action] in the Admiral Court for any matter done upon the sea, or beyond the sea, or otherwise, within the Admiral's jurisdiction should make the like oath, that his libel [action] is in that point true... But suits for matters properly determinable in the Admiral Court, are withdrawn from that Court to the Courts of the Common Law (especially to the King's Bench) by another later device... Supposing in some cases that some goods or merchandises, that indeed never were in England; and in some cases that a ship itself was lost in Cheapside in London or in some other place in Middlesex..."[295] But the parish of St. Mary-le-Bow was the most common choice in the 16th century: "Prohibitions were constantly issued to the Admiralty and other mercantile courts, while by a daring fiction which begins to appear frequently in the sixteenth century the common law courts assumed jurisdiction over acts which took place abroad, by the simple device of describing the place as being "in the parish of St Mary-le-Bow in the ward of Cheap".[296]

As far as we know, neither the true character of the Clayton suit as a bill of Middlesex by which the King's (Queen's) Bench expanded the scope of its jurisdiction nor the actual purport of the presence of the clause "to wit in the parish of St. Mary-le-Bow in the Ward of Cheap" have ever been recognized. It seems also to have eluded E.K. Chambers, who comments: "I agree with Lee that there is no ground for identifying the Willelmus Shackspere of this with the dramatist. The debt was acknowledged in Cheapside on 22 May 1592. No local description is given by which the habitation of the plaintiff can be fixed. The defendant was of Willington in Bedfordshire."[297]

As seen, Cheapside was a legal fiction. In Appendix III to Blackstone's *Commentaries* are shown several forms of a bill of Middlesex.[298] In this fictional device the residence of the plaintiff was never indicated, the place of dwelling of the defendant ever: "Whereas by our writ we have lately commanded you that you should cause Charles Long, late of Burford, gentleman... that you should take him to be safely kept, so that you might have his body before our justices at Westminster... to answer William Burton, gentleman, of a plea, that he render him two hundred pounds, which he owes him and unjustly detains..." **The same formula is found in the record of the Clayton suit: John Clayton "continues to refuse and unjustly detains them".**

Finally, the following communication was found on the Web: "We now know a few more facts about Shakespeare due to the investigation of Antwerp archives, by Frank van Nueshoorn. He discovered that Shakespeare had worked in Antwerp as an apprentice with the English Merchant adventurers in 1587. (A sizable English community lived in Antwerp in the 16th century). An entry in the ledgers of the Plantin publishing house revealed that on 9/23/1587 'Willem Shaakspeer' bought a copy of Christopher Plantin's Polyglot Bible and the municipal archives for the same year report that 'Shaakspeer' was fined by city magistrates for 'bawdy behavior' in a sailors tavern."[299] If it were so, it would be without doubt a sensible, if not sensational, contribution to Shakespeare research. The probability, however, that this merchant adventurer in Antwerp was William Shakespeare is nil.[300] Despite this, Frank von Nueshoorn might have made a marginal but valuable contribution to Shakespeare research. He just might have identified the 'Willelmus Shackspere' of the Clayton suit.

Part III
The Concealed Poet

Chapter I
To Be Or Not To Be Melicertus

Among the pamphlets that swamped the London book market in the wake of Queen Elizabeth's death and James I's accession in the Spring of 1603, one has retained the attention of the literary world more than any other. This is *England's Mourning Garment.* No author's name is mentioned on the title-page; under the epistle to the reader only a motto is found. It is the same motto which appears thrice in *Greene's Groatsworth of Wit,* namely: *Fœlicem fuisse infaustum* (to be happy one must have been unhappy). But the author does sign the *erratum* note at the end:

To the Reader

I love as little as any man to come into print: but seeing affection hath made me commit this fault, I pray you pardon it; and amend in reading the Printer's errors; where, being ill acquainted with Poetry, he hath passed Herores for Heroes; what ever else seems harsh, imagine I can write English, and make the fault not mine.

Farewell. *Hen: Chettle.*

In a poem, purposely modeled on Spenser's poem *Colin Clouts Come Home Again,* in which Spenser, returning from Ireland, greets his fellow -poets under pastoral names, the cunning imitator Chettle complains of the failure of several prominent contemporary poets to write an elegy on the deceased queen. Among these poets Shakespeare is unequivocally identified by an allusion to *The Rape of Lucrece.* The pastoral name by which Chettle addresses him is Melicert(us). However, Chettle uses the same pastoral name Melicert another time. One would naturally assume that within the same work the first and second Melicert must be the same. But the first Melicert is mentioned as having been more or less actively involved in preparations to the expedition in the Low Countries in the year 1585 or 1586, which is incompatible with the traditional time-frame of Shakespeare's flourishing. Chettle would not have used the same pastoral name for two different living persons at the same time. Either the Melicert of 1585/86 is Shakespeare himself or he had died by 1603, leaving the name vacant, so that it could be assigned to Shakespeare. To be or not to be Melicertus, that is the question. Not to be in 1603, is the orthodox condition *sine qua non* with regard to the first Melicertus. Without that it is utterly **bereft**.

Chettle himself adopts Spenser's pastoral name Colin, but Spenser had died four years before. He also uses the pastoral name Melibœus for two different identifiable persons, but one of them had died in 1603. The first Melicert seems to have been a prominent literary figure associated with Euphuism. It would make him a fair candidate for Shakespeare, and in 1603 he doubtless **is** Shakespeare. In either case we are facing an interesting problem. Either William Shakespeare frequented the court in the 1580s and thus was probably not 21-22-year old Will of Stratford. Or Shakespeare had a poetical precursor whose identity should be worth knowing. The third possibility is that Shakespeare's precursor was Shakespeare himself.

The name Melicert(us) is rife with associations. In Greek mythology he is the son of Leucothea, the White Goddess. Melicertus was also the name given to the Greek poet Simonides, whom Plato considered the foremost Greek poet of the time and Cicero called "suavis poeta,"[301] (sweet poet). Melicertus was a very suitable pastoral name for William Shakespeare, the foremost English poet of the time and, as many maintain, of all time. If the earlier Melicertus is not also Shakespeare, it seems likely that those who gave him this name thought him to be the foremost poet of the 1580s. It would therefore have been a suitable name for Edward de Vere, 17th Earl of Oxford, whom Puttenham in *The Arte of English Poesie* praised as the first among the court poets and of whom William Webbe in his *Discourse of English Poetry* (1585) wrote that "he may challenge to himself the title of the most excellent [poet at Court] among the rest."[302]

Edward de Vere being still alive in March 1603, would thus be Shakespeare himself. As it is suggested by the context that the first Melicertus was a courtier, other courtiers known to have written poetry might also qualify as Melicertus in 1585/86: Sir Walter Ralegh, Sir Edward Dyer, Fulke Greville, or Robert Sidney. But for the pastoral name Melicert to apply both to one of them and to Shakespeare as non-identical persons , the bearer of that name in 1585/86 had to be dead by 1603. All of the four mentioned alternative candidates were still alive in 1603, so one of them would be Shakespeare. The name would evidently admirably fit Sir Philip Sidney. He had died in 1586, so the pastoral name Melicertus would then have been vacant in 1603. However, he must be ruled out, being named 'Philisides' in the same context. Sir Christopher Hatton and the earl of Essex, both known to have written some poetry, were dead in 1603, yet other elements considerably impair their claim. Once again, the implacable question with which Chettle's double use of the name Melicertus confronts orthodox theory is: who is the poet dubbed Melicertus in 1585/6 that had died in 1603?

The historical period in which Chettle speaks of Melicertus is the period preceding the war with Spain, not later than 1586, Sir Philip Sidney being spoken of as alive. Again, Oxford would pretty closely fit the picture, having been involved in the preparations to the war with Spain in 1585. The thorny question of Shakespeare's pastoral name was briefly debated in 1873/4 in *Notes & Queries* and in C.M. Ingleby's *Shakespeare-Allusions Books*. Oxford's name does not show up.

The poem, pastoral names, works

However, the stanza in which Shakespeare is addressed in 1603 contains some details which are suggestive of a court poet. It reads:

Nor doth the silver tongued *Melicert*,
Drop from his honeyed muse one sable tear
To mourn her death that graced his desert,
And to his laies opened her Royal ear.
   Shepherd, remember our *Elizabeth*,
   And sing her Rape, done by that *Tarquin*, Death.

Would Chettle have been speaking "loose language" again? We have an allusion to Shakespeare's *Rape of Lucrece*. It is further said that the queen "graced" Shakespeare's "desert" and "opened her royal ear" to his poetry. The meaning of these phrases may be stretched to include other than court poets, but one would first think of a court poet, or a "companion for a king," as John Davies of Hereford wrote in his epigram to "Our English Terence, M. Will Shake-speare," a court poet whom the Queen had shown some favor.

The name Melicert already existed as a pastoral name in Robert Greene's romance *Menaphon*. In Chettle's poem most of the other poets addressed are easily identifiable, either by their sobriquet or by the work alluded to or by both. Daniel, typically, is not given a pastoral name but there is a clear allusion to his *Civil Wars*: "He that so well could sing the fatal strife/ Between the royal Roses White and Red." Typically, because in Spenser's *Colin Clouts Come Home Againe,* Daniel is not given a pastoral name either. "Then rouze thy feathers quickly *Daniel,* /And to what course thou please thy selfe advance:/But most me seems, thy accent will excell, /In Tragic plaints and passionate mischance." (ll. 424-427) Daniel seems to have stood aloof from the pastoral fashion.

Chapman is identifiable by a work, the continuation of Marlowe's translation of Musæus' *Hero and Leander,* and a name: "Neither doth *Coryn* full of worth and wit,/That finished dead *Musœus* gracious song," dead *Musœus* being Marlowe. Ben Jonson is given the name of his Roman idol: "Nor does our English *Horace,* whose steele pen/ Can draw Characters which will never die". He had been satirized as Horace in Thomas Dekker's and John Marston's play *Satiromastix* two years before. Hence, the latter two are also recognizable without difficulty as Antihorace and Melibœus respectively:"Quick *Antihorace,* though I place thee here, /Together with young *Mœlibee* thy friend."

Drayton, too, is identified through a work of his: "No less doe thou (sweete singer *Coridon*);/ The Theme exceedeth *Edwards Isabell,*/Forget her not in *Poly-Albion;*". "Edward's Isabel" is a reference to Drayton's long poem on Edward II's favourite Piers Gaveston. *Poly-Olbion* was not published until 1611/12 but as early as 1598 it was known to be in the making. Chettle takes the pastoral names or sobriquets either from existing works (*eg,* Horace for Jonson) or in relation to such works (*eg,* Antihorace for Dekker). In any case he chose the names from a literary context, and the only literary context in which the pastoral name Melicertus occurs is Greene's romance

Menaphon.

The problem with Shakespeare, at least for orthodox scholars, is that no occurrence of Shakespeare's pastoral name Melicert is known other than in Greene's novel *Menaphon*. This novel was published in 1589 with an epistle to the students of both universities by Thomas Nashe in which he speaks of "whole hamlets" or "tragical speeches," and Greene's description of Melicert indeed suits Shakespeare fairly well,[303] but the date is again wholly incompatible with orthodox theory. Greene represents Melicert as the best poet of his time at a moment that the Stratford Shakespeare would have just come to London or would have still been living in Stratford.

Shakespeare and his supposed forerunner

England's Mourning Garment is a pastoral retrospective on the reign of the deceased queen. Elizabeth Tudor overcame factional strife and re-stored peace, Chettle argues. When it comes to the war with Spain, Colin/Chettle remarks that Elizabeth has been held responsible for that war: "And albeit I know some (too humorously affected to the Roman government) make question in this place, whether her highness first brake not the truce with the *King of Spain*: to that I could answere ... that her highness suffered many wrongs before she left off the league." To which his fellow-shepherd Thenot replies: "O, saith *Thenot*, in some of those wrongs resolve us, and think it no unfitting thing, for thou that hast heard the songs of that warlike Poet *Philesides*, good *Melœbee*, and smooth tongued *Melicert*, tell us what thou hast observed in their saws, seene in thy own experience, and heard of undoubted truths touching those accidents: for that they add, I doubt not, to the glory of our *Eliza*." The three participants in the debate on the identity of Melicertus in 1873/4 were C. Elliot Browne, Brinsley Nicholson and C.M. Ingleby.

C. Elliot Browne[304]

"I know of no other mention of Shakspeare under this name, but it would seem probable from the manner of this one that he had been previously, in some way or other, identified with Melicert. The other allusions of Chettle are generally appropriate, and for most of them there is other contemporary authority...Where did Chettle get the name Melicert? It is scarcely likely that he intended to allude to the son of Ino, who was no shepherd, but it is probable, I think, that he referred to the *Melicertus* of Greene's *Menaphon,* one of the principal characters in the most popular fiction of Shakspeare's old antagonist...".

Elliot Browne then remarks that the way Greene depicted Melicertus in his novel would well fit Shakespeare: "The character was evidently a favourite with Greene, who has put into his mouth the best poetry in the book. There are certainly some points of resemblance between Melicertus and the traditional idea of Shakspeare. Melicertus is a great maker of sonnets, and after his poetical excellence, the leading quality ascribed to him is the possession of a very ready and smooth wit, which enables him to shine in the euphuistic chaffing-matches with which the work is interlarded." Elliot Browne uses exactly the same adjective for Greene's Melicertus as Chettle: "smooth wit" the one, "smooth-tongued" the other. And on the latter Melicertus he writes: "... there is another mention of Melicert and his works which has given rise to much speculation... Mr. Halliwell was the first, I believe, to point out this notice, and he considers that Shakspeare must have written some poem or ballad upon Spanish subjects, probably the Armada invasion; and Mr. R. Simpson believes that he has discovered a joint work of Shakspeare and Marston (Melibee), assisted by Rich or Gascoigne (Philesides), in a play entitled *A Larum for London*... I cannot bring myself to think that any one not labouring under the encumbrance of a theory upon the subject will ever find any trace of Shakspeare in this wretched production..." Perhaps out of politeness, Browne leaves Simpson's trio Shakespeare-Marston-Gascoigne uncommented upon. Gascoigne died in 1577, Marston was born c. 1575!

Having identified, somewhat pusillanimously, Philisides as Philip Sidney and Meliboeus as Walsingham, he goes on: "Assuming, then that Philisides was Sidney, I venture to submit the probability that Melibee and Melicert were dead Statesmen, not living poets; that, in fact, the allusions in the political portion of the work are entirely independent of those in the poetical part, and refer, perhaps to Walsingham and Burleigh, who, with Sidney, were associated together in the popular mind as the three great leaders of the anti-Spanish policy." Why Elliot Browne does not give any thought to the possibility of Melicertus being the Earl of Leicester, along with Walsingham the strongest partisan of intervention in the Low Countries, commander-in-chief of the English forces, whose nephew and sometime heir apparent Sidney was, is not altogether clear. He goes on: "There can be no question of associating Melicert and Melibee with Shakespeare and Marston as Chettle refers to a period when Shakspeare and Marston were little more than children," a statement true for Marston, who would have been ten years old, but not for Shakspere, born in 1564.

This solution is, of course, not wholly satisfactory. The author perceives it himself: "I anticipate the objection that the second part of my proposition may be said to weaken the first; that in seeking to dissever the two allusions to Melicert I am depriving the supposed allusion to Greene's hero of any significance. But this must depend in great measure upon the question whether Chettle originated the allusion, or only applied it, and in any case it must be remembered that if my guess is right, the political Meliboeus and Melicert had been dead for some years before their poetical namesakes were brought upon the stage."

But there can be little doubt that Chettle appropriated the name from Greene's *Menaphon,* as he borrows other pastoral names or sobriquets from literary contexts. Burghley's candidature thus grows very pale; he would fit because he died in 1598, but it is difficult to believe that the name given to the poet Simonides would have been associated with him. The same objection holds of course for the Earl of Leicester. Other difficulties subsist. Some of them were addressed by the two other authors.

Brinsley Nicholson[305]

Brinsley Nicholson insists that there is no reason to be in the least hesitant with the identification of Sidney in Philisides. He quotes several other instances where Sidney was referred to as Philisides, omitting the argument that the name, composed of the Greek "phileo" and the Latin "sidus," is just another form of Astrophel, Star-Lover, the name he took in his sonnet sequence *Astrophel and Stella*. Nicholson points out that a pastoral name cannot be treated as a nickname or pseudonym: "But there is a sixth and more cogent argument. It is a great mistake to suppose, that because one poet speaks of a friend, statesman, or other poet under a pastoral name, that such name became a sort of baptismal Arcadian name recognized and adopted by all. Even Spenser, though he had the authority of arch-poet, did not impose names used by all. Sidney he spoke of under Sidney's own assumed name, Astrophel, but Drayton calls him Elfin, Bryskett, Spenser's friend, Philisides, and A.W. Willie, probably from the Wiltshire stream that gave its name to Wilton, while Spenser's Willie, I believe, after fresh investigation, to be certainly, and in accordance with Malone's own belief, John Lyly. Here, however, there can be no doubt as to Philisides, for it has no meaning in Greek, English, or any other tongue, unless it be a Grecized form of Phil[ip] Sid[ney]." He delivers further evidence for identifying Meliboeus as Walsingham, as not only Thomas Watson used that name in his elegy on him but, more specifically, Spenser remembered him as "good Melibee" in *The Ruins of Time*. Hence, the two uses are well discriminated, not only because Walsingham was dead and Marston not, but also by the different epithets "good" and "young."

In the case of Melicert, however, the epithets "smooth-tongued" and "silver-tongued" are rather akin, as "smooth," "filed," "refined," "sweet," "honey-tongued" and "silver-tongued" were in current use for eloquence and poetical language. One can almost hear Brinsley Nicholson's sigh of relief at Elliot Browne's suggestion about the transferability of pastoral names: "Lastly, as to Melicert. I confess that the conjunction of Sidney, Walsingham, and Shakspeare was a strange one, I was inclined to think that Chettle could not have given the same name to two people in one book. But since reading MR. ELLIOT BROWNE'S note, and reconsidering the matter, I believe that the smooth-tongued Melicert of the Philisides and Melibee trio must have been a statesman or person of eminence, and the significant name Honeycomb or 'he of the honeycomb', agrees well with Ascham's notice of Burleigh in his Introduction to his *Scholemaster* and with the description given for instance in Chalmer's *Biography*." But C.M. Ingleby demurred.

C. M. Ingleby[306]

He mostly quotes abundantly from the two previous authors but takes issue with the identification of Melicert as Burghley (Burleigh): " Clearly, if it be a condition of identification, that all three shepherds shall be poets, or at least well-known versifiers (and this is *primá facie* the inference from Chettle's use of the word *songs*), Mr C.E. Browne's conjecture, that the "smooth-tongued Melicert" is Burghley, is put out of court. Apart from this condition, we do not understand Dr Nicholson to give Burghley the decided preference over every competitor; for manifestly Lord Buckhurst would equally well fit the place, besides satisfying the condition of being a song-writer; and for choice, perhaps we should give the preference to the latter, as the associate of Sidney and Walsingham in Chettle's prose. Meanwhile the phrase "smooth-tongued Melicert" is perhaps too vague to furnish ground for more than a plausible guess... The chief point of interest in Dr Nicholson's paper, is the doctrine, now first propounded, that literary nick-names not infrequently lapsed on the death of their owner, and were revived in certain of their survivors... Thus Walsingham and Buckhurst being dead, it is the most natural thing in the world for Chettle to bestow them on Marston and Shakspere."

Conclusion

Ingleby's condition that this Melicertus should be associated with "songs" is unnecessary. On the same grounds he rejects Burghley as candidate we would have to reject Walsingham. Walsingham has no literary record although his connection with the literary world, with Christopher Marlowe, Thomas Watson, and others, is well known. This is confirmed in Watson's elegy on him but only in the Latin version. The line " Nec pectus varia suffultum Palladis Arte" (that death could not be prevented from taking him away, though his mind was nourished by the arts of Pallas), is missing in the English version.[307] Such a connection with the literary world sufficed for one to be spoken of as a "shepherd." In Watson's elegy, others are addressed as shepherd, Hatton, for example, also Burghley and the Lord Admiral, Charles Howard of Effingham. They are given the pastoral names of Damœtas, Damon and Aegon respectively. All four names occur in Virgil's *Eclogues*.

It may be useful to look for what they represent there and how they could be related to a specific quality of the English bearers. Virgil's eclogues are composed as dialogues between two shepherds, the first eclogue between Tityrus and Melibœus, the third between Damœtas and Menalcas, the eighth between Damon and Alphesibœus; Ægon is mentioned in the third eclogue. We cannot detect any reason for the four statesmen to be so called beyond the vague, general notion that as statesmen they cared for the people like shepherds for their flock. But if Chettle meant one of them he would more likely have taken the names from Thomas Watson's elegy and not used the name Melicertus.

With his replacement of Burghley by Buckhurst Ingleby solved nothing. Based on Ingleby's own criterion Burghley, being dead in 1603, is a better candidate than Buckhurst, who, then still being alive, is thus no candidate at all. Buckhurst died five years later, in April 1608, a detail Ingleby seems to have thought not worth verifying. It looks as if he were content to have declared someone dead, true or not, so as to enable Shakespeare to take over the name. It seems difficult to detect an appropriate dead candidate, though the criterion that the Melicertus be dead does not logically follow from his being mentioned along with the dead Sidney and Walsingham. He might well have lived on. Nothing in Chettle's text suggests that he was dead. On the contrary, the use of semantically proximate adjectives in both references implies that the first and second Melicert would be identical, and would thus be consistent with the Melicertus in Greene's romance. On the other hand, Ingleby's claim has some justification. The quasi-synonymous epithets 'smooth-tongued' and 'silver-tongued' seem to point to significant literary achievement. As Ingleby wrote, 'the plot thickens'.[308]

Greene's *Menaphon* presents us with a Melicertus who accords with our traditional view of Shakespeare, sharing with him the same pastoral name. Chettle's *England's Mourning Garment* (a title borrowed from *Greene's Mourning Garment* evidencing Chettle's familiarity with Greene), takes over this name for a literary person who was somehow involved in the anti-Spanish policy of which Walsingham (Melibœus) and Sidney (Philisides) were exponents.

Greene's Menaphon

In Greek mythology Melicertus is a demi-god associated with the myth of Dionysus, hence with lyric poetry, theatre and music, and arts in general. Etymologically, too, the name evokes the idea of music and sweetness, smoothness, refinement and grace. The Greek words "meli" (honey) and "melos" (melody) have the same root. Brinsley Nicholson gives the meaning of "honeycomb". Another interpretation is "honey-cutter," a demon who gathers honey from trees and rock cavities.[309] The latter interpretation chimes in with the use of the word honey for poetry in Torquato Tasso's *Aminta* (III.i) where it is said of Elpino[310]: "E stillar melle dalle dure scorze" ("and drawing honey from the rough bark"). Regardless of which interpretation one prefers, the very name Melicertus is strongly linked with "poetry" and "sweetness," not only etymologically but also historically. As mentioned, the name (in Greek as Melikertes) was given to the Greek poet Simonides in the *Suida*,[311] a well-known Byzantine encyclopedia and familiar source for mythology in Shakespeare's time.[312]

The plot thickens. Oxford's candidature is supported by another passage in which Samela links Melicertus with Euphuism. Samela is the pastoral name Sephestia assumes in the shepherds' Arcadia. "Samela" is a transformation of "Semele" which is identical with "Selene," the Greek moon-goddess and mother of Dionysus.[313] "Sephestia" is a derivation from "sophia," (wisdom). Sephestia is the daughter of Democles, King of Arcadia, and the wife of Maximus or Maximius, as Greene also spells the name, the real name of Melicertus. The slight difference in spelling is heavy with significance.

Greene's novel is a romance. A romance does not lack psychological depth but it adheres little to psychological and empirical consistence.

The narrative is not committed to realism, let alone naturalism. As in Greene's *Pandosto* and Shakespeare's *The Winter's Tale*, the drama is set in motion by a king's jealousy. The king's decision to banish his daughter Sephestia and her husband is left unexplained, it comes down like a blow of Fortune: "But *Sephestia* thou art daughter to a King, exiled by him from the hope of a crown, banished from the pleasures of the Court to the painful fortunes of the country, parted for love from him thou canst not but love, from *Maximus*, *Sephestia*, who for thee hath suffered so many disfavors..."[314] They have been set out in a boat, are parted at sea, one thinks the other dead and at first does not recognize the other, so providing for a recurrent theme in romance, that of *anagnorisis* or re-identification.

Both have found refuge in the Arcadia of the shepherds/poets. Before even having heard Melicertus' first song praising her, Samela wonders: " May this *Melicertus* be a shepherd: or can a country cottage afford such perfection? Doth this coast bring forth such excellence? ... but his face is not enchased with any rustic proportion, his brows contain the characters of nobility, and his looks in shepherd's weeds are Lordly, his voice pleasing, his wit full of gentry: weigh all these equally, and consider, *Samela*, is it not thy *Maximus*?'[315] He is, of course, her Lord Maximus, and nothing in this description is incompatible with the Melicertus whom Chettle mentions in one breath with Sir Philip Sidney/Philisides and Sir Francis Walsingham/good Meliboeus. After Melicertus has finished his first song, he meets Samela in the fields and extols her god-like qualities, to which Samela delivers an answer which makes Melicertus wonder. "*Samela* made this reply, because she heard him so superfine, as if *Ephœbus* had learned him to refine his mother tongue, wherefore thought he had done it of an inkhorne desire to be eloquent; and *Melicertus* thinking that *Samela* had learned with *Lucilla* in *Athens* to anatomize wit, and speak none but *Similes*, imagined she smoothed her talke to be thought like *Sapho*, *Phao's* Paramour."[316] The passage contains several references to John Lyly's *Euphues: The Anatomy of Wit*. Euphues is an Athenian youth, Ephoebus an Athenian teacher, Lucilla is the heroine of Lyly's tale, and *Sapho and Phao* is one of Lyly's plays. But Lyly was not an aristocrat and is nearly as odd in conjunction with Walsingham, Sidney and the anti-Spanish campaign as Shakspere of Stratford. Oxford, on the contrary, played a role in the period leading up to the English expedition in the Low Countries and was at first nominated General of the Horse, a major command which for some reason he did not eventually assume.

Greene uses the name Arcadia in **two different senses**, in-court as the name of a **state**, out-of-court as the **world of the shepherds**, or the **literary world**. So we may understand that Melicertus/Maximus has been exiled from the court into the literary world. In the Arcadia of the shepherds, he is accounted the foremost poet, even Melicertus. Why, then, does Samela/Sephestia call him Maximus and not Maximius, as Greene consistently names him once he is back at court? "Maximus" is an epithet meaning "the greatest". When Samela speaks of him as Maximus, she does not refer so much to his social rank but to his refined language. Therefore, "Maximus" should be understood as "the most excellent poet at court," who according to Puttenham and William Webbe, was Edward de Vere. Indeed, once Melicertus/Maximus has returned to the court of Arcadia, Greene makes it clear that his true name is not Maxim**us** but Maxim**ius**. Roman gentilitial or family names were formed by adding the ending *–ius* to the root. One of the great Roman leaders in the Second Punic War was Fabius Maximus. He was thought the greatest and therefore called Maximus, "the greatest". The gentilitial name Fabius is derived from "Fab-us" (bean) by adding the ending *–ius* to the root. Maximius is the gentilitial or family name derived from the adjective "maximus". Hence, the letter "i" changes the name from an epithet to a name of an aristocratic family. Greene seems to have used it to allude to the most prestigious or one of the most prestigious aristocratic houses in England. The threefold name Melicertus/Maximus/Maximius would then again match Edward de Vere. He would have been considered as the best poet in the whole English literary world, Melicertus; he would also have been considered the best court poet (Maximus); and he was a descendant of one of the oldest English aristocratic houses (Maximius).

The dualism between court and country informs Greene's novel on the level of narration, and at the same time on the level of allegory. The allegorical thread sometimes supersedes the narrative. On the narrative level Sephestia and Maximus have been banished from court and are taking refuge in the simple world of the shepherds. On the allegorical level the world of the shepherds is the world of poetry: Maximus is a courtier and poet who has incurred disfavour and is living as a poet amidst common poets of whom Menaphon is the chief. Sephestia, wisdom, takes the name of the moon-goddess, the muse of both Melicertus and Menaphon. In a series of poetical contests, which seem mere interludes within the narrative, but on the allegorical level appear as the main theme of the novel, Melicertus and Menaphon are striving for Samela's favour, that is, for the laurel of the Muse, the prevalence in the world of poetry.

Greene was preeminent within the literary world outside the court, and this position could be allegorically grafted on Menaphon's position as chief of the shepherds. Melicertus had been a shepherd; a poet elsewhere, at court. If some features of Greene were incorporated by Menaphon, then Melicertus could have been lent some features of his rival, Shakespeare or his precursor. In wending our way back from allegory to reality we may be able to gather some information, however scarce, on the relationship between Menaphon/Greene and Melicertus, represented as the greatest poet of the time.

In the last part we receive at least a glimpse of a possible motive for the banishment of Sephestia (Samela) and Maximus (Melicertus). As in the case of Pandosto and Faunia it is incestuous love, actualized when Sephestia appears to her father Democles as a sheperdess. Democles decides to abduct Samela from the shepherds' Arcadia to the Arcadian court. Thereupon the shepherds, bereft of their muse, prepare for war against the king. The contest between Menaphon and Melicertus about the commandership of the army of the shepherds, which can again, be read as an allegory for what might have been a real source of tension in the circle of the euphuists: "What needs that question, quoth *Menaphon*, am not I the King's shepherd, and chief of all the bordering swains of *Arcadie*?" "I grant, quoth Melicertus, but am not I a Gentleman, though tired in a shepheardes skincoat; superior to thee in birth, though equal now in profession."[317] A gentleman, attired in a shepherd's skincoat, is an image for a "concealed poet" about whom we will soon learn more.

Thus Edward de Vere seems by far the most likely candidate for Melicertus. As he was still alive in 1603, he would be Shakespeare. It is incumbent upon orthodox theory to find another candidate, who, by the end of March 1603, had died.

Chapter II
The Harvey-Nashe Quarrel And *Loves Labours Lost*

"The play's the thing." Hamlet's words sound as familiar as "there's no business like show business." The play *The Mousetrap* within the play of *Hamlet* is not merely the thing. The thing has an object : to catch the conscience of the king; it is not entirely contained within its own world, it trangresses its borders and works outside its own reality. Ironically, the phrase is now being used to urge quite the opposite motion. It has become a catch phrase to intimate that it does not matter who wrote Shakespeare's plays, whether a man with the name Shakespeare or a man who called himself Shakespeare or a Mister Nobody. We have the play, let us be silently grateful and not ask irrelevant questions. The play should be entirely understood from within itself. The play is the thing with no other object than itself.

The play *Love's Labour's Lost* is perhaps not the thing, not the whole thing. This play, especially the subplot, contains puns and jokes which some scholars would like Shakespeare never to have written. "Although its situations", Alfred Harbage wrote, "are conventional, there is a curious open-endedness about them which sends the fancies groping, and although all its jokes are explicable as jokes, some of them are so execrably bad as to create *hope* for ulterior meanings."[318]

There was a time when many a scholar would have welcomed the play's removal from the canon. Richard David, the Arden editor, commences his introduction with a brief survey of its reception. "'If we were to part with any of the author's comedies it should be this,' wrote Hazlitt of *Love's Labour's Lost*, and his opinion was shared by most critics between Shakespeare's day and our own. Their reason was partly the belief that this was one of the earliest of Shakespeare's plays, if not the very earliest, a beginner's clumsy effort, full of stilted rhyming couplets and over-elaborate puns, the characters unlifelike, and the actions constantly held up for skirmishes of what the uneducated countryman from Stratford mistakenly took for wit. Pope found the comic scenes so generally barren that he cut whole pages of them out of his text, printing them at the page-foot for those curious archaelogists who might wish to see what blunders Shakespeare made before he learnt his business." [319]

The eel of Ely

The following dialogue between Don Armado and Moth is probably one of the jokes Harbage would term "execrably bad." It is, at any rate, "curiously open-ended".

Armado. Pretty and apt.
Moth. How mean you, sir? I pretty, and my saying apt? or I apt, and my saying pretty?
Armado. Thou pretty, because little.
Moth. Little pretty, because little. Wherefore apt?
Armado. And therefore apt, because quick.
Moth. Speak you this in my praise, master?
Armado. In thy condign praise.
Moth. I will praise an eel with the same praise.
Armado. That an eel is ingenious?
Moth. That an eel is quick.
Armado. I do say thou art quick in answers; thou heat´st my blood.
Moth. I am answer´d, sir.
Armado. I love not to be cross´d. (I.i.21-32)

The meaning is clear. To Don Armado ("Sir Armed"), the Spanish *miles gloriosus*, his page Moth is pretty because he is of low stature, this makes him apt because it makes him quick. Moth wants to give an eel the same praise, which infuriates Armado because he feels crossed by Moth´s praising an eel for its quickness. Imitating the above dialogue, we may ask: So what, Shakespeare? Are you funny because you are Willy and therefore witty? If the play is the whole thing, this is the very thin thing indeed.

But the play is not the whole thing. The Arden editor remarks on "an eel is quick": "There must be a topical allusion here, since Armado so much resents it." But where do we look for the source of this topicality?

Probably few commentators would deny that the subplot of the play contains several clues to the Harvey-Nashe quarrel, Don Armado representing to a certain extent Gabriel Harvey and Moth Thomas Nashe, "Moth" being perhaps an anagram of "Thom". Still, E.K. Chambers has warned against the hunt for real-life persons in the play. Though he concedes there might be "personal touches" of Harvey and Nashe in Don Armado and Moth, he considers the quest for "portraits" as "pressing the thing too far" and too often "beating the air."[320] Against this, however, it can, on the one hand, be held that a number of allusions may very well supply a profile or caricature allowing for an identification without making for a full portrait; on the other hand, that beating the air might be as effective a method to catch an eel as any other.

If we can digest the following sentence from Harvey's *Pierce's Supererogation* the eel is soon on the hook: "The Ægyptian Mercury would provide to plant his foot upon a square; and his image in Athens was quadrangular, whatsoever the figure of his hat: and although he were sometime a ball of Fortune (who can assure himself of Fortune?) yet was he never a wheel of folly, or an eel of Ely."[321] We cannot square this quadrangular image of Mercury with any cogent meaning, even if Harvey should mean the Egyptian god Anubis who was sometimes represented with a black square, signifying death, behind him and was, besides another god, Thoth, identified by the Greeks with Mercury. But a meaning can be wrested from it by representing Harvey's mental movement as a triple jump, consisting of a hop, a skip and a jump. The precise mark he wants to reach by jumping is the eel. The remark on Mercury represents the hop, that on the quadrangular hats (of Cambridge) the skip, that on the eel the jump. The quadrangular figure refers almost certainly to the pillars to which the bust of the god Hermes was affixed in Athens. From thence he can skip to the black square hat of the university of Cambridge and jump to the "eel of Ely", "mercury" suggesting the quickness of both quicksilver and eel. As to whom Harvey means by "eel of Ely" there can hardly be any doubt. The goddess Fortune may turn her wheel and toss one up and down; the wheel of folly leads to disaster by inertia; but the eel keeps its fortunes smooth in changing environments. It is in water what the chameleon is on land and the turncoat in human society. The "eel of Ely" is Dr. Turncoat, as was nicknamed Dr. Andrew Perne, vice-chancellor of Cambridge and dean of Ely, Harvey's sworn enemy, who equally flourished in the reign of the protestant zealot Edward VI, the catholic zealot Mary and the pragmatic zealot Elizabeth I. It was not this changeability which embittered Harvey, it was the fact that Dr. Perne had thwarted Harvey's academic career: the eel of Ely had **crossed** Harvey. As already noted in the preceding part, Harvey's pamphlet contains numerous pages of diatribe against the "slippery" Dr Perne. "I thank Nashe for something: Greene for more: Papp-hatchet for much more: Perne for most of all. Of him I learned to know him, to know my friends, to know the world, to know fortune, to know the mutability of times, the slipperiness of occasions..."[322] As seen, in the second of his *Three Familiar Letters*, published in 1580, Harvey calls Dr Perne "a wooden wit... a right juggler, as full of sleights... as his skin can hold."[323] But in 1593, in *Pierce's Supererogation*, the bitterness of tone is mixed with admiration. Perne, who had died four years before, "had more wit in his hoary head than six hundred of these flourishing green heads... No man could bear a heavy injury more lightly: or forbear a learned adversary more cunningly... or transform himself into all shapes more deftly... such a sly dexterity, as might quicken the dullest spirit... Some of us, by way of experiment, assayed to feel his pulse, and to tickle his wily veins in his own vein with smoothing and glosing as handsomely, but the bottom of his mind was a gulf of the main."[324] As smooth as an eel. In *Strange News*, published early in 1593, Nashe reminds Harvey of some names he has applied to Perne, one of them being "slippery eel".[325]

Despite the growing animadversion between Harvey and Nashe from the fall 1592 to the summer 1593, Harvey admired Nashe's talent and seems to have hoped to be the young man's fatherly friend. In 1592 he attests Nashe "a delicate wit", full of "quaintest inventions," and a "deviseful brain".[326] He advises him "to employ his golden talent"[327] the right way. He calls him a "springing wit".[328] This patronizing attitude in 1592 and earlier resembles that of Don Armado toward his page Moth. Only would Nashe sometimes be too quick. It is not his person,

Harvey writes, which caused him to write against him but his "rash and desperate proceeding against his well-willers."[329] In 1593 only a few undertones on Nashe's talent remain perceptible. The stress shifts to the misuse of that talent in the service of what is to Harvey base, "villain" literature. "Master Villainy became an author; and Sir Nash a gentleman."[330] The "quaintest inventions" of 1592 have become "fresh invention from the tap"[331] in 1593. Nashe's position in Harvey's fight with the ghost of Dr Perne is simple: right or wrong, the enemy of my enemy is my friend. Perne would have sensed Harvey's true nature. "The old fox Doctor *Perne* thoroughly discovered you a young fop."[332] This is repeated in 1596 in *Have With You to Saffron-Walden*: "Doctor *Perne* in this plight nor at any other time met him, but he would shake his hand and cry *vanitas vanitatum, omnia vanitas*, vanity of vanities, and all things is vanity."[333]

In 1592 Harvey complains of the practice of mocking living persons in the theatre: "... and it is the luck of some pelting comedies to busy the stage, as well as some graver tragedies."[334] In 1593 he expresses the fear of being thrown on the stage himself: "Such an antagonist has Fortune allotted me, to purge melancholy and to thrust me upon the stage."[335] Whom did Harvey mean? Probably not Nashe, though Nashe had in the meantime announced Harvey would be played by Will Kempe, the clown of the Chamberlain's Men (see next chapter). Possibly he meant Shakespeare. Harvey had been thrust upon the stage before 1593. Perhaps first in 1581 in the Latin comedy *Pedantius* acted at Cambridge. The model for Pedantius is thought to be Gabriel Harvey, though it is possible that Harvey was likened to Pedantius after the play had been staged. But he had also been caricatured about 1585 in John Lyly's comedy *Endimion*, in some aspects, particularly with respect to the subplot, comparable to Shakespeare's *Love's Labour's Lost*. The main characters of the subplot of *Endimion* are Sir Tophas, a Chaucerian figure, a warrior-like pedant like Don Armado, and his quick-witted page Epiton. Sir Tophas is hunting the monster Ovis, which is a black sheep, a reference to grammar which is also found in Shakespeare's play.[336] Sir Tophas dotingly loves the hag Dipsas, a personification of antiquity. "Argumentum ab antiquitate, My master loveth anticke worke", the page Epiton says, and "Nothing hath made my master a fool but flat scholarship." (V.ii.32 and 38). Another allusion seems leveled at Harvey in Lyly's play:

Tophas. Then I am but three quarters of a noun substantive.
But alas, *Epi*, to tell thee the truth, I am a noun
adjective.
Epiton. Why?
Tophas. Because I cannot stand without another. (III.iii.16-19)

Harvey was this "adjective", who in the 1570s and early 1580s could not stand without his friend Edmund Spenser, on whom he piggy-backed his own ambition. But Harvey was an adjective striving to take the place of the substantive. He "would have killed Spenser poetically" if he had let him.[337] One has only to read the epistle of the "wellwiller" to his *Three Familiar Letters* to realize that Harvey was using Spenser's fame for his own glory. He would have killed Nashe's talent too.

If we step out of the play to the Harvey-Nashe quarrel and replace Don Armado with Harvey and Moth with Nashe the passage on the "quick eel" becomes transparent. Like Moth in the play Thomas Nashe seems to have been of low stature. In the anonymous *The Trimming of Thomas Nash* (1597; the presumed author is Gabriel's brother Richard) he is portrayed as a little boy in chains. Harvey is attracted by Nashe's quick wit and praises him. But Nashe reminds him that Dr. Perne, the eel (of Ely), is also quick,[338] which immediately sets Harvey afire, because he does not "love to be crossed". For these lines to be amusing, the public had to be aware of the travesty of Harvey/Don Armado, Nashe/Moth, Dr. Perne, dean of Ely/eel of Ely ("eel of Ely" would have suggested itself as a sobriquet of Dr. Perne). To an informed public the allusions would be witty. Alfred Harbage rightly has called *Love's Labour's Lost* a "coterie" play, written for a select informed public in the private theatre, at an Inn of Court or at court.

Thus the play itself is, without knowledge of the context in which it was presented, no longer 'the thing' for modern readers or spectators, as it had been for that segment of the Elizabethan audience, reflecting a common experience of author, player and spectator.

Costard´s broken shin

In III.i Costard is sent for in order to carry a letter of Don Armado to Jacquenetta. Moth fetches Costard and introduces him:
    "A wonder, master! here´s a costard broken in a shin."
"Costard" means "head". A head broken in a shin does excite wonder, but at first glance the pun itself does not look that wonderful. Armado´s reaction seems to carry no senseful relation to Moth´s words:
    "Some enigma, some riddle; come, thy l´envoy; begin."

Certainly, a few lines later Armado explains that an envoy "is an epilogue or discourse to make plain some obscure precedence that hath tofore been sain." But what is this "obscure precedent"? Is it the rather unusual form "broken in a shin" for "a broken shin"? As the scene contains cross-punning between English and French words, this might be why Shakespeare chooses this curious locution. "A shin" sounds like the French **échine**, "backbone". In Nashe´s *Strange News* we find a passage which could shed light on the use of this form. Speaking of Dr Perne at whom Harvey in 1580 had been shouting in Billingsgate manner, Nashe warns him: "He that wraps himself in earth, like the Fox, to catch birds, may haps have a heavy cart go over him before he be aware and break his back."[339] Harvey´s insults against Dr Perne in his *Three Familar Letters* in 1580 did definitively break the back of his academic career. By "heavy cart" Nashe could have meant Lord Burghley, chancellor of the University. We have here a first possible, if debatable, reference to the Harvey-Nashe quarrel in scene III.i. About the other reference of "broken in a shin" we need not doubt.

    The next work Nashe published after *Strange News* is *Christ´s Tears over Jerusalem*. It must have been published between 8 September 1593, the date of registration in Stationers´ Register, and 16 September next. The "Epistle to the Reader" contained an offer of truce to Harvey. "Even of Maister Doctor *Harvey*, I heartily desire the like, whose fame and reputation though, through some precedent injurious provocations, and fervent incitements of young heads, I rashly assailed: yet now better advised, and of his perfections more confirmedly persuaded, unfeignedly I entreat of the whole world, from my pen his worths may receive no impeachment."[340]

Harvey bluntly rejected Nashe's offer by return of post in a separate pamphlet dated 16 September under the title *A New Letter of Notable Contents*. As always, some droll poems were appended, in this case three, two of them ending with a "l'envoy". Nashe's offer for peace was rejected in these words: "... or accept of a silly recantation, as it were a sory plaister to a **broken shin**, that could knock malice on the **head**, and cut the windpipe of the railing throat?"[341] [our emphases] In this sentence we find the head "Costard" and his "broken shin". It seems as if Shakespeare had re-arranged Harvey's reply.

Costard. No egma, no riddle, no l'envoy; no salve in the mail, sir.

O, sir, plantain, a plain plantain; no l'envoy, no l'envoy;
no salve, sir, but a plantain!

Armado. By virtue thou enforcest laughter; thy silly thought, my
spleen; the heaving of my lungs provokes me to ridiculous
miling. O, pardon me, my stars! Doth the inconsiderate
take salve for l'envoy, and the word 'l'envoy' for a salve?

By naming the clown Costard ("head"), having him break a shin and ask for a plantain plaister, one connexion is established with the Harvey-Nashe quarrel, another if one accepts the pun on "a shin" and **échine**, ('backbone'). But the allusions do not end there. Shakespeare returns to it. Armado asks:

Armado. But tell me: how was there a costard broken in a shin?

Moth. I will tell you sensibly.

Nashe's reply to Harvey's rebuttal in the epistle to the second issue of *Christ's Tears over Jerusalem* resounds in Moth's "I will tell you sensibly". "Thrice more convenient time I will pick out to stretch him forth limb by limb on the rack, and afield as large as *Achilles'* race to bait him to death with darts according to the custom of baiting bulls in Spain."[342] Is it merely fortuitous that in *Love's Labour's Lost* Don Armado is a Spaniard, that in the show of the Nine Worthies at the end of the play Don Armado represents Hector and Nashe announces he will drag Harvey like Achilles dragged Hector, or that in the same show Moth represents Hercules to whom Nashe is likened in Harvey's pamphlets more than once? For instance, "his Pen is his mace, his lance, his two-edged sword, his scepter, his Hercules club."[343] Or where he calls Nashe "the mighty Hercules of rhetoric and poetry"?[344] Or "Many are the miracles of right virtue. And he enters an infinite labyrinth, that goes about to praise Hercules or the Ass, whose labours exceed the labours of Hercules..."[345] Then Moth is interrupted by Costard:

"Thou hast no feeling of it, Moth; I will speak that l'envoy.

I, Costard, running out, that was safely within,

Fell over the threshold and broke my shin."

In the quatrain of the fox, the ape and the humble bee, however, it is the goose which comes out of door. The goose is Harvey. But at this point, Armado wants to drop the theme:

We will talk no more of this matter.

But Costard digs his toes in:

Till there be more matter in the shin.

No doubt, more matter in the shin is to be found outside the play.

The association between "l'envoy" and "goose" is not merely based on the French word for "goose", "oie". Moreover, what senseful way leads from "broken shin" to "l'envoy"? If we stay within the borders of the play, we have to find the senseful thing in the play. We will have to grope in the dark, while the light shines outside the play in Harvey's rejection of Nashe's truce proposal in his pamphlet *A New Letter of Notable Contents* and the odd poems with an "envoy" ending it.

"Sudden Shakespeare"[346] is clearly writing on two levels at once, in play and out of play.

Harvey, the goose

Armado. I will example it:

The fox, the ape, and the humble-bee,

Were still at odds, being but three.

There's the moral. Now the l'envoy.

The l'envoy goes:

Until the goose came out of door,

And stay'd the odds by adding four.

The couplet, called the moral, refers to Nashe's tale of the bear in *Pierce Penniless*. The couplet called "l'envoy" refers to the role the Harvey brothers Gabriel and Richard aimed at in the Martin Marprelate controversy.

Probably less than a week after the publication of *Pierce Penniless*, Harvey warned Nashe: "... they can tell parlous tales of bears and foxes, as shrewdly as *Mother Hubbard's Tale*."[347] As noted in part II.1, Spenser had run into difficulties the previous year, though probably more because of the ape than the fox. In his tale Spenser had made an ape a successful courtier. Nashe's tale of the bear in *Pierce Penniless* is about Leicester, who had died in 1588. It draws heavily upon an anonymous pamphlet *Leicester's Commonwealth* published in 1584. In it the Earl of Leicester was accused of nearly all the evils in Pandora's Box and, above all, of his ambition to get hold of the English throne in one way or another. In his "Epistle to the Readers" in *Strange News* Nashe warns his readers against doing what, actually, he is doing brazenly. His rectification represents the most common subterfuge with which authors sought to shield themselves from the charge of libel, often at the same time drawing the attention of the reader to the presence of a hidden meaning. His tale, Nashe states, was not meant individually "but generally applied to a general vice. Now a man may not talk of a dog, but it is surmised he aims at him that gives the dog in his crest."[348] The dog was the crest of the earl of Shrewsbury; no dog plays a significant part in Nashe's tale. But the bear was the crest of the Earl of Leicester. Leicester is sometimes spoken of as the bear in *Leicester's Commonwealth*. "You know the bear's love, said the gentleman, which is all for his own paunch, and so this Bearwhelp turneth all to his own commodity, and for greediness thereof will overturn all if he be not stopped or muzzled in time."[349] In Nashe's fable Leicester is marked out in almost every respect but in name. He is called the "chief Burgomaster of all the beasts under the Lion"; the use of the Dutch term for 'mayor' highlights once more that the former governor-general of the Low Countries is meant. The lion was so fond of the bear that he turned a blind eye to his crimes; the lion is the crest of the English monarchs; it cannot have been difficult for contemporaries to identify the lion as the queen and the lion's fondness for the bear as her complaisance for Leicester. In *Leicester's Commonwealth* the earl is accused of having poisoned the Earl of Essex to marry his widow; in Nashe's fable the bear poisons the stream from which the deer was wont to drink; the deer was the crest of the Earl of Essex. In *Leicester's Commonwealth* he is accused of having murdered the Duchess of Lennox (who through the descendance from Henry VII's daughter Margaret had a claim to the succession) during a visit at her house in Hackney; in Nashe's fable the bear "assailed the Unicorn as he slept in his den";[350] the unicorn was the crest of the duke of Lennox.

How closely Nashe follows *Leicester's Commonwealth* in this part of his tale appears most palpably from the account of the planned marriage between Mary Stuart and the duke of Norfolk, leading to the duke's execution in 1574, in the pamphlet and in the corresponding allegory in Nashe's fable. "But the sum of all is this, in effect, that Leicester, having a secret desire to pull down the said Duke, to the end that he might have no man above himself to hinder him in that which he most desireth, by a thousand cunning devices drew in the Duke to the cogitation of that marriage with the Queen of Scotland which afterward was the cause or occasion of his ruin".[351] Leicester would have approached the duke of Norfolk, feigning warmest friendship and highest respect, giving him a counsel "to plunge his friend over the ears in suspicion and disgrace, in such sort as he should never be able to draw himself out of the ditch again..."[352], wherein he was seconded by Sir Nicholas Throckmorton. In Nashe's fable Norfolk appears both as "fat camel and a horse"; the horse was the crest of of his first wife, Mary FitzAlan, daughter of the Earl of Arundel, whose title and crest passed to Norfolk; the "camel" probably hints at Norfolk's gullibility. The bear was longing for "horse-flesh, and went presently to a meadow, where a fat camel was grazing, whom fearing to encounter with force because he was a huge beast and well shod, he thought to betray under the colour of demanding homage."[353] The bear is advised by the ape "to dig a pit with his paws right in the way where this big-boned Gentleman should pass, that so stumbling and falling in, he might lightly skip on his back."[354]

It is probably sheer coincidence that in *Leicester's Commonwealth* the "ape" who helped the "bear" dig the pit for Norfolk, corresponds to Sir Nicholas Throckmorton (who died in 1571), whereas in Shakespeare's quatrain in *Love's Labour's Lost* the ape is the pseudonymous pamphleteer Martin Mar-prelate in 1589-90, whom many now take to be Job Throckmorton. Sir Nicholas and Job Throckmorton, however, were not related. One could presume that Nashe was using the identical surname to link Leicester with Marprelate. However, the ape disappears from Nashe's tale after the bear/Leicester has trapped the horse-camel/Norfolk. Moreover, in his anti-Martinist pamphlet *An Almond for a Parrat*, published in 1590 anonymously, but generally and for good reasons ascribed to Nashe, he seems convinced that Martin Marprelate was the Welsh divine John Penry, whom some scholars still consider to be the main author of the Marprelate tracts. Toward the end of *Strange News* he nevertheless suggests that the Fox might have had something to do with Martin Marprelate. "The tale of the bear and the fox, however it may set fools' heads a-work afar off, yet I had no concealed end in it but, in the one, to describe the right nature of a bloodthirsty tyrant,... for the other, to figure an hypocrite: let it be *Martin*, if you will, or some old dog that bites sorer than he, who secretly goes and seduces country swains.[355] The old dog which bites sorer and seduces country swains is here probably the same as the fox in the tale, namely Thomas Cartwright, protégé of Leicester and his brother, the earl of Warwick. Cartwright, the leading Calvinist adversary of John Whitgift, Archbishop of Canterbury, had been invested by Leicester with a living in Warwick.

In Nashe's tale the bear, seeing he cannot reach his ends by his accustomed methods, changes his tactics and "bethought him what a pleasant thing it was to eat nothing but honey".[356] "Honey" is a metaphor for religion. The Fox starts on a preaching tour in the country to persuade the husbandmen that they can have cheaper and purer honey than the poisoned native one by importing it from other countries like "Scotland, Denmark and some purer parts of the Seventeen Provinces."[357] The purer parts of the Seventeen Provinces are, of course, the Calvinist northern Low Countries not governed by the Spaniards. The principal bone of contention between the Anglican Church and the more radical Calvinists, including Martin Marprelate, was the office of bishop, which according to the Calvinists was of Popish origin and unwarranted by the Scripture. In Nashe's fable the Fox tries to convince the people that most of their bees are drones, "and what should such idle drones do with such stately hives, or lie sucking at such precious honeycombs".[358] Nashe's metaphor for the bishops might have been inspired by Martin Marprelate, who was used to writing "bishops" as "Bb.".

Nashe's representation of Leicester using Puritan preachers, symbolized by the Fox, as a tool to overthrow the established order and by this device to achieve the long sought-for hegemony, inverts the causal direction in which Leicester's patronage of the Puritans actually worked. It rather operated as a check on radicalism in the interest of the Royal Supremacy. Leicester's death, followed by Thomas Cartwright's eclipse, creating a vacuum into which rushed Martin Marprelate in October 1588, a month after Leicester's death. Today Job Throckmorton has emerged as the most likely candidate for Martin Marprelate. Other candidates have been contemplated by the contemporary authorities and modern scholars as well. One argument makes their candidature highly improbable. In his fourth pamphlet, *Hay, any work for Cooper*, published in March 1589, Martin himself cheerfully refutes the authorship of those who have been contemplated as authors of the Marprelate tracts. "You haue and do suspect diuers, as master Paggett / master Wiggington / master Udall / & master Penri / &c. to make Martin. If they cannot cleare their selues their sillinesse is pitifull / and they are worthy to beare Martin's punishment,"[359] an ominous statement in the light of the subsequent fate of John Penry, who was hanged, and John Udall, who died in prison. The battleground on which Martin Marprelate chose to challenge the bishops of the Anglican church was not the open battlefield of theological dispute. In a colloquial language he harassed them in a sort of humorous one-man guerilla, a railing wrestle in which the dignitaries of the Anglican church could not engage without either forsaking their dignified countenance or being wrenched in the hip by a rollicking messenger of God. Martin justified his nonconformist procedure by appeal to the will of the Lord. "The Lord being the author both of mirth and gravity, is it not lawful in itself for the truth to use either of these ways when the circumstances do make it lawful?"[360] The bishops had to look for other means, "to purge this field of such a hilding foe" (*Henry V*). If Thomas Nashe was sometimes called the English Aretine, Martin Marprelate deserves to be called the Puritan Aretine. This or a similar idea might have occurred to Richard Bancroft, then chaplain of the Archbishop of Canterbury, generally thought to be the originator of the plan to engage professional writers who could meet Martin on his own ground. One of them was Nashe, another Lyly. Anthony Munday could have been another. A series of anti-Martinist pamphlets was launched, including some plays, which are no longer extant. Henceforth Martin was called "the ape", so in a pamphlet in verses, "A Whip for an Ape", ascribed to John Lyly:

A Dizard late skipt out upon our Stage;
  But in a sacke, that no man might him sée:
And though we knowe not yet the paltrie page,
Himself hath *Martin* made his name to bée.
A proper name, and for his feates most fit;
The only thing wherein he hath shew'd wit.

    Who knoweth not, that Apes men *Martins* call;
Which beast this baggage seemes as t'were himselfe:
So as both nature, nurture, name and all
Of that's expressed in this apish elfe.
Which I'll make good to Martin Marr-als face
In thrée plaine poynts, and will not bate an ace.[361]

The strategy pleased neither all Anglicans nor all Puritans. Francis Bacon held that the jesting tone and the substitution of the pulpit by the public stage was unworthy of the Church. In two letters to Lord Burghley the Puritan Thomas Cartwright condemned "Martin's disordered discourse" and expressed his "dislike and sorrow for such kind of disorderly proceeding."[362] Thus the "fox" disagreed with the "ape" and both disagreed with the bees. "The fox, the ape, and the humble-bee/ Were still at odds, being but three."

In 1589 a fourth party entered the lists. The party was composed of the Harvey brothers Gabriel and Richard. Early in 1590 Richard Harvey published his sermon *The Lamb of God* (entered in the Stationers' Register on 23 October 1589) in an attempt, according to Nashe, "to play the Jack of both sides twixt Martin and us."[363] In his dedication to the earl of Essex Richard Harvey, surely with the silent assistance of his elder brother, censured both Martin and the anti-Martinist pamphleteers, the latter, however, in more contemptuous terms, being "unworthy any witty stage, and too piperly for *Tarleton's* mouth. Scurrility was odious even among the heathen Romans... grave matters would be debated gravely."[364] He equated Nashe to Martin for "railing incivility". Nashe would be doing for "civil learning" what Martin Marprelate was doing in religion. The same year appeared the anonymous pamphlet *Plaine Percevall, the Peace-Maker of England*, dedicated to the "new upstart Martin" but also to his adversaries "Cavaliero Pasquill,... Marforius and all Cutting Huffsnuffs" etc. Richard Harvey's authorship seems beyond doubt: he never denied Nashe's ascription to him. Richard's position was of course shared by his brother Gabriel, who wrote his own pamphlet in 1589, but did not publish it until 1593 as second part of his *Pierce's Supererogation*, unwittingly lending the title a self-ironic connotation. Gabriel Harvey's publication of his position in the Martin Marprelate controversy in 1593 was itself a supererogation. Martin Marprelate had published his last tract in September 1589, exactly four years before Gabriel Harvey brought his commentary to the printer. His position was in nothing different from that of his brother, only much later and longer. Again, his attitude to Martin (who had anyway decamped by then) was more friendly than to the other adversary, John Lyly, despite the fact that there was no substantial difference between him and Lyly on the religious issue. He, too, deplored the scurrilous level to which the debate had been pulled down. "Alas poor miserable desolate Church, had it no other builders, but such architects of their own fantasies, and such maisons of infinite contradiction."[365] And he charitably implored Martin to hold his peace. "Sweet Martin, as well Junior as Senior... and you sweet whirlwinds, that so fiercely bestir you at this instant; now, again and again, I beseech you, either be content to take a sweeter course; or take all for me."[366] Martin had fled into silence for almost four years.

But what then had moved Gabriel Harvey to publish this text? First of all, Harvey had sollicited in vain the office of Public Orator at Cambridge; a public orator is nothing without public, and Harvey wanted to go public. Shakespeare expresses this motive in his wonted pithiness and precision. Harvey had decided to 'go public', simply to 'come out of door':

Until the goose came out of door,
And stay'd the odds by adding four.

How apt and appropriate! Indeed, going public was the sole cause and staying the odds by adding up to four the sole effect of Harvey's intervention in 1593. But why the goose?

There are several ways in which Gabriel Harvey can be associated with the "goose". First, because of his fondness of "l'envoy", "oie" or "oye" being the French word for goose. Secondly, because of his "honking" verse. After he had been allowed to kiss the queen's hand at Audley End in 1578, his dark complexion prompting the queen's remark that he looked like an Italian, he composed a Latin poem "De vultu Itali" ("Concerning the look of an Italian") which was , in fact, a variation of Virgil's ninth eclogue. Harvey writes:

"Me also do the shepherds call a poet,
But I am slow to credit what they say.
O may I always recollect his warning:
Don't credit more what others say of thee
Than what thyself dost say unto thyself."[367]

Virgil:

"The muses made me
A poet too. There are songs of mine. The shepherd folk
Call me their bard – though I am not deluded by what they say.
I know I cannot be mentioned in the same breath with Cinna
Or Varius – a honking goose with silver-throated swans."[368]

In Vergil's eclogue the shepherd's humility must be understood in social, not in aesthetical terms. Cinna, Varius, Gallus, Pollio were members of the Roman nobility and therefore accounted more "refined" than the common shepherd Lycidas.[369] For Harvey's English poems, however, "honking goose" is a fit characterisation.

Finally, the Earl of Oxford would have a special reason to call Harvey the "goose". In his Latin address at Audley End in 1578 he had lauded Sidney and Oxford as excellent poets. Notwithstanding, he had urged the earl of Oxford to throw away the "insignificant pen" and to accomplish heroical feats. "Pull Hannibal up short at the gates of Britain. Defended though he be by a mighty host, let Don John of Austria come on only to be driven home again. And what if suddenly a most powerful enemy should invade our borders? If the Turk be arming his savage hosts against us?"[370] When the Gaules stood at the gates of Rome, the geese grazing before the Capitol alarmed the Romans; in 1578 at Audley End the rhetorician Harvey was playing the same role – solo. Some five years after the Spanish Armada had assailed the English coast, Harvey's military rhetoric might have called forth the name of Don Armado.

Even with the Martin Marprelate controversy being over, Harvey conserved a motive, his inmost motive, to publish his paper on the controversy. His position paper on the Marprelate affair also addressed another controversy, not on religious but on literary matters: the long-standing feud between Harvey and the Euphuists and their wider circle: John Lyly, Robert Greene, Thomas Lodge but also authors who cannot properly be considered as Euphuists like Thomas Watson, Christopher Marlowe and Thomas Nashe. And above all the Euphuists' patron -poet, the earl of Oxford.

Harvey and English literature

Apart from several scattered general declarations of allegiance to the model of the ancients, to the sacred union of poetry and virtue, in his pamphlets of 1592 and 1593, Gabriel Harvey has left us only two letters on versifying, addressed to Edmund Spenser, both published in 1580 but in two separate volumes: *Three Proper and wittie, familiar Letters: lately passed betweene two Universitie men: touching the Earthquake in April last, and our English reformed Versifying – With the Preface of a Wellwiller to both* and *Two Other very commendable Letters, of the same men's writing: both touching the foresaid Artificiall Versifying, and certain other Patriculars :*

More lately delivered unto the Printer. If it is the roots of the Harvey-Nashe quarrel we are seeking, they are here, not in the Marprelate controversy. McKerrow remarks that the "quarrel between Nashe and the Harveys seems in its origin to be an offshoot of the well-known one between Edward de Vere, Earl of Oxford, and Sir Philip Sidney in 1579, and to have arisen out of what may have been a simple misunderstanding of a harmless piece of impersonal satire."[371] This assessment cannot be accepted in its entirety. Harvey's libel "Speculum Tuscanismi" was not an "impersonal" satire. The mockery of Oxford's Italianate and effete manners was immediately followed by an umistakably personal quip.[372] The battle was continued without any visible further implication of Sidney in 1583. In his *Mamillia, second part*, registered in September 1583, Robert Greene (possibly the Earl of Oxford himself within Greene's work) wrote a witty reply to Harvey's libel, a sort of "Retro-Speculum Tuscanismi". In "Speculum Tuscanismi" Harvey had mocked womanish behaviour, the lack of manly valour, commemorating the old times of knightly ardour:

> Since *Galateo* came in, and *Tuscanisme* gan usurpe,
> Vanitie above all: Villanie next her, Stateliness Empresse.
> No man, but Minion, Stout, Lout, Plaine, swain, quoth a Lording:
> No words but valorous, no works but woomanish only.
> For life Magnificoes, not a beck but glorious in shew,
> In deede most frivolous, not a looke but Tuscanish always.

Galateo is the title of Giovanni della Casa's famous treatise on education, written in 1560, translated into English in 1576. It is difficult to understand how Harvey, who at Audley End in 1578, two years before his *Familiar Letters*, had claimed for himself the succession of Castiglione, Giovanni della Casa and Stefano Guazzo, could link this treatise with the scorned "Tuscanism" or "Italianateness". In the satire on Harvey's satire in Greene's *Mammillia II* the situation is inverted. Here the complaint was about the decline of the old female values, the masculinity of women:

> Since Ladie milde (too base in array) hath lived as an exile,
> None of account but stout: if plaine? Stale slut not a courtresse
> Dames nowadayes? fie none, sauced with conceits, quick wits very
>   wily.

Words of a Saint, but deeds guess how, feigned faith to deceive men.
Courtsies coy, no vale but a vaunt tucked up like a Tuscan.[373]

In Nashe's mind Harvey's *Familiar letters* of 1580 and his pamphlets of
1592-3 were so closely interwoven that in *Have With You to Saffron-
Walden* he four times confuses them. The 'confusion' is without doubt
on purpose; to mistake one event for the other is to underscore their
unity. As he does in his dedication of *Strange News* (1592), in which he
insinuates clearly enough that Harvey's *Four Letters* are a repetition of
his *Three Familiar Letters* in 1580: "*veterem ferendo iniuriam inuitas nouam,*
which is as much in English as, one cup of nippitaty pulls on another"[374], less freely translated, "an old injury incites a new one". In
Have With You (1596) he chooses the oblique way, conflating four times
Harvey's *Four Letters* of 1592 with the *Three Familiar Letters* of 1580:

On page 69: "... and afterward, in the year when the earthquake
was, he fell to be a familiar Epistler, & made *Paul's Churchyard* resound
or cry twang again with **four** [our emphasis] notable famous letters: in
one of which he interlaced his short but yet sharp judicial of earth-
quakes, & came very short and sharp upon my Lord of Oxford in a rattling bundle of English hexameters."[375] Nashe can not possibly have
thought that the earthquake of 1580, on which Harvey commented in
Three Familiar Letters, had happened in 1592. And in other places he is
well aware that "Speculum Tuscanismi" was written in 1580.

On page 78: "I had forgot to observe unto you, out of his first **four**
familiar Epistles, his ambitious stratagem to aspire, that whereas two
great Peers being at jar, and their quarrel continued to bloodshed, he
would needs... step in the one side, which indeed was the safer side...
and hew and slash with his Hexameters, but hewed and slashed he had
been as small as chippings, if he had not played duck Friar and hid
himself eight weeks in that nobleman's house for whom with his pen
he thus bladed. Yet nevertheless Sir *James Croft*, the old Controller, fer-
reted him out, and had him under hold in the Fleet a great while, taking that to be aimed & leveled against him, because he called him his
old Controller, which he had most venomously belched against Doctor
Perne." It is not certain that Nashe's report is in all points correct, but it

is known that Harvey was in Leicester's house for a while, after having written his hexameters against the Earl of Oxford; Nashe must also have known that all this happened in 1580. In 1592, when Harvey wrote his *Four Letters*, Dr. Perne and Sir James Croft were dead.

On page 80: "as those ragged remnants in his **four** familiar epistles twixt him and *Senior Immerito, raptim scripta, Nosti manum & stylum,* with innumerable other of his rable routs."[376] Again, the letters exchanged with Spenser were published in 1580 in *Three Familiar Letters,* the title of the pamphlet of 1592 is "Four Letters", but not "Four Familiar Letters". *Four Letters* contains in an appendix a sonnet of Spenser but no letter. Then, only the third letter of 1580 containing the libel on Oxford is subscribed "nosti manum & stylum" ["the well-known hand and pen"]. Finally, in 1592 Spenser no longer used the pseudonym Immerito. It is difficult to believe that Nashe was not aware of it (in *Pierce Penniless*, in 1592, he addresses Spenser by name, not as Immerito). But he mixes up these letters with Harvey's *Four Letters* of 1592 and his *New Letter of Notable Contents of 1593*.

On page 127 of *Have With You* he writes: "as also his writing *the* **wellwiller's Epistle** in praise of himself, before his *Four Letters* a year ago. The compositor that set it swore to me it came under his own hand."[377] "A year ago" indicates that Nashe was writing these lines in 1593 or early in 1594, two years before publication. But there is no such epistle of a welwilling friend in *Four Letters* in 1592, only in *Three Familiar Letters* in 1580.

Hence, Nashe tells us five times that the letters of 1580 and 1592-3 are parts of one and the same story. Sidney, dead for 6-7 years, had nothing to do with it. It is the earl of Oxford who stood at the center in 1580 and 1592-3 as well. Oxford did not react in 1580, except via Robert Greene in *Mammillia II.* Nor did Oxford react in 1593... except via Shakespeare, who remains unnamed in the quarrel itself.

As for Harvey, let us first hear what the Arden editor has to say. He does note that there are obvious parallels between Harvey's writings and his depiction by Nashe on the one hand, and Shakespeare's *Love's Labour's Lost* on the other. "Holofernes whom he more unmercifully mocks — and indeed the very name Holofernes might be one of the distortions to which Nashe subjects that of Harvey. Holofernes is attended by an obsequious clerical shadow, just as Gabriel was by his parson brother Richard. Armado pawns his linen, as Harvey was said to have done to pay his printer, and is stingy as Harvey to his dependants. The objections to each identification are equally extensive, not the least being the strength of the rival claim. To note only single difficulties in addition, Holofernes's precise pronunciation seems as remote from Harvey (who wrote 'dettor' and was all for modernity) as does Armado's romantic passion for Jacquenetta. In *Love's Labour's Lost* Harvey is still to seek."[378] Holofernes, though, is rather the incarnation of the pedant pure and simple, the counterpart of Sidney's Rhombus in *The Lady of May*. As such he shares some features with Harvey, the English "Tubalcain" who invented the English hexameter. But it is in Armado that Harvey is fully caricaturized. He that has still to seek him, must be very loath to find him.

Even the Arden editor cannot overlook that Armado's letters brim over with Harveian phraseology, especially the second letter of *Three Familiar Letters* on the earthquake:

"that the Earth under us quaked, and the house shaked above: besides the moving, and ratling of the table, and forms, where we sat...And the last final, which we are to judge of as advisedly, and providently, as possibly we can, by the consideration, & comparison of Circumstances, the time when: the place where: the qualities, and dispositions of the persons, amongst whom such, and such an Ominous token is given."[379]

In *Love's Labour's Lost* (I.i.227-240):

The time When? About the sixth hour; when beasts most graze, birds best peck, and men sit down to that nourishment which is called supper. So much for the time When. Now for the ground Which? which, I mean, I upon; it is ycleped thy park. Then for the place Where? where, I mean, I did encounter that obscene and most prepost'rous event that draweth from my snow-white pen the ebon-coloured ink which here thou viewest, beholdest, surveyest, or seest.'

It may be objected to it that in his letter Harvey simply applied the rules from Thomas Wilson's *Art of Rhetorique,* but the language of the whole passage is Harvey's, not Wilson's.

According to Harvey himself, he had once wielded notable influence on young people. The context suggests that these young people were authors. Harvey, according to Robert Greene's quip, was the inventor of English hexameter. It is a fact that both Philip Sidney and Edmund Spenser experimented with hexametric verse. The latter even wrote Harvey: "I like your hexameters exceedingly well, that I also ensure my pen sometime in that kind: which I find indeed, as I have heard you often defend in words, neither so hard, nor so harsh, that it will easily and fairly yield itself to our mother tongue."[380] Spenser was not writing out of mere courtesy to his friend, but nonetheless neither he nor Sidney did carry the experiment very far. Harvey, who lacked poetical talent, seems not to have understood that his failure to establish the hexameter in English poetry and himself as preceptor of English literature was due to the fact "that our vulgar *Saxon English* standing most upon words *monosyllable,* and little upon *polysyllables,* doth hardly admit the use of those fine invented feet of the Greek & Latins"[381] and not, as he thought, to the inimical endeavours of others: "I had no sooner shaken off my young troop, whom I could not associate as before, but they were festivally re-entertained by some nimble wights, that could take advantage of opportunity... like ambitious planets that enhance their own dignities by the combustion of their fellow-planets... Iwis [surely] it were purer euphuism to win honey out of the thistle... Tush, you are a silly humanitian of the old world."[382]

Euphuism was the literary current running against Harvey. It is Lyly who was his adversary as early as 1580, it was Greene whom he attacked in 1592. It was their patron, the earl of Oxford, whom he libeled in 1580. "Needs he must cast up certain crude humours of English hexameter verses that lay upon his stomach; a nobleman stood in his way as he was vomiting, and from top to toe he all to bewrayed him with Tuscanism."[383]

It was Nashe, whom he attacked in *Pierce's Supererogation.* We will soon learn who Nashe's patron was.

Literature and policy

"Industry" is a key word in Harvey's conception of society and literature. In his three pamphlets of 1592-3 he uses the word about twenty times, seventeen times in *Pierce's Supererogation* alone. Harvey prefers the active to the contemplative way of life, including poetry. To throw away the useless pen is the counsel he gave to Oxford at Audley End in 1578. It is the lack of deeds he mocks in his libel on Oxford in 1580 in his *Three Familiar Letters*. It is certainly Oxford he means when in the second part of *Pierces Supererogation*, written in 1589, he writes "It is not the first time that I have preferred a Gentleman of deeds before a Lord of words: and what if I once by way of familiar discourse said?"[384] In the same pamphlet he regrets to have been compelled to use his pen in a quarrel with Nashe instead of serving "an active and industrious world."[385] with it. He values mathematics for the practical results, hence, mathematics are "industrious".[386] Policy and industry are the essence of the new age.[387] In his *Four letters* "industry" is contrasted with poetry, Ovid is condemned as a poet who, taking too much poetical license, is obnoxious to the order of the state: "Youth is youth: & age corruptible: better a hundred Ovids were banished than the state of Augustus endangered or a sovereign empire infected... not riot but valour, not fancy but policy must strike the stroke. Gallant gentlemen, bethink yourselves of the old Roman discipline and the new Spanish industry".[388] Shakespeare seems to be poking fun at it in *Love's Labour's Lost* when he has the Spanish Don Armado close one of his letters to Jacquenetta with the phrase "Thine in the dearest design of industry". (IV.i.87). The formula is odd. The Arden editor notes that Harvey uses the word several times, but misses Harvey's "Spanish industry" and the parodying character in Shakespeare's play. The only instance he retains is Harvey's praise of Sidney as "esquire of industry".[389]

Nashe would deride the expression profusely.[390] And further, "One Ovid was too much for Rome; and one Greene too much for London: but one Nashe more intolerable than both."[391] But in "Speculum Tuscanismi", his libel on Oxford, Harvey also rubbed Greene's and Nashe's patron's nose (as will be seen) in his political credo, "Nosed like to Naso."

Thus a literary quarrel begun with a libel of Edward de Vere. In his pamphlets Nashe pours ridicule on his adversary Harvey. In the sub-plot of the play *Love's Labour's Lost* Shakespeare pokes fun at him. But not once does the name Shakespeare surface in this quarrel. It is Oxford who inhabits the centre.

Nashe's mysterious fellow-writer

An unidentified ghost frequents Harvey's pamphlet *Pierce's Supereroga-tion*. From the very beginning he sides with Nashe, alias Pierce Penni-less. He is the "old Ass" in the subtitle of *Pierce's Supererogation – A New Praise of the Old Ass*. The identity of this "old ass" has attracted little to no curiosity from literary historians, though according to Harvey this "old ass" is the dominating figure of the literary world. Why has no-one ever been eager to know who this figure was? Is it because the "old ass" has been overshadowed by the gigantic shadow of 'William Shakespeare'? But in Harvey's pamphlet William Shakespeare is a non-entity, never named, never alluded to. The old ass, on the contrary, looms large, so large that his great mantle seems worthy only of Shake-speare.

Harvey published his pamphlet in September 1593. He finished the preliminary pamphlet *A New Letter of Notables Contents*, written later but published earlier, on 16 September 1593.[392] On 21 September 1593 William Reynolds, a mentally deranged soldier, writes a letter to Lord Burghley from which it appears that by that time he had read Shake-speare's *Venus and Adonis*. "There is another boke made of Venus and Adonis wherein the queen represents the person of Venus, which queen is in great love (forsooth) with Adonis, and greatly desires to kiss him, and she woos him most entirely, teling him although she be old, yet she is lusty, fresh & moist, full of love & life (I believe a goodel more than a bushel full)... and much ado with red & white, but Adonis regarded her not, wherefore she condemns him for unkindness, those bookes are mingled with other stuff to dazzle the matter."[393] Can it be possible that in the month of September 1593 the lunatic soldier Reynolds would have read Shakespeare and that the scholar Gabriel Harvey, Edmund

Spenser's friend, would have known less than the man in the moon? In the third of his *Four Letters* written in September 1592 he mentions several authors: "Edmund Spenser, Richard Stanyhurst, Abraham Fraunce, Thomas Watson, Samuel Daniel, Thomas Nash, and the rest". Is Shakespeare simply lumped in with the nameless "rest"? Or among others who Harvey mentions in the same context: "the honorabler sons & daughters of the sweetest & divinest muses that ever sang in English or other language" whom he dares not name "for fear of suspicion of that which I abhor",[394] namely to meddle with the affairs of the nobility as he had done in 1580. In his *New Letter of Notable Contents* he names of course Nashe and Greene, and also Marlowe. In *Pierce's Supererogation*, dated 27 April 1593 (the pamphlet proper) and 16 July 1593 (the prefatory matter), but not entered in the Stationers' Register until September 1593, he mentions not only Greene, Marlowe, Nashe and Chettle but also: Thomas Deloney, Philip Stubbs, Robert Armin and 10 pages later George Gascoigne, Thomas Churchyard, Floyd, Barnabe Rich, Whetstone, Anthony Munday, Stanyhurst, Abraham Fraunce, Thomas Watson and the rather obscure Kiffin (most probably Bartholomew Griffin), William Warner, Samuel Daniel, etc.[395] It is true that he does not mention Michael Drayton, who published his sonnet cycle *Idea* and his epic poem *The Legend of Piers Gaveston* in 1593. However, the latter work cannot have been printed in September, as it was registered on 3 December 1593. *Idea* was registered on 23 April 1593, 5 days after Shakespeare's *Venus and Adonis*. In September 1593 Drayton could still be seen as a newcomer with few credentials. But Shakespeare? His *Venus and Adonis* was immediately a great success. But to Harvey the biggest figure in the world of English literature was not Shakespeare, but the "old ass". We have to wait some time to meet him again after the title-page. After a long-winded preface and a bulky load of commendatory poems the pamphlet proper starts on page 31. On page 40 the old ass is back:

> "Happy the old father, that begat, and thrice happy the sweet Muses, that suckled, and fostered young Apuleius... I go not about to discover an Ass in an Oxes hide..."

So we have an old "father" or "founder", probably the old golden ass of Apuleius, and a young ass in an Ox hide. The young ass is Nashe. Who fathered him? We will meet this ox again. We can only hope that Harvey will be less cryptic in the course of his polemic.

On page 59 the old ass is more explicitly mentioned as the companion of the young ass:

"Divers excellent men have praised the old Ass: give the young ass leave to praise himself, and to practise his minion rhetoric upon other."

Who were these divers excellent men who praised the old ass? The phrase reminds us of the "divers of worship" who we know from Chettle's apology lauded the third playwright for his "facetious grace of writing". Given the slender information it would be overrash to relate Harvey's allusion to Chettle's apology. Fortunately, Harvey will tell us more. On page 69:

"He that breedeth mountains of hope, and with much ado begetteth a molehill (shall I tell him a new tale in old English?), beginneth like a mighty Oxe, & endeth like a sory Ass."

We may understand the "new tale in old English" as the biblical new wine in the old bottles. The old tale must be about the old ass, the new tale about the young one, Thomas Nashe. Nashe would breed great hope but suffer the fate of the old ass, who began like a mighty ox but whose fortunes, apparently, had decayed. On page 79 Harvey gains in clarity:

"Marvel not, that Erasmus has penned the encomium of folly; or that so many singular learned men have laboured the commendation of the Ass: he it is, that is the godfather of writers, the superintendant of the press, the muster-maister of innumerable bands, the general of the great field: he and Nashe will confute the world... He that has christened so many notable authors; censured so many eloquent pens; enrolled so many worthy garrisons; & encamped so many noble and reverend Lords, may be bold with me. If I be an ass, I have company enough: and if I be no ass, I have favour to be enstalled in such company."

It should be clear by now that Harvey is not speaking of an imaginary figure. "Godfather of the press", "muster master", "general of the field". He certainly could be speaking of the Earl of Oxford and those known to have been his servants or followers: John Lyly, Anthony Munday, Thomas Watson, Robert Greene, Thomas Churchyard, Nashe himself. Is there anybody else who could fit the picture? Certainly not Shakespeare. And was not Melicertus, which was the pastoral name given by Chettle to Shakespeare in 1603, called by Robert Greene in his romance *Menaphon* the "general of the shepherds", or the poets? We are confronted with the same problem as in the case of Melicertus. Either the "old ass" is an important, the most important precursor of Shakespeare or he is Shakespeare himself. So it seems legitimate to continue asking questions about the old ass.

Furthermore, Harvey's report of this old ass might cause us to begin thinking about the notion of "conspiracy". Here is an important author and patron, often spoken of but never explicitly named. No conspiracy was at work, the social standards of the time were. Harvey does not grow weary of repeating that this old ass played a major role in English literature and was a close friend of Nashe, even his patron and spiritual father. Nashe is named. The old ass is never named. And has not Shakespeare been thought close to Nashe? But Nashe does not mention him. Was this Nashe's "conspiracy"???

On page 121 follows a queue of convoluted sentences the meaning of which is not easy to grasp:

"He summed all in brief, but material sum; that called *the old Ass*, the great A, and the est Amen of the *new Supererogation*. And were I here compelled to dispatch abruptly, (as I am presently called to a more commodious exercice) should I not sufficiently have discharged my task; and plentifully have commended *that famous creature*, whose praise the title of this pamphlet professes? He that would honor Alexander, may crown him the great A. of puissance: but Pyrrhus, Hannibal, Scipio, Pompey, Cæsar, divers other mighty conquerors & even some worthies would disdaine, to have him sceptered the est-Amen of Valour. What a brave and incomparable Alexander is that great A that is also the est-Amen of Supererogation."

The passage does not end here but a pause to gather breath seems welcome. The meaning is clouded in allusions which are soon dispelled, though, if we look back to Harvey's libel of Oxford, "Speculum Tuscanismi". In 1593 Harvey renews his attack against Oxford, the old ass, by attacking the young ass, Thomas Nashe. It was in "Speculum Tuscanismi" Harvey had described the earl of Oxford as "Every one A per se A, his terms, and braveries in print" and "Eyed like to Argus, eared like to Midas, nosed like to Naso,/Winged like to Mercury, fittest of a thousand to be employed,/ This, nay more than this does practice of Italy in one year. None do I name...". "A per se A" or "A per se" is the letter A standing alone, the first letter of the alphabet, meaning "incomparable" with the connotation of the beginning. The old ass is an outstanding person; "a passing singular odd man", Harvey calls him in his libel. The beginning and the end, after which there is nothing more, the "est-Amen". Yet Harvey renews his strictures of 1578 and 1580. The "old ass", too, is only "valourous" in words, not in deeds, only a "great general" in the literary world, which is why the great generals of the past would disdain him. Literary accomplishments are vain, supererogatory, if not serving a more valourous end, so Harvey's creed. And the ears of Midas, of course, were ass's ears which Apollo gave Midas when he decided a musical contest between Apollo and Pan in favour of the latter. The rest of the passage should no longer present difficulties:

"Shall I say, blessed, or peerless young Apuleius, that from the swathing bands of his infancy in print, was suckled of the sweetest nurses... and more tenderly tendered of the most delicious Muses, the most amiable Graces, and the most powerful Virtues of the said unmatchable great A., the great founder of supererogation and sole patron of such meritorious clients."

On page 261 Harvey confirms another time that the old ass and Nashe were close fellows:

"The Ox and the Ass are good fellows".

The phrase stands isolated amidst an enumeration of other beasts. But this enumeration coming from the pen of a consummate classicist like Harvey presents some peculiarities. Harvey seems to be sneaking round something he would fain express in a less veiled manner.

"Virtuous Italy in a longer term of dominion, with much ado bred two Catos, and One Regulus: but how many Sylvios, Porcios,

Brutos, Bestias, Tauros, Vitellios, Capras, Capellas, Asinios, and so
forth.
The world was never given to singularities: and no such monster, as
Excellency. He that speaketh as other use to speak, avoideth trouble:
and he that doth, as most men do, shall be least wondred at. The Ox
and the Ass are good fellows, quaint wizards..."
   We should not be deceived by Harvey's devious tactics. He feigns
speaking of politics and history, of Cato and Regulus, Brutus, Vitellius,
and Anisius. He so does, manifestly. But latently he also speaks of the
ox and the ass and of poetry. Porcius is the family name of the two Catos, porcius means pig. Vitellius ist the name of a Roman emperor,
vitellius means egg yolk, Brutus is clear enough, Capras is a family
name, capra is a goat, Asinius is a Roman family name, asinus is ass.
The ox is also present as bull, taurus. But most of the endings are
Greek. 'Os' is not a Latin but a Greek ending. Except for taurus, no approximately analogous Greek noun exists for one of the animals. Besides, the Greek did not build their family names after the names of
animals and plants as Romans did. To what other end would Harvey,
the accomplished classicist, replace the Latin ending by a Greek ending
than to insinuate that he is not really speaking of the historical figures
but of the "poetical animals", the ox and the ass? And what does Harvey mean by his warning not to try to stand out from the common lot?
He had already launched such a warning the previous year in his *Four
Letters*, interestingly by citing Ovid as the wrong example the "ass and
his fellow ox" would be following.
   Two pages later, on page 263, Harvey, finally, refers to fully identifiable events. He compares the press to a kingdom, namely the ancient
kingdom of Assyria, for the sole reason that the use of the name of this
kingdom gives him the opportunity to continue his punning on "ass".
Proud of his invention he explains the pun at considerable length. Harvey writes sonnets with footnote-sonnets and tells jokes with footnotes.
The king of Assyria or the press is Phul-Assar, that is "full ass" –
Nashe, of course. Another "noble King of Assyria" is "Lob-assar-duck",
who is clearly Henry Chettle. What Harvey means by this peculiar
name is not clear. In part II we advanced the hypothesis that Harvey

conveyed Greene's papers to the printer, and might have foisted some-thing into them before transmitting them to John Danter and Chettle; if correct, the nickname "Lob-assar-duck" for Chettle would be under-standable, as he would have made a "sitting duck" of the lob or lout Chettle. Be that as it may, Chettle is perfectly recognizable. Harvey re-fers to the passage in Chettle's tale *Kindheart's Dream* where the ghost of Robert Greene appears, urging Piers to take up his defense against Harvey's denigrations in *Four Letters*. "Pierce, more witless than penni-less; more idle than thine adversaries ill-employed; what foolish inno-cence hath made thee (infant-like) resistless to bear whatever injury Envy can impose." When Chettle wrote these lines (probably in No-vember or December 1592) he might have already been setting Nashe's reply to Harvey, *Strange News*, at John Danter's printing shop. Chettle continues, "Had not my name been *Kind-heart*, I would have sworn this has been sent to myself; for in my life I was not more penniless than at that instant. But remembering the author of the *Supplication*, I laid it aside till I had leisure to seek him." It is to these lines that Harvey re-fers: "Lob-assar-duck, another noble king of Assyria, has already of-fered fare for it, & were it not that the great Phul Assur himself had forestalled and engrossed all the commodities of Assyria... it should have gone very hard, but this redoubted Lob-assar-duck would have retailed and regrated some precious part of the said commodities and advancement."

But then Harvey also mentions a third king of the "Ass-ar" or "Ass-ur dynasty", the founder and father of Phul-Assur/Nashe. We would expect that this founder is the same as the aforesaid "godfather of the press", the "old ass" and would be called "Phul Vestustass," "full-old ass" or something similar, but Harvey writes, "Phul Assar himself, the famous son of the renowned Phul Bullochus," that is, "full bullock" or "full ox". We may definitively conclude that Nashe is the young ass, the son of the old ass, and that the old ass and the ox are one and the same father of Nashe.

Taking stock once more, we see that on the one hand it has some-times been suggested that Nashe might have had a hand in or in some way contributed to some of Shakespeare's works, especially the plays

Henry VI, Henry IV, and *Love's Labour's Lost.* A close relationship must at some time have existed between Nashe and Shakespeare. But nothing is to be learned of Shakespeare from Nashe. On the other hand, there is an author who occupies this place left vacant by Shakespeare and is called the Old Ass, alias Ox.

On page 265 Nashe is again designated as the "heir apparent of the old Ass." And on page 322 we meet Nashe and Chettle again as members of a quintet. The other members are Christopher Marlowe, Robert Greene, and Apis lapis. Nashe is accused by Harvey of having "shamefully misused every friend or acquaintance, as he has served some of his favorablest patrons (whom for certain respects I am not to name), M. Apis lapis, Greene, Marlowe, Chettle, and whom not?". But M. Apis lapis is not named either. For which "respects"? Moreover, Apis lapis is not only an author but also a patron, the patron to whom Nashe dedicated *Strange News* the year before. We have just met Chettle and Nashe as kings of the "Assyrian dynasty" or the press. Greene and Marlowe were not named there. They were dead by September 1593. So, it is logical to take the name Apis lapis chosen by Nashe as the third of Harvey's "Ass-yrian dynasty of the press", Phul Bullochus, full ox. And so Harvey authenticates the analysis of some Oxfordians[396], who have argued that Apis lapis, alias Master William, does indeed mean Master Beeston(e) but at the same time signifies "stoned bull," Apis meaning the sacred Egyptian bull and "stone" "stoned" or "castrated", hence bullock or ox. Apparently, Harvey also understood it so, naming him in one place Apis lapis, in another "Phul Bullochus".

But where is William Shakespeare? He was not absent. He **was** a party to the Harvey-Nashe quarrel. As William Shakespe[a]re on the title-page of *Love's Labour's Lost.* Shakespeare must have been intimately acquainted with Harvey and Nashe. In his second letter of *Four Letters* Harvey speaks of the "banquet of pickled herrings and Renish wine" which would have been the immediate cause of Greene's mortal illness. Harvey knows that Nashe was present at that "banquet". "Alas, even his fellow-writer, a proper young man if advised in time, that was a principal guest at that fatal banquet..."[397] The phrasing implies that there were some other guests besides Nashe. Which Nashe confirms in

Strange News. "I and one of my fellows, *Will. Monox* (hast thou never heard of him and his great dagger?) were in company with him a month before he died, at that fatal banquet of Rhenish wine and pickled herring (if thou will needs have it so)."[398] Nashe's comment suggests that the "banquet of Rhenish wine and pickled herrings" should perhaps be understood rather metaphorically.[399] In 1593 Harvey himself several times puns on the word "ox." But in September 1592, in his *Four Letters*, he dares not name this Will. Monox, he even dares not state there was a third person. So to speak, Harvey could not pronounce the word "three". Remembering that "tapster", "literature from the tavern", and "villanism" were terms which Harvey regularly applied to the kind of literature Nashe and his ilk produced, we may reread the following passage in *Love's Labour's Lost* which Alfred Harbage and others would probably place into the category of stale jokes. The passage looks indeed pale and relatively witless... until we see Don Armado as Harvey and Moth as Nashe. Moth/Nashe teases Armado/Harvey by asking to what amounts three times one and two plus one (deuce-ace). Like Harvey in his *Four letters*, Armado shies away from saying "three":

Armado. I have promised to study three years with the Duke.

Moth. You may do it in an hour, sir.

Armado. Impossible.

Moth. How many is one thrice told?

Armado. I am ill at reck´ning; it fitteth the spirit of a tapster.

Moth. You are a gentleman and a gamester, sir.

Armado. I confess both; they are both the varnish of a complete man.

Moth. Then I am sure you know how much the gross sum of deuce-ace amounts to.

Armado. It doth amount to one more than two.

Moth. Which the base vulgar do call three.

Armado. True. (I.ii.34-46)

In September 1592 Harvey could not say three. In September 1593, probably encouraged by Nashe's own pert allusions to Oxford, he feels much surer and, following Nashe's example, alludes to Oxford with a veil through which it is still possible for us to see.

Chapter III
The Dedication Of "Strange News"

Early in 1593 Thomas Nashe published *Strange News* in reply to Gabriel Harvey's *Four Letters*. Anthony Burgess's dictum about *Greene's Groatsworth of Wit*[400] (that the text "needs slow digestion"), is partly also true for *Strange News*, especially the dedication, but whereas the former text, apparently being about Shakespeare, has induced more overheated speculation than "slow digestion", the latter, apparently **not** being about Shakespeare (only about Thomas Nashe and some unidentified person nicknamed "Apis lapis" or "Maister William Beeston"), has been the object of more sober examination. To begin with, we have McKerrow's landmark edition of Nashe's complete works (1904-1910) supplemented by F.P. Wilson in 1958. Then, we have Charles Nicholl's excellent study[401], and numerous articles. Nevertheless, all of them leave us in the lurch with respect to the crucial question, the identity of Apis lapis. McKerrow notes:

"This evidently conceals the name 'Beeston', and from l. 7 we learn that the person's Christian name was William, but the only William Beeston known seems to be an actor who was alive as late as 1652 [authors' note: in fact as late as **1682**] and who is therefore out of question... From ll. 21-2 it would appear that the dedicatee was already a man of ripe age."[402]

Nicholl simply collates the elements from Nashe's dedication but has nothing noteworthy to add about the identity of Apis lapis, William Beeston, Will. Monox, or Lord Vaux of Lambeth, all mysterious names which occur in Nashe's *Strange News* and all presumably representing real persons.[403]

Another author observes that Apis lapis must have taken issue with a passage in Nashe's dedication which was cancelled from the second edition, but fails to examine this passage.[404] It seems as if any interest in the identity of an Elizabethan literary life soon slackens when Shakespeare does not seem to be involved. Yet, at the end of the previous chapter we have identified Apis lapis as Edward de Vere, Earl of Oxford, who is, according to the *Encyclopædia Britannica,* the leading candidate for the authorship of the Shakespearean canon next to Shakspere himself.

This identification rests upon an alternative interpretation of the nonce pseudonym "Apis lapis" and Gabriel Harvey's confirmation of it by using the name Apis lapis in one place and Phull Bullochus, "full ox," in another. As seen, Harvey speaks in one context of five authors: Marlowe, Greene, Chettle, Nashe, and the mysterious Apis lapis; in the other context, speaking of authors still alive, which in September 1593 excludes Greene and Marlowe, he nicknames Chettle 'Lob-assar-duck,' Nashe 'Phul Assar,' and the mysterious man not Apis lapis, but 'Phul Bullochus.' The latter is the founding father of a "literary dynasty," Nashe's "father". It is difficult to conceive of Shakspere of Stratford, born in 1564, as the spiritual father of Thomas Nashe, born in 1567. It is nearly as difficult to visualize the 28-year-old William Shakspere as William Beeston, being, as McKerrow notes, probably "a man of ripe age", which would set the mark from forty years upward. In 1592 the Earl of Oxford was 42 years old.

Nevertheless, it cannot completely be ruled out that Harvey meant two different persons by "Phull Bullochus" and "Apis lapis". Besides, it is also noteworthy that the first syllable of "Bee-stone" builds a link to the "honeycomb" or "honey-cutter", that is, Melicertus, the name given by Robert Greene to a concealed poet, taken over by Chettle for an unidentified court-poet about 1585 and, identifiably, for Shakespeare in 1603. But neither this Melicertus of 1585 nor the 'William Beeston' of 1592 has ever been identified. What can be confidently stated at this stage is that Apis lapis, alias M. William Beeston, is not Shakspere of Stratford. Despite all this, Penny McCarthy has recently claimed that Apis lapis, gentle Master William, is none other than William Shakspere of Stratford.[405]

Apis lapis, William Beeston, gentle M. William.

Nashe's dedication opens:

To the most copious carminist

> of our time, and famous persecutor of *Priscian*, his
> very friend, Master *Apis lapis*: *Thomas Nashe* wish-
> *eth new strings to his old tawny purse, and*
> *all honourable increase of acquain-*
> *tance in the cellar.*

"*Gentle M.* William, *that learned writer*, Rhenish wine & sugar, *in the first book of his comment* upon Red-noses, *hath this saying*, veterem ferendo iniuriam inuitas nouam, *which is as much in English as, one cup of nippitate pulls on another. In moist consideration whereof, as also in zealous regard of that high countenance you show unto scholars, I am bold, instead of new wine, to carouse to you a cup of news, which, if your Worship (according to your wonted* Chaucerism*) shall accept in good part, I'll be your daily orator to pray that that pure sanguine complexion of yours may never be famished with pot-luck, that you may taste till your last gasp, and live to see the confusion of both your special enemies, small beer and grammar rules.*"

But what are we to make of "Gentle M. William, that learned writer Rhenish Wine & Sugar, in the first book of his Comment upon Red Noses"? McKerrow notes: "I do not know whether anything is meant by this 'learned writer.'"[406] Penny McCarthy, however, believes that Nashe is referring to Falstaff's comments upon Bardolph's red nose in the first part of *Henry IV*, a play which according to orthodox chronology Shakespeare had still to write (1597/98):

> "And what a sentence! The combination of 'Rhenish wine & Sugar,' 'first book' and 'red noses' is highly evocative of *Henry IV*, part 1 (i.e. first book), in which Sir John Sack and Sugar (Falstaff) comments on Bardolph's red nose. I suggest the syntactical false alley is deliberate: we are meant to hear M. William as addressee. But even disallowing that supposition, the notion that Apis lapis is Shakespeare becomes more plausible within a page of text."[407]

From a rigid empirical position, this identification would have to be rejected. Falstaff is called "Jack Sack and Sugar" in *1 Henry IV* (I.ii.110), a scene from which Bardolph is absent, and Falstaff's comments in III.iii (ll. 1-49) are not only on Bardolph's red nose but, more generally, about his red face. But Nashe's text, veering between earnestness and jest, fact and encryption, is moving below the radar of strict empiricism. Sack and Rhenish wine being white wines, "William Rhenish Wine and Sugar" may be considered as a variant of "John Sack and Sugar". Then, the contempt for "small beer", a phrase also twice used by Prince Hal (II.ii.6 and 11), is evocative of Falstaff's creed in 2 *Henry IV*, IV.iii.121-4: "If I had a thousand sons, the first human principle I would teach them should be to forswear thin potations, and to addict themselves to sack." Such allusions from Nashe to Shakespeare (as in the case of Ben Jonson's early comedies) are anathema to the orthodox chronology. But it is an indisputable fact that both Nashe and Ben Jonson do refer bitwise to existing plays and other works, mainly to Shakespearean plays.

Nashe alludes to *Titus Andronicus* in *The Unfortunate Traveller* in 1594 and to *Romeo and Juliet* in *Have With You to Saffron Walden* in 1596, Ben Jonson to *Romeo and Juliet* and *Much Ado About Nothing* in *Poetaster* in 1601.[408] No problem exists for the orthodox chronology in these cases, as the publication and/or orthodox dating of these plays precede the Nashian and Jonsonian bits; but in several instances the very same kind of allusions precede the orthodox dates by many years. Thus our only option (if we insist on the orthodox dating scheme) is to chart the influence from the other direction, viewing Shakespeare as a cutter and paster of other writers' bits, gathering them together like a squirrel its nuts — truly a nutty idea of his creativity.

Correspondences between Nashe and Shakespeare

Parallels between Nashe and Shakespeare, especially the two *Henry IV* plays, have been the subject of various essays and notes. As in the majority of cases such parallels precede the dates of the orthodox chronology, the borrower, if borrowing there really is, must be Shakespeare. G. Harold Metz gives a short survey of the hunt for correspondences between Nashe's and Shakespeare's vocabulary. "Critics who believe that Shakespeare is the borrower place some reliance on similar possible borrowings from Nashe in other Shakespearean plays. York cites George C. Coffmann, who finds parallels in passages in *1 Henry IV* and

The Unfortunate Traveller concerned with Pegasus and "estriches." Schrickx notes Dover Wilson's twenty parallels in his New Cambridge edition of the same play; his own *Shakespeare's Early Contemporaries* for a "further echo" from Nashe in *2 Henry IV*; Davenport's discovery of parallels in *Hamlet* from Nashe's *Pierce Penniless*; and Frank Bradbrook's possible Shakespearean borrowings from *Christ's Tears over Jerusalem* in *Antony and Cleopatra* and *The Tempest*."[409] The strictest advocate of a unilateral axis of dependence from Nashe to Shakespeare is J.J.M. Tobin, who in a series of contributions, mostly to *Notes & Queries* between 1980 and 1992, finds Nashe's influence on Shakespeare in nearly every play.

To vindicate the all-out validity of his thesis that Shakespeare systematically borrowed from Nashe's works, Tobin has to recur to some ad hoc hypotheses. Particularly threatening to his thesis is *Two Gentlemen of Verona*, dated 1594, in which, according to Tobin, Shakespeare would have borrowed from Nashe's *Have With You to Saffron Walden*, published late in 1596. Nashe can hardly have started writing *HWYSW* before finishing *The Unfortunate Traveller*, entered in the *Stationer's Register* in September 1593 and published in 1594. Furthermore, Nashe's pamphlet mentions the death of Anthony Chute, a minor author and literary foe of Nashe's. Chute was still alive in May 1594. How could Shakespeare have borrowed in 1594 from a work which Nashe had probably not yet commenced? Tobin quickly dispenses with the chronological difficulty by postulating Shakespeare's revision of the play after 1596.

Even if one is prepared to concede this ungainly makeshift, Tobin's thesis, like so many other quests for verbal correspondences, suffers from overweight. Too many parallels are meaningless. Moreover, the underlying conception tends to substitute the zealous endeavours of the source-digger for the creative work of the author. One illustrative example is a passage in Nashe's *Have With You to Saffron-Walden* from which, according to Tobin, Shakespeare would have borrowed three times in *Two Gentlemen of Verona* [emphases ours]:

"I should have believed, if, immediately upon the **nicke** of it, I had not seene him shrug his shoulders and talke of going to *Bathe*, and after, like a true Pandar (so much the fitter to be one of *Gabriel's* Patrons), grew in commending to young gentlemen two or three of the most detested loathsome whores about *London* , for peereless beautous **paragons** & the pleasingest wenches in the world: whereby I guessed, his judgment might be infected as well as his body; & he that would not **sticke** so to extoll stale rotten lac'd mutton, will, like a true *Milanese* , suck figs out of an ass's fundament, or do anything."

The word "stick" occurs in *TGV*, I.i.101-2:

Proteus. Here's too small a pasture for such store of muttons.

Speed. If the ground be overcharg'd, you were best stick her.

The meaning is that if there is not enough pasture, the mutton should be "stabbed", "slaughtered." Shakespeare uses the word in the same sense in *As You Like It*, I.ii.242: "My father's rough and envious disposition/ Sticks me at heart" and in *Troilus and Cressida*, III.ii.195: "To stick the heart of falsehood." This is not at all the sense in which Nashe uses it. In Nashe's phrase the meaning is "not hesitate" , as in Shakespeare elsewhere, for instance in *2 Henry IV*, I.ii.22, where Falstaff says of Prince Hal: "he will not stick to say his face is a face royal."

The same applies for the word "nick". Shakespeare uses it in IV.ii.69-73 in the sense of "notch"; "out of all nick" means "without in the least calculating", "unconditionally":

Julia. I would always have one play but one thing.

But, Host, doth this Sir Proteus, that we talk on,

Often resort unto this gentlewoman?

Host. I tell you what Launce, his man, told me: he lov'd her out of

all nick.

In Nashe's use "nick" means "instantaneous". As can hardly be expected otherwise, both Nashe and Shakespeare use the word "paragon" with the same meaning:

Proteus. Enough; I read your fortune in your eye.

Was this the idol that you worship so?

Valentine. Even she; and is she not a heavenly saint?

Proteus. No; but she is an earthly paragon. (II.ii.138-142)

Shakespeare's use of the word arises out of the context, as does Nashe's use of "stick" and "nick". The idea of borrowing in either direction is meaningless. It seems possible, however, that in the case of 'paragon,' there was borrowing, but by Nashe from Shakespeare. It is not the word "paragon" by itself that nurses this suspicion, though, it is the occurrence in Nashe's passage of the phrase "lac'd mutton" together with "Milanese".

Shakespeare's play is about Proteus and Valentine, two Veronese gentlemen, travelling to the court of the emperor in Milan. The phrase "laced mutton" is part and parcel of a long punning bout on the different meanings of "mutton" between Proteus and his servant Speed in I.i.89-97:

> *Proteus*. The sheep for fodder follow the shepherd; the shepherd for
> food follows not the sheep: thou for wages followest thy master;
> thy master for wages follows not thee. Therefore, thou art a
> sheep.
> *Speed*. Such another proof will make me cry 'baa.'
> *Proteus*. But dost thou hear? Gav'st thou my letter to Julia?
> *Speed*. Ay, sir; I, a lost mutton, gave your letter to her, a lac'd
> mutton; and she, a lac'd mutton, gave me, a lost mutton, nothing
> for my labour.

It is out-of-the-way to suppose that Shakespeare would have revised the whole passage after having read the phrase "lac'd mutton" in Nashe's pamphlet. On the contrary, it is not improbable that Nashe would have had Shakespeare's play in mind and that this engendered the subsequent association with Milan. Without the reference to the play, Nashe's phrase about the "Milanese" looks out of joint with the the expression "lac'd mutton". Because this example argues the opposite direction of borrowing, Tobin prefers to omit the only example in the passage which might suggest an actual influence.

Notwithstanding the fact that Tobin's hunting for parallels between Nashe and Shakespeare overshoots the mark, a certain number of cases he submits are not so easy to dismiss. But here, too, the coherence of Nashe's text is a derivative from the *ensemble* within which they occur in Shakespeare's plays , some of which he would still have had to write if the orthodox chronology were reliable, which as a consequence, in some cases baffles any meaningful notion of creativity. McCarthy demonstrates how outlandish such assumptions to save the orthodox dates are. One of her examples is particularly illustrative. Nashe describes Harvey's voluminous pamphlet *Pierce's Supererogation* in terms reminiscent of Falstaff's vocabulary as "... an unconscionable vast gorbellied volume... far more boisterous and cumbersome than a pair of Swissers omnipotent galeaze breeches... You may believe me if you will, I was fain to lift my chamber door off the hinges, only to let it in, it was so fulsome a fat *Bonarobe* and terrible *Rouncevall*. Once I thought to have called in a cooper... and bid him hoop it about like the tree at *Gray's Inn* gate..."[410]

"The parallels in Shakespeare are manifest", McCarthy notes. In *1Henry IV*, I.ii, Falstaff uses the phrase "omnipotent villain" (l. 106), Poins speaks of Falstaff's "incomprehensible lies" (l. 181), Falstaff describes himself as "corpulent" (II.iv.416), addresses some travellers as "gorbellied knaves" (II.ii.84) and in *2 Henry IV* Justice Shallow remembers his youth at the Inns of Court when he knew where to find the bonarobes (III.ii.23) and fought with one Samson Stockfish behind Gray's Inn (III.ii.31-2).[411] But she rejects James M. Tobin's thesis that Shakespeare created the Fat Knight on the outlines of Nashe's description of a bulky pamphlet.[412]

The old and the lusty lad of the castle

When in *1 Henry IV*, I.ii.41, Prince Hal addresses Falstaff as "my old lad of the castle," he is punning on Falstaff's former name Sir John Oldcastle. Orthodox chronology ignores that the same allusion is made by Harvey in September 1592. In his *Four Letters* he utters his contempt about the "rapping bable of some old lads of the castle."[413] One year later, in his *New Letter of Notable Contents* he levels at "the long tongues of the Steelyard."[414] He surely aims at the same literary duo, Nashe and his fellow-author Apis lapis, possibly also at John Lyly.

The Steelyard was a place on the north bank of the Thames inhabited by German merchants and associated with Rhenish wine in Thomas Dekker's *Westward Ho!* and Barnaby Barnes' *The Devil's Charter*. The Steelyard is mentioned as "one of the four houses in *London* that do sell Rhenish wine."[415] The German Hanse merchants had been granted the right to delegate an alderman, who was a citizen of London, into the London Council. In his dedication to Apis lapis, Nashe jokes that Apis lapis will "be called shortly upon to be the Alderman of the Steelyard,"[416] which suggests that Nashe and Apis lapis were regular consumers of Rhenish wine there. So, Harvey's "long tongues of the Steelyard" include Apis lapis, alias "William Rhenish Wine and Sugar." In using the expression "old lads of the castle," however, Harvey more specifically refers to scene I.ii in *1 Henry IV* in which both phrases "old lad of the castle" and "John Sack and Sugar" occur.

Another reference by Harvey to the play seems probable. Harvey entreats Nashe "to keep the huge main shot of his rattling babies for buckram giants."[417] Eight instances of "buckram" are found in Shakespeare, seven of them in one single scene (II.iv) of *1 Henry IV*, where Falstaff reports his fight with the two "buckram rogues," who in the course of his tale increase their number successively to four, seven, nine and eleven. By urging Nashe to reserve his railing for buckram giants, Harvey hints at the Falstaffian character of that railing and, besides, expresses in other words the advice given in the letter *Greene's Groatsworth of Wit* to "young Juvenal" not "to inveigh against vain men."

Old and young Apuleius

Occasionally Nashe's prose comes fairly close to Falstaff's satirical comments, both in style and content. In the play *Summer's Last Will and Testament*, published in 1600 but written in 1592/3, the Roman god Bacchus, mythological inventor of the wine (his Greek name *Dionysos* means 'god of wine') reproves the personified Summer in the following terms:

"Never cup of *Nipitaty* [strong ale] in London come near thy niggardly habitation. I beseech the gods of good fellowship, thou may'st fall into a consumption with drinking small beer. Every day may'st thou eat fish, and let it stick in the mid'st of thy maw, for want of a cup of wine to swim away in... And to conclude, pine away in melancholyand sorrow, before thou hast the fourth part of a dram of my juice to cheer up thy spirits."[418]

Compare this with Falstaff's soliloquy in defiance of the Duke of Lancaster's chill rebuttal of his request to speak in his favour at Court (IV.iii.84-91):

"I would you had but the wit; 'twere better than your dukedom. Good faith, this same young sober-blooded boy doth not love me; nor a man cannot make him laugh- but that's no marvel; he drinks no wine. There's never none of these demure boys come to any proof; for thin drink doth so over-cool their blood, and making many fish-meals, that they fall into a kind of male green-sickness; and then, when they marry, they get wenches."

But who emulates whom? In one of the more elegant allegories, of which he was sometimes able, suggesting how excellent an author he could have been had he freed himself from the pressure of overcompensating for his low origin (which often caused his powers of introspection to extrovert and evaporate into the very thin air of grandiloquence), Gabriel Harvey gives us the answer: it is the "**lusty lad** of the castle" who emulates the "**old lad** of the castle"(emphases ours).

In a long invective in *Pierce's Supererogation* he calls Nashe "young Apuleius." If there was a "young Apuleius," there must have been and "old Apuleius." Harvey certainly does not mean the second-century author of the *Metamorphoses*, better known as *The Golden Ass*, but "the old father, that begat., and ... the sweet Muses, that suckled and fostered young Apuleius."[419] We have met "Nashe's father" before. Phull-Assar, Full-Ass, Nashe was, Harvey writes, the son of the famous Phull Bullochus, Full-Ox; we have met the "old ass" as the godfather of so many authors. "Old Apuleius" is most likely the selfsame person, that is, the "old ass." Harvey confirms it a few pages later, when he delineates the distinction between "young Apuleius" and "old Apuleius": "But the old ass was an infant in wit and a grammar scholar in Art: ... Unico Aretino will scourge Princes: and here is a lusty lad of the castle, that will bind bears, and ride golden asses to death."[420] "Unico Aretino", as seen, is Nashe; the "lusty lad of the castle" is also Nashe.

Nashe had tried to "bind bears" in his fable in *Pierce Penniless*, that is, to bind bears, the Earl of Leicester, to the stake, put them in the pillory, exposing him, in that he undertakes "to describe the right nature of a bloodthirsty tyrant."[421] There is no mystery in this exchange between Harvey and Nashe. It all revolves around the "old ass", "old Apuleius", though the latter epithet is not used by Harvey.

But how should we understand the phrase that Nashe, the "lusty lad of the castle," will ride "golden asses to death?" It seems as if the "golden ass" of 1593 would be the same as the one to whom Harvey vaguely alludes in 1577 in his Latin essay *Rhetor*.

"For as I look around at everyone here, I nowhere spot that "ass with a lyre," born for the stables and not the schools. Forgive me, if I declare that I do see some Apuleiuses--but why do I say some?-- rather I see one such, or even perhaps a second (I dare not add still another), who is delighted by his own peculiar style of speaking, a style I am not suggesting is asinine, but rather insufficiently Ciceronian. I name no names; I anticipate a metamorphosis. Not a change from asses into men, but from Apuleiuses into Ciceros."[422]

Apuleius' *Metamorphoses*, written in the second century A.D., is a satirical romance about a young man Lucius transformed into an ass by the charms of an earthly Venus, called Fotis. Though outwardly an ass, Lucius conserves his human intellectual faculties. The romance ends with Lucius recovering his human shape by eating the roses the goddess Isis reaches him. Nowhere in the tale is there any question of a "golden" ass. The alternate and better-known title *The Golden Ass* is most likely based on a note by Apuleius' countryman Saint Augustine some three centuries later: "sicut Apuleius in libris quos 'Asini Aurei' titulo inscripsit..."[423] The epithet "golden" does not relate to any tribulation suffered by the hero of the novel but to the literary quality of the novel. One of the meanings of the latin "aureus" is "of great excellency and beauty."[424] The alternate title "Golden Ass" is to be understood as a tribute to the outstanding literary quality of the work. Hence, Harvey does not use the epithet "golden ass" in a pejorative sense but as a synonym of literary excellence. In *Four Letters* he notes: "Even Lucian's true tales are spiced with conceit: and neither his nor Apuleius's ass is altogether an ass. It is a piece of cunning in the most fabulous legends..."[425] Nevertheless, Harvey, the rhetorician, places rhetoric above poetry in general and lyrics in particular. To him the Apuleian style is "insufficiently Ciceronian," contrary to Sir Philip Sidney, who in his *Apology for Poetry* puts poetry on the throne of rhetoric, which he demonstrates by Menenius Agrippa's famous tale of the belly and the body and Nathan's parable of the rich man who sacrifices the poor's man sole sheep (2 Samuel, 12), whence Sidney concludes that "the Poet doth draw the mind more effectually than any other art doth..."[426]

It would be interesting to know who the one poet is that Harvey recognizes in 1577 as the unique or nearly unique Apuleius. If he is the same "golden ass" Harvey in 1593 says Nashe "will ride to death", then this "Apuleius" of 1577 is the golden ass that in 1593 has become the "old ass".

In 1577 the only point of reference[427] seems to be the three Apuleius sonnets among the "Divers excellent Devises by Sundry Gentlemen" in the original edition of *A Hundreth Sundrie Flowres*.[428] Twenty-two-year-old Edward de Vere is certainly one plausible candidate for the authorship of these three sonnets. A line in Harvey's satire "Speculum Tuscanismi" in 1580 adds some more weight to the hypothesis that it was Oxford to whom Harvey referred as Apuleius in his *Rhetor* in 1577. In this satirical poem Harvey characterizes Oxford as: "*Eyed*, like to *Argus*, *Eared*, like to *Midas*, *Nosed*, like to *Naso*." The reference to the Phrygian king Midas assembles the two elements of "golden ass".

One story about Midas relates that all that he touched was changed into gold, another story that he was given asses' ears by Apollo for having decided a musical contest between Apollo and Pan in favour of the latter. It should be remembered that the epithet "golden ass" was, in fact, an epithet for poetical excellence. As early as 1577, certainly in his *Gratulationes Valdinensis* in 1578, again in "Speculum Tuscanismi" in 1580 and in *Pierce's Supererogation – A New Praise of the Old Ass*, the pedantic scholar Gabriel Harvey acknowledged Oxford's great poetical talent. Indeed, he whose name had almost become a by-word for pedantism among his contemporaries was in this respect less pedantic than some scholars today. And what of Harvey's characterization of Oxford as "nosed like to Naso," that is, Publius Naso Ovidius, whose soul, Meres was to write in 1598, lived on in "mellifluous & honey-tongued Shakespeare?" It is easy to downplay Harvey's comparison as a mockery, it is as easy to refute this belittling interpretation. Harvey's reproach of Oxford in "Speculum Tuscanismi" was not that his poetry lacked quality, on the contrary, in 1580 and repeatedly in 1592/3 he acknowledges its excellence. But he rejects the subject of Oxford's poetry as not sufficiently "valorous" or "heroical." Moreover, in 1592/3 he accuses him, Lyly, Greene and Nashe of taking too many liberties. But for a similar reason Harvey could not accept Ovid as a model of poetry: "better an hundred Ovids were banished than the state of Augustus endangered, or a sovereign empire infected."[429]

The sense of Harvey's 'prophecy' seems to be that Nashe, the "lusty lad of the castle," will exceed the Falstaffian railing of the "old golden ass" to the point of making his model look pale in comparison, of "riding the golden ass to death", possibly with an additional malicious hint of Oxford's decayed estate, to which he palpably alludes in his *Four Letters*, when he counsels Nashe to "enchant some magnificent Mæcenas"[430] and warn him of the fate of the poet-soldier Thomas Churchyard:

"I would think the Counter [the prison for debtors], M. *Churchyard*, his hostess *Penia* and such other sensible lessons, might sufficiently have taught him that Penniless is not lawless: and that a poet's or painter's license is a poor security to privilege debt or defamation."[431]

In 1592, Thomas Churchyard had been compelled to seek sanctuary against arrest for debt, because Oxford was not able to keep his promise to pay Churchyard's rent to his hostess Julia Penn.[432]

How the impossibility of linking Shakespeare to Apis lapis is "overcome".

Though not all of McCarthy's parallels may be equally convincing, some of them suffice to fully justify her refutation of Tobin's representation of Shakespeare as the borrower. "To Tobin's principle of core magnets, then, I oppose the principle of the second law of thermody-namics. How unlikely it is that from the chaos of Nashe's remarks there should emerge the solid figure of Falstaff!"[433] She therefore claims that Apis lapis, Gentle Master William Beeston, and Shakespeare are identi-cal. But her attempt to link the latter (as William of Stratford) with the former is vitiated from the very beginning and swerves out of rail to end up an amorphous heap of bizarre associations. She thus supplies her own verification of the second law of thermodynamics, which states that the decrease of entropy or disorder in one particular system will always be exceeded by an increase in the whole of the surrounding systems. McCarthy's elimination of entropy in Tobin's system is more than compensated by the entropy she herself generates by the attempt to link up Apis lapis with Shakspere. Her attempt is based on Gabriel Harvey's sneer that Nashe has "robbed William the Conqueror of his surname, and in the very first page of his Strange News chopped off the head of four Letters at a blow"[434]:

Here is an attempt at an answer: Nashe left off the first "L" of "Lapis Lapis," so that this William became apparently "Bee stone," not "Stone stone" or "Stones." And what might "Stones" imply? Nashe took as his scriptural text for his oddly off-key sermonizing *Christs Tears Over Jerusalem* (1593/4) a verse from Matthew's gospel: "Stones gather desolation." Shakespeare's tomb-stone in Stratford Church has the inscription "Bleste be ye man that spares these stones." These puzzles may find their secret rationale in a nick-name. As for "William the Conqueror," everyone knows the anecdote in John Manningham's diary about Richard Burbage's thwarted assignation with a woman, and the message that gave the identity of his rival Shakespeare: "William the Conqueror came before Richard."[435]

To McCarthy's attempt, partially based on the third line of the quatrain on Shakspere's tomb, we may oppose the first line of that quatrain: "Good frend for Iesus sake forbeare!" By "four letters" Harvey means his own pamphlet published in the form of four letters, not "four char-acters." A secret nickname is postulated and reference is made to a story which scholars have discarded as a "myth." Further, it is possible to understand "Conqueror" as but another way of expressing Nashe's "supererogation," his "overbearing" according to Harvey, as an alternative for other warrior-like metaphors, in which Harvey delights, such as "Hercules," "King Phul Assur," "doughty warrior," and so on. If "William the Conqueror" is Gentle M. William, than he is rather Harvey's "old and golden ass," Nashe's fellow-author.

McCarthy's criterion against Tobin's having Shakespeare scour Nashe for suitable morsels, sometimes fetching a phrase from Nashe's manuscript at deadline, can be turned against her own assimilation of Apis lapis to William Shakspere of Stratford: "I also propose a new axiom: *the lectio facetior* or "wittier reading." An analogue to the well-established critical principle of *lectio difficilior*,[436] a more difficult reading. But: how could Nashe have foreseen in 1592 the doggerel quatrain on Shakspere's tomb in 1616? Like a rolling stone of associations from atop the mountain of revelation, she has no eye for the surrounding landscape, the information contained in Nashe's dedication. What does it mean that Apis lapis kept three daughters in his house? Shakspere of Stratford had only two. Why would Shakspere and Gabriel Harvey have been set off as antagonists, as suggested by the matching of the three sons of John Harvey, the "honest man of Saffron-Walden," with the **three** daughters of Apis lapis? Was Shakespeare a generous patron of scholars and poets, as Nashe states? And above all, why was this passage cancelled in the dedication of the second edition?

Obviously, Apis lapis/William Beeston was not so well pleased with Nashe's pert allusions. He must have felt publicly exposed; if he had not feared recognition, there would have been no need for the ensuing cancellation and apology. Nashe's visor was judged too transparent to contemporaries. Should it be too opaque to us? And again the question: why would Shakspere of Stratford have needed a visor? Why he and not Nashe or Harvey? Was it because he was, in the words of Harvey, one of the "honorabler sons of the Muses"?[437] Was gentle Master William of gentle birth? A member of the gentry? Nashe is not at all parsimonious with clues that indeed he was.

Liberality and hospitality

Gentle M. William has been "such an infinite Mæcenas to learned men, that almost every man has "tasted of the cool streams of his liberality," even "sumners," and Nashe could also witness to his "hospitality" but that is recorded in the "Archdeacon's court." The words "hospitality" and "liberality" are absent from the second dedication; as are the words "sumner" and "Archdeacon's court". Scholars have failed to pinpoint these cancellations, which lead us in but few removes to the man. In the sixteeenth century they were, indeed, reliable identifiers, first, generally, of M. William Beeston's social rank, then, particularly, of his being exceptionally liberal and 'hospital' himself.

The pairs "liberality/hospitality" and "sumner/Archdeacons's court" tie up the second and third paragraph and need to be analyzed jointly. Unlike today, the words were not just adjectives applicable to any member of society: in the 16th and 17th centuries they were hallmarks of the aristocracy. The mere use of these words by Nashe should have induced scholars to do what they never did: to look first for Master William Beeston, gentle M. William, among the nobility.

Aristocratic society was based on honor and reputation. "A by-product of this cult of reputation was an insistence upon the aristocratic virtue of generosity... The prime test of rank was liberality, the pagan virtue of open-handedness... Memorial inscriptions upon tombs are reliable evidence of aspirations, if not of achievements, and they are almost unanimous in their harping upon the open-handedness of the deceased, both in entertainment of equals and in charitable gifts to inferiors... John Dutton of Sherborne, Glos., who survived the Restoration, was 'noted for his great hospitallitye.' Sir Henry Poole of Sapperton, Glos., did not hesitate to boast that he was 'much given to Hospitallity'..."[438] However, rather than a by-product, as Stone terms it, liberality and hospitality were constitutive elements of the aristocratic ideology; rather than a cult, it was a culture by which the aristocracy marked itself off from the other social classes, especially from the merchants. As seen in Part I, chapter I, merchants were considered to be acquisitive and profit-oriented, guided by their own selfish interest, not liberal-

and hospitality-minded, not, like the aristocracy, heedful of the overall interest of the commonwealth. Though like all ideologies this aristocratic attitude ought to be taken with a pinch of salt – the court aristocracy and the gentry too looked to their own interests but their main channels were royal grants and landed property – it was not dead letter either. It was sufficiently put into practice to shape social perception.

In France an anonymous citizen put it pithily: "Le marchand acquère, l'officier conserve, le noble dissipe." ["The merchant acquires, the officer keeps, the nobleman spends."][439] In his report of the three Frobisher expeditions 1576-1578 captain George Best complains of the merchants, "which never regard virtue without sure, certain, and present gains" and turned a deaf ear to Frobisher's request for funding; had it not been for the court, "from whence, as from the fountain of our commonwealth, all good causes have their chief increase and maintenance," the expeditions would never have materialized.[440] Incidentally, the Earl of Oxford was an enthusiastic backer of Martin Frobisher in what would have been his fourth expedition had he not resigned his command, precisely because the objective of the expedition was diverted from the exploratory to the mercantile.. "Here is no answer come from my L. of friends here, as yet I have not more need Sir Francis Walsingham, nor any of the rest but my L. of Oxford, who bears me in hand; he will buy the Edward Bonaventure."[441] The debate between an unknown member of the gentry and a merchant in the Parliament of 1597 about the enclosures hinged on the dichotomy between common wealth and private wealth, liberality/hospitality and private gain.[442] In the counsels to his son Robert, Lord Burghley advises him to keep hospitality "according to the measure of thy estate."[443]

Burghley's son-in-law, the Earl of Oxford, did not follow that rule. He was certainly liberal, which in this case means "generous in spending" and which Gabriel Harvey calls "magnificent," having more or less the same meaning as 'liberal.' Harvey writes that Oxford "in the prime of his gallantest youth... bestowed Angels upon me in Christ's College in Cambridge, and otherwise vouchsafed me many gracious favours..."[444] Like Apis lapis, Oxford displayed a "high countenance unto scholars."

The same generosity is attested Ver, the spring, in Nashe's play *Summer's Last Will and Testament*, written in 1592 or 1593 but published in 1600 (likely the year of Nashe's death). It is a play about the succession of the seasons. Spring, Autumn, Winter; Vertumnus and Sol, the Roman god of the seasons and the sun respectively, Solstitium (solstice), Bacchus, the hunter Orion and Harvest, are called to account by Summer. Of the four seasons only the spring is given its Latin name, *Ver*. 'Ver' is an alternative spelling of Oxford's family name. In Nashe's play Ver has nothing left, he has spent it all: "...what I had, I have spent on good fellows; in these sports you have seen, which are proper to the Spring, and others of like sort (as giving wenches green gowns, making garlands for fencers and tricking up children gay) have I bestowed all my flowery treasure and flower of my youth."[445] The phrase "tricking up children gay" can perhaps be understoood as an allusion to the Earl of Oxford's theatre company of children in the 1580s.[446] The passage on Ver/Spring contains allusions to the Earl of Oxford and Shakespeare alike. In the play Ver sings a song reminiscent of one written by Edward de Vere:

> Falangtado, Falangtado, to wear the black and yellow:
> Falangtado, Falangtado, my mates are gone, I'll follow.

The couplet conflates two alternating refrains in Edward de Vere's song "A crown of bays shall that man wear":

> For black and tawny will I wear,
> Which mourning colors be.

and:

> Ah a lalantida, my dear dame
> Hath thus tormented me.

As on some other occasions where Nashe mentions the Earl of Oxford or alludes to him, Shakespeare's voice can be heard in the background. Here, in Nashe's play, it is Ver's song :

> Spring, the sweet spring, is the year's pleasant King,
> Then blooms each thing, then maids dance in a ring,
> Cold does not sting, the pretty birds do sing,
> Cuckoo, jugge, jugge, pu wee, to witta woo.

which calls to mind Shakespeare's closing songs in *Love's Labour's Lost*:

SPRING
When shepherds pipe on oaten straws,
And merry larks are ploughmen's clocks;
When turtles tread, and rooks and daws,
And maidens bleach their summer smocks;
The cuckoo then on every tree
Mocks married men, for thus sings he:
'Cuckoo;
Cuckoo, cuckoo'– O word of fear,
Unpleasing to a married ear!

Here we can catch a glimpse of William Beeston, the "copious carmin-ist". McKerrow notes that A.B. Grosart took the meaning of "carminist" to be "poesy-maker and adds: "I am by no means sure that this is the sense intended, but can suggest nothing better."[447] The meaning, though, seems obvious. *Carmen* (pl. *carmina)* is the Latin word for song, but it was also used (Horace, Catull) for lyric poetry. Nashe addresses Master William as the most prolific writer of songs and poetry. This insight does not carry us far. For one thing, many song lyrics are extant, very few authors are known. "It was not in accordance with the custom of the time to print in the music-books the name of the author of the lyrics. This was not done even in the case of those poems of which we can actually identify the author; and the presumption is, therefore, that many of these charming verses were written by the great Elizabethan poets, some of them perhaps by Shakespeare himself. This probability is not inconsistent with the fact that the poems do not happen to have survived apart from the song books."[448]

Yet, some of them have survived, partly under Shakespeare's name in *The Passionate Pilgrim,* partly under Oxford's name in manuscripts, among the latter the popular "My mind to me a kingdom is", twice al-luded to by Ben Jonson.[449] Edward de Vere is known to have been a writer of song texts, about a dozen can be attributed to him. It is further known that he was a prodigious patron of scholars and poets, as is re-peated in the next paragraph. The "wonted Chaucerism" hardly needs to be insisted on, several scholars have emphasized Shakespeare's debt to Chaucer. Harold Bloom considers the Bible and Chaucer as Shake-speare's two main sources. In 1569 Edward de Vere bought a Geneva Bible, Chaucer's works and, besides, Plutarch's *Lives* in French and two Italian books.[450]

But that 'William Beeston' was a prolific poet ("copious carminist") there can surely be no doubt. Nashe writes: "Proceed to cherish thy surpassing carminical art of memory with full cups (as thou dost); let Chaucer be new scoured against the day of battle, and Terence come but in now and then with the snuff of a sentence..." Even so, Charles Nicholl in his Oxford Dictionary of National Biography entry on Nashe, opines: "Another early benefactor was William Beeston, probably a lawyer"! Why? Because of two passages which allude to law courts; but these lines contain nothing to justify the assumption that William Beeston was a lawyer. Nashe writes: "I would speak in commendation of your hospitality likewise, but that it is chronicled in the archdeacon's court" (William Beeston is said to have been "summoned to the Archdeacon's court" not as a lawyer but for a reason we will explore presently) and "I heard say, when this last term was removed to Hertford, you fell into a great study and care by yourself to what place the Steelyard should be removed." The sense here is that the law-term (according to McKerrow the Michaelmas term of 1592) was removed from Westminster to Hertford because of the plague, making 'William Beeston' fear the Steelyard might also be removed, so this remark is more about the Steelyard than the court, and it is a reference also found in Harvey. The Steelyard (in the neighbourhood of the Blackfriars), where the German Hanse resided, also had a Rhenish wine tavern, where according to Harvey, Nashe and his fellow poets would meet. In "A New Letter of Notable Contents" (Harvey, Works, ed. A.B. Grosart, I. 283), Harvey writes: "I fit thee with a Similitude for thy capacity: or belch a new Confutation against the long tongues of the *Stilliarde*, and some twenty *Tavernes in London*. Thus with clear allusions to Master William Beeston as a poet and two other statements with no clear evidence of his being a lawyer, Nicholl, flying in the face of what Nashe tells us, confidently (and inexplicably) infers that William Beeston was "probably" a lawyer.

Sumner and Archdeacon´s court

In the first edition paragraphs 2 and 3 read:

"It is not unknown to report, what a famous pottle-pot Patron you have been to old Poets in your days, & how many pounds you have spent (and, as it were, thrown into the fire) upon the dirt of wisdom, called Alchemy. *Yea, you have been such an infinite* Mecænas *to learned men, that not any that belong to them (as Sumners, and who not) but have tasted of the cool streams of your liberality.*

I would speak in commendation of your hospitality likewise, but that is chronicled in the Archdeacon´s Court, and the fruits it brought forth, as I guess, are of age to speake for themselves. Why should virtue be smothered by blind circumstance? An honest man of Saffron Walden kept three sons at the University together a long time; *and you kept three maids together in your house a long time. A charitable deed, & worthy to be registered in red letters."*

In the second edition the part between *"Yea, you have been such an infinite* Maecenas *to learned men"* and *"red letters"* was replaced by:

"Yea, you are such an infinite Mecaenas to learned men, that there is not that morsel of meat they can carve you, but you will eat for their sakes, and accept very thankfully. Think not, though under correction of your boon companionship, I am disposed to be a little pleasant, I condemn you of any immoderation either in eating or drinking, for I know your government and carriage to be every way **canonical** *[our emphasis]. Verily, verily, all poor scholars acknowledge you as their patron, providitore, and supporter, for there cannot a thread-bare cloak sooner peep forth, but you straight press it to be an outbrother of your bounty: three decayed students you kept attending upon you a long time."*

In the revised dedication Apis lapis is attested "canonical behavior". Apparently, the behavior suggested in the first dedication was not so canonical. Which is why William Beeston received the visit of a "sumner to let him taste of his liberality" and was recorded in the Archdeacon´s court in "red letters."

A "sumner" was a summoner to an ecclestiacal court. A good account of sumners and the jurisdiction of the Archdeacon´s Court is given by Geoffrey Chaucer in "The Freres Tale" (in *Canterbury Tales*):

Once on a time there dwelt in my country
An archdeacon, a man of high degree,
Who boldly executed the Church's frown
In punishment of fornication known,
And of witchcraft and of all known bawdry,
And defamation and adultery
Of church-wardens, and of fake testaments
And contracts, and the lack of sacraments,
And usury and simony also.
But unto lechers gave he greatest woe;

Chaucer's account is confirmed by a document published in *Notes & Queries*.[451] The time referred to in the document is the beginning of the 16th century. The Archdeacon's Court had not only jurisdiction over the clergy but in some matters also over the laity. Though the 16th and 17th century saw a shift of competences towards the common law courts, ecclesiastical courts still retained notable powers in behavioral matters.[452] The document notes: "The third part of our charge is concerning the life and conversation of the lay people of the parish you come from". 'Conversation' is to be understood here in its usual broad 16th-century sense of 'behavior.' The document sums up: witchcraft, usury, incest, sacrilege, adultery, fornication, testamentary fraud, tithes, unlawful marriage, swearing, etc. A large part of the competences concerned extra-matrimonial sexual relations, including bastardy.[453]

Nashe's exuberant praise of Apis lapis' liberality, which would even have extended to sumners (summoners of the Archdeacons Court), can only be meant ironically. First, it can be ruled out that Oxford, a peer, would have been summoned to this court for "lechery" or "fornication." But the term as such, especially within the context of progeniture, conjures up the idea of a bastard child. The only meaning can be that Apis lapis would have had to pay a sumner, so letting even "him taste of his liberality." In other words, for some reason or another he had to appear before the Archdeacon's court. This kind of "hospitality" is "chronicled in the Archdeacon's court" and "the fruites it brought foorth (as I guess) are of age to speake for themselves."

Nashe is alluding to an illegitimate child, now old enough to express his own wishes. In 1593, Edward Vere, Oxford's and Anne Vavasour's natural son, was about twelve years old, old enough to speak for himself.

It seems that Apis lapis/Oxford felt uneasy about Nashe's allusion to one of the most troubled periods of his life. The birth of his natural son was followed by feuds with Ann Vavasour's family, in the course of which Oxford not only fell from favor at Court but was dangerously wounded. There was another and probably even stronger reason. Certainly, Oxford had three daughters (Nashe calls them "maids"). But they were not, as Nashe writes, kept in his house for a long time but in fact, since the death of his wife Anne in 1588, were housed in the home of their grandfather Lord Burghley.

We know that Oxford regretted this alienation and was taking steps to restrengthen the paternal bond with his children. In a letter of 18 May 1591[454] he writes to Lord Burghley: "The effect hereof is I would be glad to have an equal care with your Lordship over my children, and if I may obtain this reasonable suit of her majesty, granting me nothing but what she has done to others and mean persons, and nothing but that I shall pay for it, then, those lands which are in Essex as Hedingham, Bretts and the rest whatsoever, which will come to some 5 or 600*l* by year, upon your Lordship's friendly help towards my purchases, in Denbigh, shall be presently delivered in possession to you, for their use... So shall my children be provided for, myself at length settled in quiet, and I hope your lordship contented, remaining no cause for you to think me an evil father... For to tell the truth I am weary of an unsettled life, which is the very pestilence that happens unto courtiers, that propound to themselves no end of their time, therein bestowed."

Oxford also might not have wished to become too deeply and too openly involved in the Harvey-Nashe quarrel, for Gabriel Harvey's animadversion against him was well known. Juxtaposing the three sons a honest man of Saffron-Walden (John Harvey) kept at the university of Cambridge and Oxford's three daughters, was to mark them out as the principal antagonists in the literary contention known to posterity as the Harvey-Nashe quarrel.

8. Nashe suggests that Apis lapis write or rewrite a play featuring Harvey

The next paragraphs in the dedication which should arrest our attention are 9-11 and the first part of paragraph 12. Not only does Nashe ask his patron Apis lapis to shield him from envy, which was almost a stock formula in dedications. But he also urges him to defend himself and suggests the way it could be done, namely by bringing Harvey on the stage. If Apis lapis is Shakespeare, the candidate which suggests itself for the play Nashe is alluding to is *Love's Labour's Lost*:

"*What say you, Master* Apis lapis, *will you, with your eloquence and credit, shield me from carpers? Have you any odd shreds of Latin to make this letter-monger a coxcomb of?*"

"It stands you in hand to arm yourself against him, for he speaks against conycatchers, and you are a conycatcher, as conycatching is divided into three parts: the verser, the setter, and the barnacle."

"*A* Setter *I am sure you are not, for you are no musician, nor a* Barnacle, *for you never were of the order of the Barnardines, but the* Verser *I cannot acquit you of, for M.* Vaux *of* Lambeth *brings in sore evidence of a breakfast you won of him one morning at an unlawful game called riming. What lies not in you to amend, play the doctor and defend.*"

"A fellow that I am to talk with by and by, being told that his father was a rope-maker, excused the matter after this sort: And hath never saint had reprobate to his father? They are his own words; he cannot go from them. You see here he makes a reprobate and a rope-maker, voces conuertibiles. Go to, take example by him to wash out dirt with ink, and run up to the knees in the channel if you be once wetshod."

Nashe's pamphlet *Strange News* contains at least four clues to *Love's Labour's Lost*, one in the pamphlet proper, three in the above paragraphs. First, in the last of these paragraphs Nashe harps on the word "reprobate", a word that Harvey used to excuse his low descent. Harvey wanted to be recognized as a gentleman. He liked warrior-like rhetoric. And he imitated the Petrarchan vein by inventing a gentlewoman who took up his defence against Nashe. This gentlewoman is none other than Gabriel Harvey himself. At least in his imagination could Harvey claim "gentle blood" through his spiritual union with his own creature, "the gentlewoman." In *Love's Labor's Lost* Shakespeare fulfills Harvey's wish in the personage of the Spanish Don Armado, a "gentleman and a gamester," a soldier and a rhetorician, but a "Don." However, the gentlewoman is turned into a country girl, and like the real Harvey his own descent, so does Don Armado term his love for the country girl "reprobate"(I.ii.56).

Secondly, Nashe asks whether Apis lapis has not some odd shreds of Latin to make a cockscomb of Harvey and adds that Apis lapis should defend himself. Again, if Apis lapis is Shakespeare, where or when did Harvey attack him? And where did Shakespeare counter-attack? He clearly attacked Oxford directly in 1580, and, as seen, under-cover also in 1592-3, whereas Shakespeare poked fun at Harvey– in Nashe's words "washed out dirt with ink" – with the character of Don Armado in *Love's Labour's Lost*. We are looking for Shakespeare, but it is Oxford who crosses our paths. It is noteworthy that Shakespeare's only plays with such odd shreds of Latin are *Merry Wives of Windsor* and *LLL*.

Thirdly, Nashe invites Apis lapis to use his talent and "to amend, play the doctor and defend." The phrase "to play the doctor" suggests that Nashe is thinking of a play in which some character would imper-sonate or caricaturize Harvey, the fear of which Harvey expressed in his pamphlets. The verb "defend" refers back to Nashe's calling upon Apis lapis to defend himself. "Amend" confirms what some scholars have assumed: that *Love's Labour's Lost* is, an older play which Shake-speare amended mainly by adapting the subplot to the Harvey-Nashe quarrel.[455]

Finally, within the pamphlet we obtain the information that such a play was planned, that it would be acted by Shakespeare's company the Lord Chamberlain's Men, and that Will Kempe, the company's clown, would play the part lampooning Harvey. To Harvey's expres-sion of regret of having been prevented by Greene's death from seeking remedy in law against him, Nashe replies, "What action will it bear? *Nihil pro nihilo*, none in law. What it will do upon the stage I cannot tell, for there a man may make action besides his part when he hath nothing at all to say, and if there, it is but a clownish action that it will bear, for what can be made of a rope-maker more than a clown? *Will Kempe*, I mistrust it will fall to thy lot for a merriment one of these days.[456]

"Conycatching literature" is, besides "tapster," "villainous," etc. another of Harvey's depreciatory terms for the kind of literature Nashe was writing. According to Robert Greene's description the setter is the one who first approaches the victim to extract as much information from him as possible. "At that word out flies the **setter**, and overtaking the man, begins to salute him thus: Sir, God save you, you are welcome to *London*, how doth all our good friend in the country, I hope they be all in health? The country man seeing a man so courteous he knows not, halfe in a brown study at this strange salutation, perhaps make him this answer. Sir, all our friend in the countrie are well, thankes bee to God, but truly I know you not, you must pardon me."[457] The setter then informs the verser who tries to win the "cony" over for some play at card or dices, "but if he smack the setter, and smells a rat by his clawing, and will not drink with him, then away goes the setter, and discourses to the **verser** the name of the man, the parish he dwells in..." If they have, finally, succeeded in enticing the "cony" into drinking with them and playing at cards or dice, a third man joins the company, feigning to be a stranger to the verser and setter but assisting them in cozening the victim. If the barnacle feigns to be drunken he is called **barnard**. [our emphases] But Nashe does not use the words in the meaning they had in thieves' slang. Apis lapis is not a setter because he does not compose music; he is no barnacle or barnard because he does not observe Saint Barnard's rules of asceticism. He is, however, a verser, a poet.

The "unlawful game of rhyming" is a quip at the rejection of rhyming by the classicists, foremost among them Harvey. "Lord Vaux of Lambeth" is an excellent example of how Nashe's zigzagging between fancy and fact, jest and earnestness, defies the empirist. On this name McKerrow notes: "I could learn nothing of him."[458] He is almost certainly Lord William Vaux of Harrowden (d. 1595), son of the poet Lord Thomas Vaux (d. 1556), an acquaintance of Oxford's. As a recusant he had to appear regularly before the Privy Council. Other recusants, occasionally perhaps also Lord Vaux, were summoned to Lambeth Palace, the Archbishop of Canterbury's London residence. Nashe irreverently insinuates that Lord Vaux of Harrowden, being more often at Lambeth Palace than at Harrowden, would be more properly called Vaux of Lambeth.

9. Nashe announces the printing of Love's Labour's Lost.

Who will doubt that it is *Love's Labour's Lost* which Nashe toward the end of *Have With You to Saffron-Walden* says has been printed? The passage on p. 133 bears some resemblance to scene III.i of the play, which opens with a sustained mocking gallop on the word "l'envoy." Nashe's ride on the same word can be likened to a rodeo:

"Oo yes, be it known, I can rhyme as well as the Doctor, for a sample whereof, in stead of his *Noddy Nash, whom everie swash*, and his *occasionall admonitionative Sonnet*, his *Apostrophe Sonnet*, and tiny titmouse *Lenvoy*, like a welt at the edge of a garment, his goggle-eyed *Sonnet of Gorgon* and *the wonderful year*, and another *Lenvoy* for the chape of it, his *Stanza declarative*, *Writers post-script in meeter*, his *knitting up Cloase*, and a *third Lenvoy*, like a fart after a good stool..."[459]

Nashe's *Have With You to Saffron Walden* was printed by John Danter, who was also the printer of the 1597 quarto of *Romeo and Juliet*. In 1599 a new edition of the play was published by Cuthbert Burby and printed by Thomas Creede. The title-page stated that the play was "Newly corrected, amended and augmented." In 1598 *Love's Labour's Lost* was published by the same Cuthbert Burby; the printer was William White. On the title-page, similarly, we find: "Newly corrected and augmented." Scholars have taken this as certain evidence for the existence of an earlier version of *Love's Labour's Lost* and presumed the same John Danter as printer. Nashe confirms it:

"In stead of all these (I say) here is the stuff or label of a rime or two, the trick or habit of which I got by looking on a red nose balladmaker that resorted to our printing-house."[460]

The "red-nose ballad-maker" reminds "Master William and the first book of his comments upon red noses", Shakespeare. And further:

"They are to the tune of *Labore Dolore*, or the Parlament tune of a pot of ale and nutmegs and ginger, or *Elderton's* ancient note of *meeting the devil in conjure house lane*."[461]

Again, the obvious answer to what this tune of *Labore Dolore* might be, has been drowned in a stream of speculation. McKerrow notes: "I can learn nothing of any such tunes."[462] A.E.H. Swaen's solution quoted in the supplement of 1958 to McKerrow's original edition is far-fetched and explains nothing: "He takes 'Labore' to mean the rustic dance *La Borée*, i.e. *la bourrée*,... and 'Dolore' to be on par with the *dolorosa* of, for example, 'Pavana dolorosa'."[463] But what labour is more dolorous than love's labour when lost?

Similar guesses have been made at Nashe's quatrain, nobody – as far as we know – has ever thought of the obvious, Shakespeare's quatrain on the fox, the ape and the humble bee:

The fox, the ape, and the humble bee,
Were still at odds, being but three.
Until the goose came out of door,
And stay'd the odds by adding four.

Nashe's quatrain has the same meter. "If you hit it right," Nashe writes, "it will go marvellous sweetly":

 Gabriel Harvey, fames duckling,
 hey noddie, noddie, noddie:
 Is made a gosling and a suckling,
 hey noddie, noddie, noddie"[464]

Apis lapis, gentle Master William, is Edward de Vere, Earl of Oxford. And Apis lapis, gentle Master William is, Penny McCarthy maintains, William Shakespeare. And Nashe still has more to say about it.

Chapter IV
Thomas Nashe's Testimony: A Certain Knight

"Save for a **passing** [authors' emphasis] reference to a certain knight whom we cannot identify, but who may possibly be Sir Fulke Greville, as 'our Patron', we have no evidence that Nashe was at this time or later in receipt of any assistance from the great, and no knowledge at all how he was living."[465] But Nashe's patron was perhaps no knight. Nashe might just have chosen the title "knight" to insert some misdirection, sufficient to camouflage the identity of the person of whom he was speaking, but insufficient for genuine concealment. McKerrow himself concedes this possibility in the context of the authorship of the anonymous anti-Marprelate tracts. "It may be argued that if the writers of the pamphlets wished to conceal their identity, any apparent indications of authorship which they contain may, with the exception of such involuntary ones as are inherent in the style itself, be mere **blinds** inserted with the deliberate intention of misleading **a too curious inquirer**... [authors' emphases] So when he apparently identifies himself with Oxford, it may be to prevent readers from searching for him among Cambridge men... It may be so: the objection is in a sense unanswerable."[466]

To speak of the Earl of Oxford as a "knight" would be to cast only a thin veil over his identity. Did not Puttenham in *The Arte of English Poesie* call the Earl of Oxford "that noble Gentleman"? "Gentleman" was not used exclusively to designate a position between yeoman and esquire in the nomenclature of titles, which was, it should be remembered, not the only criterion of social status. Behavior was another major factor in the attribution of social rank. 'Gentleman' also denoted a man of refined culture, of "honest" behavior, of "civil conversation." In a similar way, a knight was one obliged to uphold the chivalric ideal. Philip Sidney, for example, was without doubt a "knight" in 1578, the year to which Nashe refers, though not in a technical sense already knighted; in this sense Oxford, though an earl, was a knight in 1578. And for that matter, in January 1581 Sidney and Oxford were jousting side by side as the Blue Knight and the Knight of the Tree of the Sun respectively (see Appendix III).

McKerrow did not prove himself "a too curious inquirer" and was "blinded" to such a degree as to call Nashe's reference "passing" and to contemplate the possibility that Fulke Greville would have patronized Nashe; Fulke Greville who, though a courtier, was neither a knight in 1578 nor possibly even in 1596, the year Nashe was writing. Again, it is not the fact that Greville was not a knight which invalidates McKerrow's timidly advanced hypothesis. It is not even that Greville was a professed enemy of the public stage and has a very poor record as patron of literary works. McKerrow's timid hypothesis is uniquely based on Greville's friendship with Sidney. For the same reason he could also have suggested Sir Edward Dyer. But what ultimately eliminates both Greville and Dyer is the context clearly established by Nashe's report. The knight had, Nashe writes, enjoyed royal favor in his youth and had lost it. Greville was not in disgrace, Dyer possibly was by 1596. But the knight of whom Nashe is speaking is also said to have "repurified Poetry from Art's pedantism," which echoes the praise bestowed in the dedication of *Strange News* to Apis lapis, alias Master William Beeston: "However I write merrily, I love and admire thy pleasant witty humour, which no care or cross can make conversable. Still be constant to thy content, love poetry, hate pedantism."

Still stronger evidence exists that the knight Nashe means is Edward de Vere, Earl of Oxford. Indeed, irrefutable evidence. On pages 75-77 of *Have With You to Saffron Walden,* Nashe comments on Gabriel Harvey's behavior during the Queen's visit to Audley End in July 1578. This is the context McKerrow failed to examine. At Audley End Harvey addressed Latin orations to the Queen, Lord Burghley, the Earl of Leicester; speeches he published as books I, II and III of his *Gratulationes Valdinenses* soon afterwards. Book IV contains his other speeches on the same occasion, to the Earl of Oxford, Sir Christopher Hatton and Philip Sidney. Nashe's "passing" remark unequivocally refers to Harvey's orations on that occasion. He reproaches Harvey for having given but little praise to the great leaders of the realm: the Queen, Lord Burghley, the Earl of Leicester and, probably Sir Christopher Hatton; and to have taken a somewhat condescending attitude toward Sidney and his "companion":

> "Ceremonies of reverence to the greatest States (as it were not the fashion of his country) he was very parsimonious and niggardly of, & would make no bones to take the wall of *Sir Philip Sidney* and another honourable Knight (his companion) about Court yet attending..."[467]

This knight had been in favor at court and Nashe wishes him to recover it. This knight was still alive. In 1596 Sidney, Leicester and Hatton were dead; Burghley had not lost the queen's favor and could hardly be described as Sidney's companion. The only candidate left is the Earl of Oxford. True, Harvey lauded Oxford and Sidney as highly talented poets and most promising courtiers. But Harvey never could slough off his patronizing hide. In a sequel to his eulogy on Sidney, he somewhat insolently proclaims himself the fourth in a line of preceptors of courtly manners: Castiglione (*Book of the Courtier*), Giovanni della Casa (*Galateo*), Stefano Guazzo (*La Civil Conversatione*), and Harvey (he possibly meant his *Gratulationes Valdinenses*). He urges Oxford "to throw away the pen" and to take to a more active life. Thus Nashe tells us that Harvey took "the wall of" Sidney and Oxford in this behavior at Audley End, meaning that even as he honoured them he nonetheless attempted to place himself in a superior position.

A "passing reference", McKerrow notes. Passing?? Would we not have expected Nashe, who must have known and admired Shakespeare but never names him — have we nothing to wonder at here? — would we not have expected Nashe to refer to **Shakespeare** as "our first Orpheus" and "the quintessence of invention?" Yet it is in these terms Nashe eulogizes another, the Earl of Oxford. And it is not the praise of an obsequious dedication to a socially superior patron, but another greeting, rather stealthily whispered, devotely offered during a pious rest along the road of a sneering and jeering report about his pedantic adversary Gabriel Harvey; exempt from the gaudy ornaments and windy clamour of a public laudation, free of fulsome stereotypes, a salute, an exhortation, an incantation that this "knight" might become owner of his own invention.

Here is Nashe's prayer, which is also a prayer for our intellectual salvation, our redemption from buzzing maybe's and must-be's, for the conversion of ululating self-complacency into silent piety, in this our time a prayer for a miracle; one we hope is still within the compass of human cognition and volition, and a triumph Time should no longer stave off, to steer clear of pedantism:

"… to take the wall of *Sir Philip Sidney* and another honourable Knight (his companion) about Court yet attending; to whom I wish no better fortune than the forelocks of Fortune he had hold of in his youth, & no higher fame than he hath purchased himself by his pen; being the first (in our language) I have encountered, that repurified Poetry from Art's pedantism, & that instructed it to speak courtly. Our Patron, our *Phœbus*, our first *Orpheus* or quintessence of invention he is; wherefore, either let us jointly invent some worthy subject to eternize him, or let war call back barbarism from the *Danes*, *Picts*, and *Saxons*, to suppress our frolick spirits, and the least spark of more elevated sense amongst us finally be quenched and die, ere we can set up brazen pillars for our names and sciences, to preserve them from the deluge of ignorance."[468]

Appendix III
Speech Spoken At The Tryumph
Before The Queen´s Most Excellent Majestie,
By The Page To The Right Noble Champion,
The Earl Of Oxenford.

BY THE TILT *stood a statelie Tent of Orange tawny Taffeta, curiously embroydered with Silver, & pendants on the Pinnacles very slightly to behold. From forth this Tent came the noble Earl of Oxenford in rich gilt Armour, and sat down under a great high Bay-tree, the whole stock, branches and leaves whereof were all gilded over, that nothing but Gold could be discerned. By the Tree stood twelve tilting staves, all which likewise were gilded clean over. After a solemn sound of most sweet Musique, he mounted on his Courser, verie richly caparisoned, when his page ascending the stairs where her Highness stood in the window, delivered to her by speech this Oration following.*

THIS KNIGHT (most fair and fortunate Princess) living of a long time in a Grove, where every graft being green, he thought every root to be precious, found at the last as great diversity of troubles as of Trees: the Oak to be so stubborn that nothing could cause it to bend: the Reed so shaking, that every blast made it to bow; the Juniper sweet, but too low for succour; the Cypress fair, but without fruit; the Walnut tree to be as unwholesome to lie under, as the bud of the Fig-tree unpleasant to taste; the Tree that bore the best fruit, to be fullest of Caterpillars, and all to be infected with worms; the Ash for Ravens to breed; the Elm to build: the Elder to be full of pith and no perfection, and all Trees that were not fertile, to be fit for fuel, and they that were fruitful, but for the time to please the fancy. Which trying, he forsook the wood, and lived a while in the plain Champion: where, how he was tormented, it were too long to tell, but let this suffice, that he was troubled, when every Moat fell in his eye in the day, and every Ant disquieted him in the night: where, if the wind blew, he had nothing to shield him but head and shoulders, if the Sun blazed, he could find the shadow of nothing but himself, when seeing himself so destitute of help, he became desperate of hope.

Thus wandering a weary way, he espied at the last a Tree so beauti-ful, that his eyes were dazzled with the brightness, which as he was going unto, he met by good fortune a Pilgrim or Hermit, he knew not well, who being apparelled as though he were to travel into all Coun-tries, but so aged as though he were to live continually in a Cave. Of this old Sire he demanded what Tree it was, who taking this Knight by the hand, began in these words both to utter the name and nature of the Tree.

This Tree fair Knight is called the Tree of the Sun, whose nature is always to stand alone, not suffering a companion, being it self without comparison: of which kind, there are no more in the earth than Suns in the Element. The world can hold but one Phoenix, one Alexander, one Sun-Tree, in top contrarie to all Trees: it is strongest, & so statelie to behold, that the more other shrubs shrink for duty, the higher it exal-teth it self in Majestie.

For as the clear beams of the Sun, cause all the stars to lose their light, so the brightness of this golden Tree, eclipseth the commendation of all other Plants. The leaves of pure Gold, the bark no worse, the buds pearls, the body Chrisocolla, the Sap Nectar, the root so noble as it springeth from two Turkeies (Turquoises), both so perfect, as neither can stain the other, each contending once for superiority, and now both constrained to be equals. Vestas birth sitteth in the midst, whereat Cu-pid is ever drawing, but dares not shoot, being amazed at the princely and perfect Majesty.

The shadows hath as strange properties as contrarieties, cooling those that be hot with a temperate calm, and heating those that be cold with a moderate warmth, not unlike that Sun whereof it taketh the name, which melteth Wax, and hardeneth Clay, or pure fire, which causeth the gold to shine, and the straw to smother, or sweet perfumes, which feedeth the Bee, and killeth the Beetle.

No poison commeth near it, nor any vermin that hath a sting. Who so goeth about to lop it, lanceth himself, and the Sun will not shine on that creature that casteth a false eye on that Tree, no wind can so much as wag a leaf, it springeth in spite of Autumnus and continueth all the year as it were Ver.

If, Sir Knight you demand what fruit it beareth, I answer, such, as the elder it is, the younger it seemeth, always ripe, yet ever green. Virtue, Sir Knight, more nourishing to honest thoughts, than the beauty delightful to amorous eyes; where the Graces are as thick in virtue, as the Grapes are on the Vine.

This fruit fatteneth, but never feeds, wherewith this Tree is so loaden, as you cannot touch that place which virtue hath not tempered. If you enquire whether any grafts may be gotten, it were as much as to crave slips of the Sun, or a Mould to cast a new Moon. To conclude, such a Tree as it is, as he hath longest known it, can sooner marvel at it than describe it, for the further he wadeth in the praise, the shorter he cometh of the perfection...

http://www.sourcetext.com/sourcebook/library/barrell/21-40/35showman.htm

Appendix IV
Table Of Roberts' Printings
Set up From Arber Vol. v. pp. 25-213

Year	Publisher	Author	Work
1593	Ling & Busby	Michael Drayton	Piers Gaveston
	Andrew Wise	Thomas Nash	Christ's tears over Jerusalem
1594	-	Henry Constable	1. Diana (Sonnets)
			2. Quatorzains
	N. Ling	Michael Drayton	Idea's Mirror
	Ling & Busby	Michael Drayton	Matilda
	Ling & Busby	Robert Garnier	Cornelia
			(Translated by Thoms Kyd)
	Hardy	George Gifford	A Treatise of True Fortitude
	Andrew Wise	Thomas Nashe	Christ's Tears over Jerusalem (reissue)
	Waterson	Samuel Daniel	Delia and Rosamond (augmented)
1595	-	George Chapman	1. Ovid's Banquet of Sense
			2. A Coronet of Mistress Philosophy
			3. Phillis and Flora
		Walter Map.	(Transl. Chapman)
	-	Samuel Daniel	1. Delia and Rosamond (augmented)
			2. Cleopatra
	John Busby	Michael Drayton	Endymion and Phoebe
	Roberts	Gervase Markham	Tragedy of Richard Grenville
		Andrew Maunsell	The Catalogue of English Printed Books, Part II. The Sciences Mathematical, Physic and Surgery
	G. Cawood	Robert Southwell	St Peter's Complaint. With other Poems
1596	Ling	Sir John Davies	Orchestra or a Poem of Dancing
	Ling	Michael Drayton	Mortimeriados
	Ling	Michael Drayton	1. Robert Duke of Normandy
			2. Matilda (corrected)
			3. Piers Gaveston (correct.)
	M. Lownes	Gervase Markham	The Poem of Poems

Year	Publisher	Author	Title
1597	Ling	Nicholas Breton	Wit's Trenchmour in a Conference had betwixt a Scholar and an Angler
	N. Ling	John Bodenham	Politeupheuia. Wit's Commonwealth
	Ling	Michael Drayton	England's Heroical Epistles
	Millington	Madame Geneviève	Virtue's Tears for the Loss of Henry III; and of Walter Devereux slain before Rouen
	H. Lownes	Petau Maulette	(Translation: Gervase Markham)
		-	1. Of Love's Complaints 2. The Legend of Orpheus and Eurydice
	Blackman	Antoine Guérin	A tragical Discourse of two lovers. Affrican and Mensola (Transl. by John Goubourne)
1598	Ling	Evrard Guilpin	Skialetheia or a Shadow of Truth, and certain Epigrams and Satires
	Ling & Flasket	Luis de Granada	The Sinner's Guide (Book I) (translated by Francis Meres)
	E. Mattes	W. K. Kinsayder (pseud. of John Marston)	The Metamorphoses of Pygmalion's Image; and certain Satires
	John Busby	W. K. Kinsayder (pseud. of John Marston)	The Scourge of Villany. Three bookes of Satires.
		Andrew Maunsell	The Catalogue of English Printed Books, Part II. The Sciences Mathematical, Physic and Surgery
	G. Cawood	Robert Southwell	St Peter's Complaint. With other Poems
1599	-	Henri Estienne	A World of Wonders (transl. R. C.)
	Ling	Nicholas Ling	Wit's Theatre of the little World
	-	Gervase Markham	How to choose Horses
	Roberts	W.K. Kinsayder (pseud. of John Marston)	The Scourge of Villany. Satires (2nd Ed.)
	Roberts	Nicholas Breton	The History of Don Frederigo di Terra Nova (a Novel)
	Edward White	-	The lamentable Tragedy of Master Arden of Faversham

1600	Flasket	-	England's Helicon (collected and Ed. by John Bodenham)
	Hayes	William Shakespeare	The Merchant of Venice
	-	William Shakespeare	The Merchant of Venice (2nd Ed.)
	-	William Shakespeare	A Midsummer Night's Dream
	Edward White	William Shakespeare	Titus Andronicus
1601			
1602			
1603	Roberts	Samuel Harsnett	A Declaration of the Popish Impostures, practised by Edmunds alias William Weston, and divers Romish Priests
1604	N. Ling	William Shakespeare	Hamlet

Endnotes

1   Rabb, Theodore K. *Enterprise & Empire, Merchant and Gentry Investment in the Expansion of England, 1575-1630.* Cambridge, MA: Harvard University Press, 1967, p. 35.

2   *Ibid.*, pp. 37-8

3   From Greg, W.W., *A Companion to Arber,* Oxford: At the Clarendon Press, Oxford, 1967, pp. 144-5.

4   Quoted from Magendie, Maurice. *La Politesse Mondaine et les théories de l'honnêteté. En France au XVIE siècle, de 1600 à 1660.* Geneva: Slatkine Reprint, 1970 (original edition of 1925), pp. 60-1.

5   Pelorson, Jean-Marc, *Les Letrados – juristes castillans sous Philippe III. Recherches sur leur place dans la société, la culture et l'état.* Poitiers, 1980, p. 208.

6   Hexter, H.J. "The Education of the Aristocracy in the Renaissance" in *The Journal of Modern History,* Vol. XXII, March 1950, Number 1, p. 2.

7   *Ibid.*, p.8, n.16. Hexter refers to Oliver Cromwell, *Writings and speeches,* ed. W. C. Abbott, Cambridge, Mass., 1937-47, I, 27-8.

8   Ascham, Roger. *The Scholemaster.* Menston (Yorkshire): Scolar Press. Facsimile of the original edition of 1570, p. 14a.

9   Elias, Norbert. *The Court Society.* Oxford: Blackwell Publishers, reprint of 2000; and *The Civilizing Process,* Oxford: B. Blackwell, 1983.

10 Ben Jonson, *Poetaster.* Edited by Tom Cain. The Revels Plays. Manchester University Press, 1995

11 *Ibid.*, p. 4.

12 For instance Max Weber. *Economy and Society.* Edited by Guenther Roth and Claus Wittich. New York: Bedminister Press, 1968, *passim.*

13 Aylmer, G.E. *The King´s Servants – The Civil Service of Charles I 1625-1642.* London and Boston: Routledge & Kegan Paul, revised edition 1974 (original edition 1961), p. 162.

14 Burke, Peter. *The Fortunes of the Courtier. The European Reception of Castiglione´s Cortegiano.* Cambridge: Polity Press in association with Blackwell Publishers Ltd. 1995, pp. 39-40.

15 *Ibid.*, p. 31.

16 Castiglione, Baldesar. *The Book of the Courtier.* Translated and with an introduction by George Bull. Penguin Classics. London: Penguin Books Ltd. 1967, Book IV, p. 284.

17 La Bruyère. *Les Caractères.* Paris. Classiques Français, 1993 (first edition 1688), p. 214.

18 Castiglione, *Book of Courtier,* p. 70.

19 Burke, *The Fortunes*, p. 32.

20 Mariscal, George, *Contradictory subjects: Quevedo, Cervantes, and seventeenth-century Spanish culture.* Ithaca: Cornell University Press, 1999, p.101.

21 Pedraza, Felipe B. y Rodríguez, Milagros, *Manuel de literatura española*, II. Renacimiento, Navarra: CÉNLIS, Edíciones, S.L., 1980, p. 534.

22 *The Poems of Edmund Waller.* Edited by G. Thorn Drury. London: Larence & Bullen, 1893.

23 Rees, Joan. Fulke Greville, Lord Brooke, 1554-1628 – A Critical Biography. London: Routledge & Kegan Paul. 1971, p. x. "There was until recently, when they were acquired by the British Museum, a collection of bound volumes of his works at Warwick Castle consisting of scribal copies with corrections in Greville's own hand. It appears that Greville kept his works by him and added to them and revised them over a period of years, perhaps right up to the time of his death, but we do not know when the Warwick transcripts were made nor at what dates Greville made his corrections. Every work, consequently, is composed of a number of strata and it is impossible now to recognize and date these."

24 Sir Philip Sidney. "An Apology for Poetry" in Gregory Smith. *Elizabethan Critical Essays.* 2 vol. London: Oxford University Press, vol. I, p. 194.

25 *The Arte of English Poesie*, by George Puttenham. Edited by Gladys Doidge Willcock and Alice Walker. Cambridge: At the University Press, 1936, p. 61.

26 Honigmann, E.A.J. and Brock, Susan (eds.). *Playhouse Wills 1558-1642.* Manchester and New York: Manchester University Press, 1993, p. 74.

27 Chambers, E.K., *William Shakespeare – A Study of Fact and Problems.* 2 vols. Oxford: At the Clarendon Press, 1930, Vol. II. 91.

28 *Ibid.*, II.118-27.

29 *Ibid.*, II.114-6.

30 *Ibid.*, II.107.

31 *Ibid.*, II.101.

32 *Ibid.*, II.87-90.

33 *Ibid.*, I.341.

34 Arber, E., Transcript *of the Registers of the Company of Stationers, 1554-1640.* Edited by E. Arber. 5 vols., London 1875-94, vol. I.xli

35 Pollard, A.W. "Authors, Players, and Pirates in Shakespeare's Day" in *Shakespeare's Fight with the Pirates and the Problems of the Transmission of his Text.* Cambridge: Cambridge University Press. 1967 (1st edition 1920), pp. 26-52

36 Blayney, Peter W.M. "The Publication of Playbooks" in Cox, John D. and Kastan, David Scott (ed.) *A New History of Early English Drama.* New York:

Columbia University Press, 1997, p.386.

37 See Patterson, Lyman Ray. *Copyright in Historical Perspective*, Nashville: Vanderbilt University Press, 1968.

38 See Part II.

39 Greg, Walter W. *Some Aspects and Problems of London Publishing between 1550 and 1650.*, Oxford: At the Clarendon Press, 1956, p. 115

40 The Arden *Hamlet*, Edited by Harold Jenkins, 1982, p. 15. "The books which he entered on the Stationers' Register include just five plays; all were entered during the period 1598-1603, all belonged to the Lord Chamberlain's Company, and four of the five were registered with the stipulation that they were not to be printed till further authority had been obtained. The exception in the case of Hamlet may be more apparent than real; for although there was no express proviso, Roberts did defer printing." Again, *Hamlet* was neither a real nor an apparent exception. *Hamlet* needed no "further authority" because it had already acquired it when registered.

41 Chambers, *Shakespeare*, I.146.

42 Pollard, A.W. "Authors", p. 44.

43 Sisson C.J. "The Laws of Elizabethan Copyright: the Stationers' View", *The Library*, Vol. XV, 5th series, 1960, pp. 19-20.

44 Blayney, p.383.

45 *Ibid.*, p. 387.

46 Arber III.222.

47 Arber II.514.

48 Arber III.37.

49 Arber III.207 and 223.

50 Arber III.60.

51 Arber III.175.

52 Arber III.168.

53 Blayney's intuition that the wardens, on notice by Roberts, expected more plays of the Chamberlain's Men to be registered in the ensuing period, is difficult to verify but could one day prove correct. However, it would only apply to plays registered by James Roberts, not by other stationers. The plays were prenoted for checking of entries to Roberts.

54 Arber III.204.

55 Arber III.146.

56 Greg, *Some Aspects and Problems*, pp. 120-1

57 Only one other work was printed by Roberts, Samuel Harsnett's *A Declaration of the Popish Impostures, practised by Edmunds alias William Weston, and divers Romish Priests.* Even this work shows a certain relationship with a

play of Shakespeare, namely *King Lear*, with which it shares a description of the exorcizing of devils. But it may be merely a coincidence that James Roberts also printed this.

58 Greg, *Some Aspects and Problems*, pp. 71-2.

59 Chambers. *Shakespeare*, I.146.

60 Kirschbaum, Leo. *Shakespeare and the Stationers*. Columbus: The Ohio State University Press, 1955, p. 205.

61 Greg. *Some Aspects and Problems*, p. 44.

62 The so-called *Court Books B* and *C*. *Records of the Court of the Stationers' Company 1576 to 1602 ~ from Register B*. Edited by W.W. Greg & E. Boswell. London: The Bibliographical Society, 1930, and *Records of the Court of the Stationers' Company 1576 to 1602 ~ from Register C*. Edited by William A. Jackson. London: The Bibliographical Society, 1957.

63 Chambers, *The Elizabethan Stage*. 4 vol. Oxford: Clarendon Press. 1923. III.188.

64 *Ibid.*, p. 60. Kirschbaum adds another case in March 1597.

65 Greg, *Some Aspects and Problems*, p. 109.

66 Arber III.478.

67 Arber II. 568 and 569.

68 Arber II. 564.

69 Arber IV.59.

70 Greg. *Some Aspects and Problems*, p. 107.

71 Arber II.43.

72 *Court Book B*, p. 25.

73 Holdsworth, W. S. *A History of English Law*, 17 vol., London: Methuen. 1924. Vol. VI, p. 365

74 Arber I.111.

75 Patterson, p. 90.

76 Arber II.16.

77 *Court Book B*, p.3.

78 *Ibid.*, p. 4.

79 Arber III.334.

80 *Court Book B*, p. 42.

81 *Ibid.*, p. 44.

82 *Ibid.*, p. 45.

83 *Ibid.*, p. 51.

84 *Court Book C*, p. 8.

85 *Hamlet*. The Arden Shakespeare (ed.) Harold Jenkins. London: Routledge, 1982 (reprinted 1990), pp. 15-17.

86   The case of Bacon's *Essays* in 1597, see Arber II.78 and II.79. Other cases
     Arber IV.209 (the author Downam against William Bladon), also see *Re-
     cords of the Court of the Stationers' Company 1602 to 1640.* (Court Book C). p.
     70: the author John Hayward against the stationers William Stansby and
     Ambrose Garbrand and p. 191: the author Thomas Farnaby against the
     stationers Ralph Roundwait and Christopher Meredith.
87   *CSP, Domestic Series, of the reign of Edward VI, Mary, Elizabeth.* Ed. by Robert
     Lemon. First published London 1856-1872. Kraus Reprint, Nendeln, Liech-
     tenstein, 1967.
88   Looney, John Thomas. *Shakespeare Identified*, Vol. II, edited by Ruth Loyd
     Miller. Port Washington, NY: Kennikat Press Corp., 1975, pp. 106-121.
89   Baldwin, J. F. *The King's Council in England during the Middle Ages.* Oxford:
     At The Clarendon Press, 1969 (1st edition 1913), p. 191.
90   Virgoe, R. "The Composition of the King's Council, 1437-1461" in *Bulletin
     of the Institute of Historical Research*, Vol. XLIII, 1970.p. 145.
91   Starkey, David (ed.). *The English Court: from the Wars of the Roses to the Civil
     War*. London: Longman Group UK Limited. 1987, p. 115.
92   *The Letters of John Chamberlain*. Edited by Norman Egbert McClure. 2 vol.
     Philadelphia: The American Philosophical Society. 1939. Vol. II, p. 18
93   *Ibid.*, Vol. I, p. 619.
94   Taylor, Gary. *Reinventing Shakespeare*. London: The Hogarth Press. 1990, p.
     380.
95   Meres, Francis. *Palladis Tamia. Wits Treasury.* Printed by P. Short for
     Cuthbert Burbie. 1598. Facsimile Reprint of the Church copy in the Henry
     E. Huntington Library. Introduction by Don C. Allen, p. vii.
96   Entry on Meres by Dr. David Kathman, *Oxford Dictionary of National Biogra-
     phy.*
97   Bentley, Gerald Eades. "John Cotgrave's *English Treasury of Wit and Lan-
     guage* and the Elizabethan Drama" in *Studies in Philology*, Vol. XL, 1943, p.
     186.
98   Smith, G. Gregory. *Elizabethan Critical Essays.*, vol. I, p. xiii and p. xxi.
99   Webbe, William. "A Discourse of English Poetry" in Gregory Smith, *Critical
     Essays*, Vol. I, p. 231.
100 Allen, Don C. "The classical scholarship of Francis Meres" in *PMLA*, Vo.
     XLVIII, March 1933, Number 1, pp. 418-425.
101 accessed on the Web under bibserv21.bib.uni-mannheim.de
102 Allen, "The Classical Scholarship of Francis Meres", p. 425.
103 *Ibid.*
104 *Ibid.*

105 The booklist of the stationer Christopher Hunt seems to indicate that the title was known. But so little is further known about this list that it seems premature to consider it definitive evidence for the existence of such a title.

106 Powell, Enoch. *Francis Meres and the Authorship Question.* A paper delivered to the de Vere Society, Oxford, on the twenty-fifth of February 1988 by the Rt. Hon. J. Enoch Powell (unpublished manuscript).

107 Hieatt, Kent A. *Short Time's Endless Monument,* Columbia: Columbia University Press, 1960, p. 6.

108 Fowler, Alistair. **Spenser and the Number of Time**, London, 1964, p. 179.

109 *Ibid.*, pp.179-180.

110 Clearly unaware that, as Stefano Guazzo writes, "civil" does not appertain to the "city" and would not be contemporaneously understood as pertaining to 'city,' Lukas Erne argued that the phrase "the quality he professes" referred to Peele as a "city poet," and stated that this was "a reading which may be given greater weight by Greene's preceding adjective, 'civill.'" Cited by Brian Vickers in *Shakespeare, Co-Author: a historical study of five collaborative plays.* Oxford: Oxford University Press, 2004, p. 141, from Lukas Erne, 'Biography and Mythography: Rereading Chettle's Alleged Apology to Shakespeare,' ES 79 (1998): 438. Compounding the inaccuracy, it is to be noted that the word 'civill' does not occur in the letter in *Groatsworth*, nor is it, strictly spoken, Chettle's "preceding adjective," but his "succeeding predicate" in the introduction to *Kindheart's Dream.* Chettle says "he has seen his demeanor no less civill." It is surprisng that Prof. Vickers would not have commented upon Erne's error.

111 Chambers, E.K.: *Shakespeare* Vol. I, pp. 58-59.

112 Carroll, D. Allen: "Reading the 1592 *Groatsworth* attack on Shakespeare" in *Tennessee Law Review*, Vol. 72, Fall 2004, pp. 292-3.

113 Heywood, Thomas: *An Apology for Actors,* New York: Garland Publ., 1973. "And this is the action behoovefull in any that professe this quality." (p. 29). "... the King of Denmarke... entertained into his service a company of English actors... the Duke of Brunswicke and the Landgrave of Hessen retaine in their courts certaine of ours of the same quality." (p. 40). "I hope there is no man of so unsensible a spirit, that can inveigh against the true and direct use of this quality." (p. 50)

114 Carroll. "Reading the 1592 *Groatsworth* attack", p. 293.

115 *Ibid.*

116 Nashe, Thomas: *Works*, ed. R. B. McKerrow and F. P. Wilson, 5 vols. Oxford: Basil Blackwell, 1958, vol. I, p. 154).

117 *The Works of Gabriel Harvey*, ed. A.B.Grosart, 1884-5, 3 vols., New York:

AMS Press, 1966, vol. 2, p. 75.

118 *Ibid.*

119 Blagden, Cyprian: *The Stationers' Company – A History, 1403-1959.* London: Allen & Unwin, 1960, p. 44.

120 Henry Conway was freed of the company in 1559/60 and must have been about 56 years old in 1592. Watkins was probably about the same age. Neither he nor Conway were founding members of the company in 1557 but he, too, was a freeman shortly after 1557. Possibly Conway's health did not allow him fully to discharge his upper wardenship and Watkins acted as his substitute, the first time on July 22, 1591, the last time on June 27, 1593. From then until his death (1598 or 1599) there was only one other licensing by Watkins, along with the incumbent wardens on August 27, 1596. Blagden's observation is restricted to Conway's two-year term as upper warden.

121 Arber II.619.

122 *Greene's Groatsworth of Wit*, Attributed to Henry Chettle and Robert Greene, edited by D. Allen Carroll, Medieval and Renaissance Text Studies, Binghamton, NY, 1993, pp. 107-8.

123 Blayney, Peter W. "Publication of Playbooks", p. 399

124 *Court Book B*, p. 46.

125 Arber II.411.

126 Arber III.397.

127 *Greene's Groatsworth of Wit. Bought with a Million of Repentance* (1592). Attributed to Henry Chettle and Robert Greene. Edited by D. Allen Carroll. Medieval & Renaissance Text Studies. Binghamton, New York, 1994, p. 124.

128 Harvey, *Works*, I.170.

129 *Ibid.*, I.196-7.

130 *Ibid,.* I.217-8

131 *Ibid.*, I.219-20.

132 *Ibid.*, I.214.

133 *Ibid.*, I. 200

134 *Ibid.*, p. 199. The abused author meant here is John Harvey, the youngest of the three Harvey brothers who studied in Cambridge. He had died shortly before (July 1592).

135 *Nashe*, V.177.

136 *Ibid.*, pp. 179-80.

137 *Nashe*, IV.320.

138 *Nashe*, II.196-7.

139 Probably "match his mare", kiss his own mare, wife, which was to be his own.

140 Nashe, V., "Supplement to McKerrow's Edition of Nashe", pp. 76-7.

141 Nashe, III.21.

142 Harvey, *Works*, I.181.

143 Nashe, I.279-80.

144 Brown, John Russel in the introduction to the Arden edition of *The Merchant of Venice*, 1985, p. xii.

145 Arber, III.37.

146 Nashe, I.256.

147 *Ibid.*, III.57.

148 Harvey, I.208.

149 Harvey, I.160.

150 *Ibid.*, I.167-8.

151 *Ibid.*, I. 176.

152 Nashe, I.198.

153 *Ibid.*, I.269.

154 *Ibid.*, I. 218.

155 *Ibid.*, I.164.

156 *Ibid.*, I.289.

157 *The Complete Works of Thomas Lodge*, 4 vols., ed. Edmund W. Gosse, New York: Russell & Russel Inc, 1963, vol. 4, p. 63. Lodge precedes here Richard Barnfield and Francis Meres by two years in lionizing Spenser, Daniel and Drayton as the three oustanding contemporary lyrics; it will be remarked that despite the great resonance of Shakespeare's *Venus and Adonis* (1593) and *The Rape of Lucrece* (1594), he is not mentioned by Lodge.

158 Nashe, I.284-5.

159 *Ibid.*, III.324.

160 Millar, Roland: *The Piltdown Men*, London: Victor Gollancz, 1972, p. 207.

161 Harvey, II.124.

162 *Ibid.*, I. 185.

163 Nashe, vol. V, Supplement, p. 18.

164 *Ibid.*, IV.78-9.

165 Nashe, V.111-2. The editor McKerrow notes: "...there seems to be evidence that it was usual practice to keep note-books in which striking phrases, images or examples met with in the course of reading might be treasured for future use." A confirmation is found in Nashe's *Have With You to Saffron-Walden*. "That word Aphorisms *Greene's* executors may claim from him; for while he liv'd he had no goods nor chattles in commoner use than it." (III.44)

166 Thomas, Sidney: "The Printing of *Greenes Groatsworth of Witte* and *Kind-*

Harts Dreame in *Studies in Bibliography*, 19, 1966, pp. 196-7.

167 Carroll, D. Allen, *Groatsworth*, 1994, p. 48, n. 2.

168 Arber, II.779.

169 Arber, II. 780.

170 Arber, II. 782.

171 Arber II.502.

172 Arber II.504.

173 Arber II.564, 569, 588.

174 *The First and Second Parts of John Hayward's* The Life and Raigne of King Henrie IIII, ed. John J. Manning, Camden Series, Vol. 42, London 1991, p. 22.

175 *Ibid.*, p. 29.

176 Nashe, III. 135. In a letter, which Nashe publishes in *Have With You to Saffron-Walden*, Thorius accuses Harvey of having forged his commendatory poem to Harvey's *Pierce's Supererogation*.

177 Greene, *Life and Works*, "Francesco's Fortunes", Vol. 8, pp. 132-33.

178 *Ibid.*, p. 132.

179 Nashe, III.311.

180 Lyly, John: "Euphues & His England" in *Euphues: The Anatomy of Wit – Euphues & His England*, ed. M.W. Croll and Harry Clemons. New York: Russell & Russell Inc, 1964, p. 241-2.

181 *Ibid.*, p. 209.

182 *Ibid.*, p. 239.

183 *Ibid.*, p. 249.

184 *Ibid.*, p. 250.

185 Lievsay, John L. *Stefano Guazzo and the English Renaissance 1575-1675*. Chapel Hill: The University of North Carolina Press, 1960, p. 34.

186 Ibid., p. 35.

187 Ibid., p. 85.

188 Stanton, Domna C. *The Aristocrat as Art. A Study of the Honnête Homme and the Dandy in Seventeenth- and Nineteenth-Century French Literature*. New York: Columbia University Press, 1980, p. 131.

189 Wilson, John Dover: "Malone and the Upstart Crow," in *Shakespeare Survey*, Vol. 4, 1951, pp. 61-2.

190 Burke, *The Fortunes*, pp. 10-11.

191 Most of his *Dialoghi* were written between 1579 and 1586.

192 Tasso, Torquato: "Il Forno ovvero della Nobiltà" in *Dialoghi di Torquato Tasso*, 3 vols., Pisa: Presso Niccolò Capurro, 1822, Tomo I, p. 54.

193 *Mémoires du Vicomte de Turenne, depuis Duc de Bouillon, 1565-1586*, publiés

pour la Société de l'Histoire de France par le Comte de Baguenault de Puchesse, Paris, 1801, p. 116.

194 Strype, John: *Annals of the Reformation and of Establishment of Religion*, 4 vols., Reprint of original edition, Oxford 1824, New York: Burt Franklin, 1966, Vol. Iv.2, pp. 506-8.

195 Elyot, Thomas: *The Boke of the Governor*, ed. Ben Ross Schneider Jr., http://darkwing.uoregon.edu/~rbear/ren.htm, Renascence Editions.

196 Burke, Peter, *The Fortunes*, p. 87

197 Elyot, *The Boke*, Book I, p. 27.

198 *Ibid.*, p. 66.

199 *Ibid.*, pp. 91-2.

200 Ascham, *The Scholemaster*, p. 17.

201 Herrup, Cynthia. "'To Pluck Bright Honour from the Pale-Faced Moon': Gender and Honour in the Castlehaven Story" in *Transactions of the Royal Historical Society*, sixth series. Cambridge University Press. 1996, p. 143.

202 *Ibid.*, p. 147.

203 *The Art of English Poesie*, p. 186.

204 *Ibid.*, p. 276.

205 Javitch, Daniel: *Poetry and Courtliness in Renaissance England*. Princeton: Princeton University Press, 1978, p. 50.

206 *Ibid.*

207 *Ibid.*, p.180.

208 *Ibid.*, p. 182.

209 Nashe, IV.178, n. 297.

210 Ascham, *Scholemaster*, p. 26b.

211 *Ibid.*, p. 27a.

212 *Ibid.*, p. 28b.

213 Strype, *Annals*, III.2, p. 477.

214 Harvey, *Works*, I.86.

215 Harvey, Gabriel: *Letter-book of Gabriel Harvey, A.D. 1573-1580*, ed. E.J.L. Scott, printed for the Camden Society, 1884, p.99.

216 Harvey, *Works*, I. 72-3.

217 *Ibid.*, I.206.

218 *Ibid.*, p. 182.

219 *Ibid.*, p. 183.

220 Holdsworth, William S.: "Defamation in the sixteenth and seventeenth centuries" in *Law Quarterly Review*, No. CLX, October 1924, p. 401.

221 *Ibid.*, p. 398.

222 Pollard, A.F: "Council, Star Chamber, and Privy Council under the Tu-

dors" in *EHR*, vol. xxxvii, 1922, p. 338.

223 Holdsworth, William S.: "Defamation", July 1924, p. 305.

224 Plucknett, T. F. T.: *A Concise History of the Common Law*, fifth edition, London: Butterworth & Co. Ltd. First edition 1929, p. 486.

225 Greville, Fulke: "The Life of the Renowned Sir Philip Sidney" in *Complete Works*, ed. Alexander B. Grosart, 4 vols., New York: AMS Press, 1966, vol. IV, p. 69.

226 Plucknett, *Concise History*, p. 487.

227 *The Complete Works of John Lyly*, ed. R. Warwick Bond, 3 vols., Oxford: At the Clarendon Press, 1902, vol. 3, p. 400.

228 Harvey, *Works*, I.184.

229 *Ibid*., p. 184.

230 *Ibid*, II.122.

231 *Ibid*., I. 183-4.

232 Austen, Warren B.: "William Withie's Notebook" in *Review of English Studies*, Vol. 23, 1947, p. 303.

233 *The Arte of English Poesie*, p. 63 and p. 61.

234 Vickers, *Shakespeare, Co-Author*, p. 141.

235 *The Oxford Companion to the English Language*, ed. Tom McArthur, Oxford: Oxford University Press, 1992.

236 Lodge, Thomas: *Works*, Vol. I, p. 23 and p. 34.

237 Greville, *Complete Works*, Vol. 3, p. 112 and p. 149.

238 *Greene's Groatsworth*. Edited by D. Allen Carroll, p. 87.

239 *Ibid*., p. 90.

240 Nashe, I.215.

241 *Ibid*., I.296.

242 *Dictionary of National Biography*.

243 Chambers, E.K.: *Elizabethan Stage*, Vol. III, p. 314 and p. 338.

244 In 1599 several actors, among them Will Kempe, left the Chamberlain's Men for another company. It is about that time the London-based Earl of Oxford's Men appears. It is not realistic to suppose that these men would have joined the Earl of Worcester's Men, who till 1600 are traced in the province only. Early in 1602 the companies of the two earls were amalgamated, and we see appear as payees the names of William Kempe, Robert Pallant, John Duke, and Christopher Beeston, who in 1598 still belonged to the Chamberlain's Men.

245 Gurr, Andrew: *Shakespearian playing companies*, Oxford: Clarendon Press, 1996, p. 270.

246 Carroll: "Reading the 1592 *Groatsworth* attack", p. 286.

247 *Henslowe Papers,* ed. Walter W. Greg, Appendix III, p. 155.

248 *Ibid.,* Appendix II, p. 144.

249 *Dictionary of National Biography.*

250 Nashe, I.212.

251 Chambers. *Shakespeare,* I.290-3.

252 *Ibid.,* 290-1.

253 Greg, Walter W. *The editorial Problem in Shakespeare. A survey of the foundation of the text.* Oxford: Clarendon Press, 1951, pp. 185-188.

254 *The Third Part of Henry VI.* Ed. John Dover Wilson. Cambridge edition, 1952.

255 Chambers, *Eliz. Stage,* II.128.

256 Eccles, Mark. "Elizabethan Authors" in *Notes & Queries,* June 1993, p. 168.

257 Greg. *Editorial Problem,* p. 188.

258 Dr. Allison Gaw's conclusion (based upon careful examination of all available evidence of the possible time-frame in which Shakespeare could have revised Marlowe's work), was that "certainly up to the end of 1592, and probably up to June, 1594, Shakespeare had not made any interpolation whatever..and that Greene's reference in early September of 1592 therefore has no bearing whatever upon the subject." (*The Origin and Development of I Henry VI.* Los Angeles: The University of Southern California, 1926, p. 162). Earlier in the book, Gaw writes: It is usually taken for granted that Greene, in quoting it, is referring to Shakespeare's 'plagiarism' of it in 3 Henry VI. But the whole theory of such an accusation is, as Dr. Brooke has shown, utterly baseless"(p.75). Dr. Gaw's footnote cites Dr. C. F. Tucker Brooke's *Authorship of 2 and 3 Henry VI,* 164-71.

259 Greg, W.W. *Editorial Problem,* p. 189.

260 Greer, Clayton A. "The York and Lancaster Quarto-Folio Sequence" in *PMLA,* XLVIII (1933), 655-704.

261 Greer, Clayton A. "More About the Actor-Reporter Theory in 'The Contention' and 'The True Tragedy'" in *Notes & Queries,* February, 1957, pp. 52-3.

262 Greer, in *PMLA,* p. 700.

263 *Ibid.,* p. 701.

264 *3 Henry VI* was for the most part ascribed to Marlowe by F.G. Fleay as early as 1886, and Dr. Allison Gaw's 1920 study concurs, citing Dr. C. F. Tucker Brooke's 1912 study that named Marlowe the primary author of *Contention* and *True Tragedy,* arguing that 2 and 3 *Henry VI* were "based upon more perfect transcripts of the earlier Marlowan plays, and that the revision was solely the work of Shakespeare." Gaw also noted that in one "brief scene" of *1 Henry VI* (Act I, sc.1 165-77) "we have ten echoes from *Tamburlaine, the Contention, the True Tragedy, Edward II, The Jew of Malta,* and *Lucan...* The

mind of the man who wrote the scene was permeated with the style, thought, and tricks of phraseology of Marlowe." He added that Dr. Brooke had "recognized a number of the [same] parallels." In 1993 a stylometric analysis led Merriam and Matthew to the conclusion that *Contention* and *True Tragedy* were authorial versions by Marlowe.

265 From Seneca. *Thyestes*, ll. 613-4. "He whom the dawning day has seen exalted/The departing day has seen downfallen."

266 From Ovid, *Heroides*, II.66. "The gods grant that this may be the peak of thy glory."

267 *The Reports of John Spelman*, ed. for the Selden Society by J.H. Baker, London 1978, Vol. II, p. 93.

268 Holdsworth, *History*. Vol. IX, 1st ed. 1926, 3rd ed. 1944, p.260.

269 *Reports of John Spelman*, Vol. II, p. 163.

270 Blackstone, William, *Commentaries*, II.360.

271 Blackstone, *Comm.*, II.359; Holdsworth, *History*, Vol. III, p. 119, n. 8.

272 Holdsworth, III.114.

273 The Statute De Donis is also called the Second Statute of Westminster or 13º Edward I, c.1. On the names of statutes see *Stephen's Commentaries on the Laws of England*. Seventeenth Edition. 4 Vol. Thoroughly revised and modernised, and brought down to the present time under the general editorship of Edward Jenks, Esq. London: Butterworth & Co, 1922. Vol. I, p.43. "In the early days of Parliament, when the King's Court was constantly moving from place to place, it seems to have been the fashion to name Acts of Parliament after the places at which they were enacted. Thus, amongst our oldest statutes, we get the Statute of Merton (1235), the Statute of Marlborough (1267), the Statute of Westminster (1275), and the Statute of Winchester (1285). But, when Parliament finally settled down at Westminster, this practice became obviously impossible; although the First, Second and Third Statutes of Westminster survive to show an attempt to continue it. Then there was a period during which statutes were named after their subject-matter, as, for example, the Statute of Mortmain and the Statute of Maintenance, or, in still cruder fashion (perhaps borrowed from the Papal Chancery), by the initial words of the enactment, e.g. the Statute De Donis Conditionalibus, or the Statute Quia Emptores. But the increasing complexity of Parliamentary legislation soon put a stop to both these methods; and the practice then arose, and continued for many centuries, of quoting Acts of Parliaments by the regnal year of the kings, and the chapter of the session. Thus — '27 Hen. VIII.c.10,'..."

274 Holdsworth, *History*, III.112-3.

275 Holdsworth, III, p. 81-2.

276 Holdsworth, III.114-5.

277 Blackstone, II.349.

278 Trevor-Roper, H.R. "An Anatomy Anatomized" in *The Economic Historic Review*, Second Series,Vol. III, No. 3, 1951, pp. 281-2. The Staple towns were established by Statute 27º Edw. III, stat. 2 (1353-4). Originally, they numbered 15 (10 in England, 4 in Ireland, 1 in Wales). Their function was to export staple goods: wool, woolfels, tin, and lead. See Brodhurst, Spencer. "The Merchants of the Staple" in *LQR*, Vol. 55, Jan. 1901, p. 68.

279 *Hamlet*. The Arden Shakespeare. Edited by Harold Jenkins. London: Routledge. 1990, pp. 386-7.

280 Nashe, I.164.

281 Blackstone, IV.343.

282 Baker, J. H. "New Light in Slade´s Case" Part II, in *The Cambridge Law Journal*, 29 (2) Nov. 1971, p. 228.

283 *The Works of Francis Bacon*. James Spedding, Robert Leslie Ellis, and Douglas Denon Heath, eds. 14 vols. London: Longman, 1857-1859. Vol. XII, pp. 250-1.

284 Bacon, *Works*. Vol. VII, pp. 465-6. As Spedding notes, "tunnel" was also written "tinnel" or "tenell", the latter being the word used in 2º Stat. Rich. II, c.3, and the translation in Russhead´s Statutes is "lodging". The verge was a radius of twelve miles around the place where the King resided.

285 Holdsworth, Vol. I, pp. 219-224.

286 *Ibid*., pp. 219-20.

287 *Ibid*., p. 220.

288 Chambers, *Shakespeare*, Vol. II, pp. 113-118.

289 Holdsworth, Vol. I, p. 220.

290 *Ibid*., pp. 220-1.

291 Holdsworth, Vol. IX , p. 141.

292 *Ibid*., p. 140

293 *Ibid*., n. 5, p. 140

294 *Ibid*.

295 Knafla, Louis A. *Law and Politics in Jacobean England – The Tracts of Lord Chancellor Ellesmere*. Cambridge: Cambridge University Press, 1977, pp. 293-4. Not only the common law courts but also the Court of the City of London seems to have used this device. About 1570 the queen addressed a letter to the Mayor and Sheriffs of London, in which she considers it ´very strange´ that they are taking on themselves to try cases on contracts arising upon and beyond the seas, which properly belong to ´our Court of Admi-

ralty,' feigning the same to have been done within some parish or ward of London, and directs them to desist." Carter, A.T. "Early History of the Law Merchant in England" in *LQR*, No. 67, July 1901, p. 244.

296 Plucknett, T.F.T. *A Concise History of the Common Law*, p. 663.

297 Chambers, E.K. *Shakespeare*, II.52.

298 "The sheriff is commanded that he take Charles Long, late of Burford, in the county of Oxford, if he may be found in his bailiwick, and him safely keep, so that he may have his body before the lord the king at Westminster, on Wednesday next after fifteen days of Easter, to answer William Burton, gentleman, of a plea of trespass; [and also to a bill of the said William against the aforesaid Charles, for two hundred pounds of debt..." IV, Appendix p. xviii. The locality of the plaintiff was never stated. The clause "and also" ("æc etiam"), the explicit mention that the object of the action was, in fact, not a trespass but a debt, was a later (17th century) requirement.

299 Website http://musea.digitalchainsaw.com/84artsur.html.

300 The Antwerp authorities seem to have understood the name as "Jack-spear" or "Jacques-Pierre". "Willem" is the usual Dutch form of "William", "Shaak" or "Jaak" is a form of "Jacques" or "James", whereas "speer" is "spear". Though "Peer" is a shortened form of "Peter" it is not a usual one.

301 *De natura deorum*, I. 22. The way Cicero comments on Simonides is not without reminiscences of how Ben Jonson values Shakespeare in the First Folio. "Sed Simonides arbitror – non enim poeta solum suavis, verum etiam ceteroqui doctus sapiensque traditur – quia multa venirent in mentem acuta atque subtilia.." "Simonides is not only a sweet poet but, besides, a learned and wise man having many acute and subtle observations."

302 Smith, Gregory, *Critical Essays*, Vol. I, p. 243.

303 The allusion is, of course, a vague one. But it has an analogue in a similar vague passage in Thomas Lodge's *Wit's Misery and the World's Madness*, 1596. Dealing with the vice of jealousy Lodge addresses the "divine wits" of his own time: Lily, Spenser, Daniel, Drayton, Thomas Nashe. Notoriously absent is — in 1596 — Shakespeare. But at the end of the previous paragraph Lodge alludes to Hamlet. "... he walks for the most part in black under color of gravity, & looks as pale as the Visard of the ghost which cried so miserably at the Theatre like an oyster wife, *Hamlet, revenge*." *The Complete Works*. vol. 4, pp. 62-3.

304 On Shakspeare's Pastoral Name in *Notes and Queries* 4th S. XII, Dec. 27, 1873, p. 509-10.

305 On Shakspeare's Pastoral Name in *Notes and Queries* 5th S. I, Feb. 7, 1874, p.109-11.

306 Ingleby, C. M. *Shakspere-Allusion Books*. Published by The New Shakspere Society. London: N. Trübner & Co., 1874, pp.xiv-xxi.

307 D. W. Thomson Vessey, Thomas Watson's Melibœus in *The Bard*, Vol. 1, No. 4, 1977, p. 163.

308 Ingleby, *Shakspere Allusion-Books*, p. xv.

309 *Pauly's Real-Encyclopädie der classischen Altertumswissenschaft*. Vol. 15.I. edited by Wilhelm Kroll. Stuttgart: J.B. Metzlerscher Verlag. 1931, pp. 514-521.

310 *The name Elpino, 'the pine-tree' carries an association with honey.* It is the pastoral name Tasso gives to Giovanbattista Pigna, secretary of state at the court of the Este in Ferrara, a man, it would seem, with little of literary value on record. It is interesting that the name 'Elphin' was also given to Philip Sidney, possibly in reference to Tasso's *Aminta*.

311 Suidas Anth. Pal. IX 571.184 II.1.45, quoted from *Pauly's Real-Encyclopädie*.

312 The name was long mistaken for the author of the work.; it is now generally accepted that we have not to do with an author's name but with a word signifying 'bulwark', in the sense of 'bulwark against ignorance', denoting the encyclopedy itself. Anatole Fraunce, in *Countesse of Pembrokes Ivychurch*, leave G, has: 'Suida's faith, that in truth, they (mermaids) certaine blinde and dangerous rocks...'. Similarly Richard Linche in *The fountain of ancient fiction*, London 1599, P: '*Suida* and *Fancrinus* report of one Lamia, who was a most lovely and beautous woman...'

313 Other names for the moon-goddess Elizabethans were using are Cynthia and Luna. The following self-description of Melicertus is perhaps not without some biographical interest: '*Melicertus* no niggarde in discoverie of his fortunes, began thus. I tell thee, *Doron*, before I kept sheepe in *Arcadie*, I was a Shepheard else where, so famous for my flockes, as *Menaphon* for his foldes; beloved of the Nymphes, as hee likte of the Countrey Damzells; coveting in my loves to use *Cupids* wings, to soare high in my desires, though my selfe were borne to base fortunes. .. I fixte mine eyes on a Nymph whose parentage was great, but her beautie fare more excellent: her birth was by manie degrees greater than mine, and my woorth by manie discents lesse than hers: yet knowing *Venus* loved *Adonis*, and *Luna Endymion*; that *Cupide* had boltes feathered with the plumes of a Crowe, as well as the pennes of an Eagle, I attempted and courted her: I found her lookes lightening disdaine, and her forhead to conteine favours for others, and frownes for me...' (p. 67)

314 *Ibid.*, p. 46.
315 Greene, *Life and Complete Works of*, Vol. 6, p. 79.
316 *Ibid.* , p. 82.
317 *Ibid.*, p. 121.
318 Harbage, Alfred. *"Love´s Labour´s Lost* and the Early Shakespeare" in *Philological Quarterly*, XLI, 1962, p. 23.
319 *Love´s Labour´s Lost,* The Arden Shakespeare, ed. Richard David, 1968, p. xiii.
320 Chambers, E.K.: *Shakespeare*, I. 336-7.
321 Harvey, *Works*, II.56.
322 *Ibid.*, II.296.
323 *Ibid.*, I.72.
324 *Ibid.*, pp. II.295-6.
325 Nashe, I.283.
326 Harvey, *Works,* I.196.
327 *Ibid.*, I. 217.
328 *Ibid.*, I. 219.
329 *Ibid.*, I.220.
330 *Ibid.*, II.41.
331 *Ibid.*, II.44
332 Nashe, I.295.
333 *Ibid.*, III.79.
334 Harvey, I. 223.
335 *Ibid.*, II.273.
336 V.i.43-53. The puns on "sheep" and "oueia", the Spanish word for sheep, used as a mnemonic for the vowels in Vives´ *Exercitatio Linguae.* F. A. Yates. *A Study of* Love´s Labour´s Lost. Cambridge: At the University Press, 1936, pp. 57 ff.
337 Lewis, C. S. *English Literature in the Sixteenth Century – Excluding Drama.* Oxford: At the Clarendon Press, 1954, p. 355.
338 Harvey´s own words, Perne was "not rash, but quick", *Works*, II. 298.
339 Nashe, I.260.
340 *Ibid.*, II.12.
341 Harvey, *Works*, I.276.
342 Nashe, II. 181.
343 Harvey, *Works*, I.233.
344 *Ibid.*, II.114.
345 *Ibid.*, II.265.
346 Davis, Philip. *Sudden Shakespeare – The Shaping of Shakespeare´s Creative*

Thought. London: Athlone. 1996.

347 Harvey, *Works*, I.205.

348 Nashe, I.260-1.

349 http://home.iprolink.ch/dpeck/write_leic-comm3.htm, Scanned and reprinted from Dwight Peck (ed.). *Leicester´s Commonwealth*. Athens and London: Ohio University Press, 1985, p. 6.

350 Nashe, I. 223.

351 *Leicester´s Commonwealth*, p. 64.

352 *Ibid.*, p. 65.

353 Nashe, I.221.

354 Nashe, I.222.

355 *Ibid.*, I. 321.

356 *Ibid.*, I.223.

357 *Ibid.*, I.224.

358 *Ibid.*, I.224.

359 *The Marprelate Tracts*. Ed. John D. Lewis. www.anglicanlibrary.org/marprelate, p. 87.

360 *Ibid.*, p. 83.

361 *The Complete Works of John Lyly*, R. Warwick Bond (ed.), 3 vols., Oxford: At the Clarendon Press, 1902, Vo. III, p. 418.

362 Strype, *Annals*, Vol. III.2, p. 67 and p. 73.

363 Nashe, I.270.

364 Nashe, V.177.

365 Harvey, *Works*, II.133.

366 *Ibid.*, II.205.

367 *Ibid.*, I.xl.

368 Virgil. *Eclogues*. Translated by C. Day Lewis. Oxford: At the Alden Press. 1963, p. 42. The lines in the original are: "Nam neque adhuc Vario videor, nec dicere Cinna/digna, sed argutos inter strepere anser olores."

369 A similar attitude is adopted by Edmund Spenser in his dedicatory poems to Lord Buckhurst and Sir Walter Raleigh prefacing his *Fairie Queen*. To Lord Buckhurst: "But sith thou maist not so, give leave a while/ To baser wit his power therein to spend,/Whose grosse defaults thy daintie pen may file,/And unadvised oversights amend." To Ralegh: "To thee that are the sommer´s Nightingale,/Thy soveraine Goddess most deare delight,/Why doe I send this rustic Madrigale,/ That may thy tunefull eare unseason quite?"

370 Ward, B.M. *The Seventeenth Earl of Oxford, 1550-1604*. London: John Murray. 1928, p. 158; Ogburn, Charlton. *The Mysterious William Shakespeare*. McLean,

VA: EPM Publications, Inc. 1984, p. 597.

371 Nashe, V.73.

372 See Part II, chapter 2.

373 Greene, *Life and Complete Works*, Vol. 2, p. 219.

374 Nashe, I.255.

375 *Ibid.*, 69.

376 *Ibid.*, 80.

377 *Ibid.*, III.127.

378 *Love's Labour's Lost*, Arden edition, p. xxxvii.

379 Harvey, I. 41 and 63.

380 *Ibid.*, I.35.

381 *Art of English Poesie*, pp. 112-3.

382 *Ibid.*, II.227.

383 Nashe, I.295.

384 Harvey, *Works*, II.200.

385 *Ibid.*, II.34.

386 *Ibid.*, II.74.

387 *Ibid.*, II.95.

388 *Ibid.*, I.191-2. In his play **Poetaster** (1601) Ben Jonson takes a similar Augustan stand. Augustus banishes Ovid on grounds similar to those implied in Harvey's rejection of Ovid.

389 *Ibid.*, II.102.

390 Nashe, III.49-50.

391 Harvey, *Works*, II.94.

392 *Pierce's Supererogation* consists of three parts. Part 1 and 3 are directed against Nashe. These parts are dated 27 April 1593 by Harvey. Part 2, a reply to Lyly's lambasting of Harvey in the anti-Martiniest pamphlet *Papp with a Hatchet*, is separately dated 5 November 1589. The prefatory matter to *Pierce's Supererogation* is dated 16 July 1593. *A New Letter of Notable Contents* is dated 16 September 1593. It constitutes a reply to Nashe's peace proposal in the preface to the first edition of *Christ's Tears over Jerusalem*. Nashe's work must already have been printed when it was entered in the Stationers' Register on 8 September 1583 and published immediately afterwards, otherwise Harvey could not have responded on 16 September.

393 Duncan-Jones, Katherine. "Much Ado With Red and White: The Earliest Readers of Shakespeare's *Venus and Adonis* (1593) in *The Review of English Studies*, New Series, Volume XLIV, Number 176, November 1993, p. 488 (modernized spelling).

394 Harvey, *Works*, I. 218-9.

395 *Ibid.*, II. 280 and 290.

396 Phillips, Gerald W. *Lord Burghley in Shakespeare*, London: Thornton-Butterworth, 1936, p. 62; Barrell, Charles Wisner. "New Milestone in Shakespeare Research – Contemporary Proof that the Poet Earl of Oxford's Literary Nickname Was 'Gentle Master William'", *The Shakespeare Fellowship Quarterly*, October 1944; Ogburn, Charlton. *The Mysterious William Shakespeare*. McLean, VA: EPM Publications, Inc. 1984, p. 725.

397 Harvey, *Works*, I.170.

398 Nashe, I.287-8.

399 Rhenish wine or white wine seems to have been a drink of literati and contain an allusion to Falstaff (see next chapter); "pickle-herring" was perhaps a poor poet's meal.

400 Burgess, Anthony. *Shakespeare*. New York: Alfred Knopf, 1970, p. 108; quoted from Carroll, D.C., 1994, p. 131.

401 Nicholl, Charles. *A Cup of News: the Life of Thomas Nashe*. London: Routledge & Kegan Paul. 1984.

402 Nashe, IV.154.

403 Nicholl, *Cup of News*, p. 44-5.

404 Hilliard, Stephen S. *The singularity of Thomas Nashe*. Lincoln: Univ. Of Nebraska Press. 1986, p. 189.

405 McCarthy, Penny. "Some *quises* and *quems*: Shakespeare's true debt to Nashe", *Shakespeare Yearbook* 2004, Mellen Press, Lewiston, NY, pp. 175-192.

406 Nashe, IV.154.

407 McCarthy, pp. 186-7.

408 In *Poetaster*, II.ii, the singer Hermogenes is urged on to sing and is at first reluctant; the passage (ll. 94-151) is a long drawn out imitation of a similar situation in *Much Ado About Nothing*, II.iii, where Balthasar is called upon to sing (ll.37-60); IV.x is an imitation of the balcony scene (II.ii) in *Romeo and Juliet*. The allusion to *Timon of Athens*, I.ii, in Jonson's *Poetaster*, II.ii, could not be clearer. The usual argument against such parallels that poets shared a common vocabulary and the direction of borrowing is often uncertain, however justified it might sometimes be, is wholly ineffectual here: Jonson adds that the quote is from a play. Jonson's play was written end 1601. The orthodox date for *Timon of Athens* is 1608!

409 Metz, G. H. *Shakespeare's Earliest Tragedy – Studies in* Titus Andronicus. London: Associated University Press. 1996, p. 251.

410 Nashe, III.35.6.

411 McCarthy, p. 180.

412 Tobin, J. J. M. "Texture as Well as Structure: More Sources for Riverside

Shakespeare" in Thomas Moisan and Douglas Bruster, eds. *In the Company of Shakespeare: Essays on English Renaissance Literature in Honor of G. Blakemore Evans.* London: Associated University Presses, 2002, p.102.

413 Harvey, *Works*, I.225.
414 *Ibid.*, I.283.
415 Mc Kerrow's annotation in Nashe, IV.132.
416 Nashe, I.256.
417 Harvey, *Works*, I.205.
418 *Ibid.*, III.268.
419 Harvey, *Works*, II.40.
420 *Ibid.*, p. 44.
421 Nashe, I.321.
422 *Gabriel Harvey's Rhetor.* Translated from Latin and edited by Mark Reynolds. http://comp.uark.edu/~mreynold/rhetor.html. 2001, p. 12
423 *Paulys Real-Encyclopädie der Classischen Altertumswissenschaft.* Vol. 2. Edited by Georg Wissowa. Stuttgart: J.B. Metzlerscher Verlag. 1896, p. 250.
424 *Oxford Latin Dictionary*, At the Clarendon Press, 1968,
425 Harvey, *Works*. I.200. Lucian is the satirist Lucian of Samosata, a contemporary of Apuleius, to whom, most probably incorrectly, is ascribed a work *Lucios or the Ass*, a similar story in which the hero is called Lucius of Patriae. It is by no means certain that the name Lucius of Patriae is the name of the author of this other novel about a man transformed into an ass.
426 Smith, Gregory. *Critical Essays*, I.174-5.
427 We are indebted to Kurt Kreiler for having drawn our attention to this.
428 *A Hundreth Sundry Flowres – From the Original Edition of 1573.* Edited by Ruth Loyd Miller. Jennings, LA: Kennikat Press Corporation, 1975, pp. 184-6.
429 Harvey, *Works*. I.192.
430 *Ibid.*, I.197.
431 *Ibid.*, I.199.
432 Moore Smith, G.C., "Taking Lodgings in 1591" in *RES*, Vol. VIII, 1932, pp. 447-450.
433 McCarthy, p. 181.
434 Harvey, *Works*. II.49.
435 *Ibid.*, pp. 187-8.
436 *Ibid.*, p. 181.
437 Harvey, *Works*, I. 219.
438 Stone, Lawrence. *The Crisis of the Aristocracy 1558-1641*. Oxford: Clarendon Press, 1965, pp.42-3.

439 Huppert, George. *Les Bourgeois-Gentilshommes*. Chicago: The University of Chicago Press, 1977, p. 120.

440 Best, George. *The Three Voyages of Martin Frobisher*, issued by the Hakluyt Society, 1867, reprint by Burt Franklin, New York, pp. 70-1.

441 Quoted from Taylor, Eva G. R. *The Troublesome Voyage of Captain Edward Fenton – 1582-1583*. Edited for The Hakluyt Society. Cambridge: Cambridge University Press, 1959, p. 16.

442 Neale, J. E. *Elizabeth and Her Parliaments, 1559-1601*, 2 vol., London: Jonathan Cape, 1957, vol. 2, pp. 340-3.

443 Strype, *Annals*, IV.1, p. 476.

444 Harvey, *Works*, I.184.

445 Nashe, III.240-1.

446 Nashe, III.323. Preface to Greene's *Menaphon*: "Sundry other sweet Gentlemen I do know, that have vaunted their pens in private devices, and tricked up a company of taffata fools with their feathers..."

447 Nashe, IV.154.

448 Fellowes, Edmund Horace. *The English Madrigal Composers*. Oxford: At the Clarendon Press, 1921, p. 142.

449 *The Case is Altered*, I.i and *Every Man Out of His Humour*, I.i. For the ascription to the earl of Oxford, see May, Steven W. "The Authorship of 'My mind to me a kingdom is'", *RES*, New Series, Vol. XXVI, Number 104, Nov. 1975, pp. 385-394.

450 Looney, John Thomas. *"Shakespeare" Identified in Edward de Vere, Seventeenth Earl of Oxford*. Port Washington: Kennekat Press for Minos Publishing Company, Jennings, LA. 1975, p. 473.

451 *Notes & Queries* 2nd Series IX, 1860, 135-7. "Ante-Reformation Archdeacon's Charge and Inquisition."

452 Holdsworth, W. S., Defamation, pp. 302-315, and pp. 397-412; the same, The State and Religious Nonconformity: An Historical Retrospect in: *The Law Quarterly Review*, Vol. CXLIV, 1920, S. 339-358; Kent, Joan R., Attitudes of members of the house of Commons to the regulation of 'personal conduct' in late Elizabethan and early Stuart England, in: *Bulletin of the Institute of Historical Research*, Vol. XLVI No. 13, May 1973, S. 41-71.

453 Furnivall, Frederick J., *Child-Marriages, Divorces, and Ratifications, &c. in the Diocese of Chester, A.D. 1561-6*, London 1897; Hodge, C.E., Cases from a fifteenth century Archdeacon's Court, in *The Law Quarterly Review*, Vol. CIXIV, 1933, 268-274.

454 BL Lansdowne 68[/6].

455 Harbage, A., "*Love's Labour's Lost* and the early Shakespeare", pp. 18ff.

456 Nashe, I. 286-7.
457 Greene, Robert. "The Art of Conny-catching" in *The Life and Complete Works*. Vol. X. , pp. 16-17.
458 Nashe, IV.156.
459 *Ibid.*, III.133.
460 *Ibid.*
461 *Ibid.*
462 *Ibid.*, IV.369.
463 *Ibid.*, V. Supplement, p. 52.
464 *Ibid.*, III.133
465 Nashe, V.28.
466 *Ibid.*, V.51.
467 Nashe. *Complete Works*. III.76.
468 Nashe, III.77.